TRUE TO THE TREFOIL

A CELEBRATION OF FICTIONAL GIRL GUIDES

edited by

TIG TH(

Girls Gone By Publishers

Published by

Girls Gone By Publishers
4 Rock Terrace
Coleford
Bath
Somerset
BA3 5NF

FIRST EDITION
Text © authors as listed under Contents 2010
Photograph p76 © Ruth Jolly
Photographs pp111–118 © Alison McCallum
Photograph p174 © Tig Thomas
Design and layout © Girls Gone By Publishers 2010
Cover design © Girls Gone By Publishers 2010

Edited by Tig Thomas

Cover design and adaptation by Adrianne Fitzpatrick and Ken Websdale
Typeset by Books to Treasure
Printed by CPI Antony Rowe

ISBN 978-1-84745-080-7

Presenting the Colours

A Good Deed

Adventure in the Ruins

Camping fun

Lord and Lady Baden-Powell

CONTENTS

(CONT.)

"We have a Girl Guide Company in the school, Judy. Most of us belong. If you aren't one already we hope you will, for it's a splendid thing. The trefoil is our badge—see!" and she unfastened the little Guide badge she wore pinning her tie and handed it to Judy.

"What does it mean?" queried Judy, as she looked wonderingly at the metal trefoil with its G.G. and motto on the scroll beneath.

"The badge, d'you mean? It means the three promises—three leaves, d'you see?"

Judy, the Guide, Elinor M Brent-Dyer, 1928

INTRODUCTION

I n 1910 true-hearted and healthy-bodied Guides emerged on the fictional landscape to stand alongside their schoolgirl sisters, and brought a tang of fresh air and woodsmoke into the girls' story. Where schoolgirls had more or less to remain within bounds, Guides were free to roam across the landscape, pitching their tents, scrambling down cliffs and performing extraordinary deeds with their loyal patrols. The combination of a deep commitment to personal honour and an unlimited freedom for adventure made Guides a perfectly pitched subject for girls' fiction in the early years of the twentieth century. *True to the Trefoil* takes an affectionate look at the authors and themes that moulded the Guiding genre, and the story behind the movement that inspired them.

To understand Guiding fiction, it helps to have knowledge of the history behind it. As I was researching this book, it astonished me to discover how few people still knew about Baden-Powell. 'Why would I have heard of a soldier from 100 years ago who founded a movement I don't belong to?' one thirteen-year-old friend asked me, puzzled. 'Baking-Powder?' said the assistant on the enquiry desk at the National Portrait Gallery (which would have amused Baden-Powell, who urged friends to call him Bathing-Towel). This book includes a short history of the movement and an account of one real-life company, to give a context to the fiction. It ends with a brief biography of the man Guides call the Founder.

The bulk of the book, however, is dedicated to celebrating the writers who engaged with Guiding. We've attempted, as Baden-Powell always urged, to 'Look Wide' and discuss many different aspects of Guiding fiction, from Guiding novels and plays to short stories in annuals and in Guiding magazines.

The Guiding genre is not a large one, but it contributed to and invigorated many other forms of children's writing. It might be argued, for example (and I would have a go, although I've not attempted it here), that Arthur Ransome took the Guiding theme and transformed it into the adventure story, with his small groups of children bonded by a common name (Swallows, Eels) who practise fire lighting, camping, signalling, woodcraft, and develop a variety of specialist skills. Certainly many writers seized the opportunity to make use of this new movement, and *True to the Trefoil* looks at how some of the most popular incorporated Guiding into their already existing series.

When I was thirteen I discovered what I thought was the most wonderful book in the world: Baden-Powell's *Scouting for Boys*. I had never read anything like it and I longed to mix up dampers on my coat lining, and make a camp candlestick by standing a glass bottle in the hot ashes of a camp fire, with a little water in its bottom; whereupon, so Baden-Powell assured me, the bottle would crack cleanly along the line of the water level. From Baden-Powell's vision, I moved on to Guiding fiction, discovering a company of stalwart girls who shared my thrill at being given such a big adventure to undertake. Their adventures and personalities still have the power to grip: Cherry and her uncaptained patrol trying their utmost to keep their Company going; Ethne, sitting alone in the upstairs room of her strict great-aunt, sustained by

Guiding principles; dear Catherine, listening entranced while a commissioner introduces her to the ideals of Service; and even Patrol Leader Judy, equally insouciant when brisking up her uncle's supper or dealing with a baby in a fit while buried under a landslide. These girls and many others live vividly in the pages of Guiding fiction, a genre which lasted less than fifty years but made a considerable contribution to popular children's books and still has an appeal for many readers. Those fictional members of the Poppies and Pimpernels, the Jills and Judys with their cheery faces, egalitarian approaches and capable way with a three-cornered bandage, still have much to offer a reader today, and it has been a great pleasure to celebrate their adventures and aspirations.

Tig Thomas

SCOUTING FOR GIRLS

Tig Thomas

In 1908, Robert Stephenson Smyth Baden-Powell (B-P), hero of Mafeking, instituted the Boy Scout movement in Britain, drawing on his training as an army scout to introduce the notions of camping, woodcraft, tracking and general preparedness to a generation of enthusiastic boys. It was a huge success, and the movement grew rapidly.

Girls, naturally, soon became interested, and initially he was happy to recruit them, cheerfully saying, 'I have had several rather pathetic letters from little girls asking if they may share the delights of a scouting life with the boys. But of course they may! I am always glad to hear of girls' patrols being formed.' But something changed—perhaps through a conversation with his mother, who deeply disapproved of the idea of Scouting girls, perhaps from an awareness that such a thing would not do at all in Edwardian society. In 1909 the first Boy Scout rally took place in Crystal Palace, attended by 1,000 boys—and, famously, a few girls. Baden-Powell realised he would have to put his mind to the problem. He wrote an article for the magazine for Scout Leaders, entitled 'A Scheme of training for Girl Guides'. Always adept at summing up a situation, he expressed his characteristic sensitivity to the concerns of different people: 'You do not want to make tomboys of refined girls, yet you want to attract, and thus raise, the slum-girl from the gutter.'

In the scheme, he says that alongside the 200,000 Boy Scouts, there were 6,000 girls who had registered themselves 'without any encouragement' as Girl Scouts. Some of them, indeed, had ingeniously acquired badges and other kit by signing their applications to headquarters only with their initials. Who was to know that G Smith was Georgina and not George?

His article was followed by two small booklets, known as 'Pamphlet A' and 'Pamphlet B'. Where boys had been encouraged to form their own troops, he suggests Guide companies should be started by groups of ladies forming a committee who would then 'get hold of the right kind of young ladies to act as captains and apportion to these their recruiting districts'.

Despite this sop to the proprieties, he caught the changing mood of the times. Middle-class girls were moving out from the protective atmosphere of the Victorian schoolroom. The Girls' Public Day School Trust had created the big high schools with their prefectorial systems, where all classes of girl mingled in an athletic and competitive environment. There was a need for an equivalent activity out of school hours. The Girls' Friendly Society and the Girls' Brigade (Girls' Guildry in Scotland) had been established, but were rather staid, overtly Christian organisations which emphasised the womanly virtues. B-P's movement was to offer girls the same opportunities for leadership and vigorous action in their leisure hours that they already enjoyed in their schools.

B-P withheld from girls the coveted title of Girl Scouts, recognising, no doubt rightly, that using that name would not only add fuel to people's fears that he was training up hoydens, but also that many Boy Scouts would be deterred by a mixed-sex organisation. He chose the new name from the famous corps of Guides, Indian soldiers of the north-west frontier, who were, as he said, 'a force distinguished for their general handiness and resourcefulness'. No doubt to reassure the doubters, the skills he then enumerated were the soldier Guides' abilities to 'tend the sick, cook and build a camp'—in happy contrast, the current Girlguiding UK website says of the original soldier Guides that 'their main task was to go on very dangerous expeditions'. In another concession to the older generation, B-P acknowledged the difficulty of allowing girls to roam around the country seeking out adventures: 'The daily "good turn" which a

Guide would have to perform in accordance with the rule of the Boy Scouts, can take the form of helping parents or neighbours in household work, or sick rooms.' Patrols were to be called after flower names—birds, trees and animals were added later.

Despite these modifications, B-P laid just as serious expectations on the girls as on his Scouts. Apart from alterations to allow for the different gender, the Girl Guide Law was exactly the same as the Scouts', except for two words: the Eighth Law states that a Scout smiles and whistles under all difficulties; the Guide is instructed to smile and *sing*; and while the Tenth Law says that a Scout is *clean* in thought, word and deed, a Guide is pure (although some early references do change it to clean).

Nor did B-P let the girls off lightly in terms of the challenges he put before them: the first list of badges for which they might compete includes electrician, gymnast, telegraphist, sailor and signaller. Other badges' requirements were

The west window of St James's church, Paddington, the parish in which B-P was born

modified: 'Florist—as for boys plus flower growing and making up bouquets etc.' He also added new ones, such as Nursing Sister. The uniform was at this stage very unspecific, being confined to an overshirt and neckerchief of company colour with a dark blue skirt (the Boy Scouts' khaki was seen as too military a colour for girls). A cape is also mentioned, and at this stage the headgear is an intriguing red biretta. Petticoats were *not* allowed, and girls whose mothers would not let them leave the house without them were told to tuck them into their knickers.

The cape, one imagines, disappeared fairly quickly. The biretta is a little mysterious. The cheering image of the early Guides dressed as cardinals must yield to the assumption that he is describing a tam, or beret, the least cumbersome hat a girl could wear, in an age when some sort of head covering had to be worn outdoors at all times. One of the earliest captains describes her girls following the instructions from headquarters and wearing red tam-o'-shanters well stuffed with paper to make them stand up. While the girls' uniform seems to have been settled on fairly quickly, there was a great deal of discussion about what the adult leaders should wear. Hats with a cockade of black cock's feathers were chosen, and some touches of militarism prevailed: cords were used to denote rank, and officials were to be called captains and lieutenants.

Agnes Baden-Powell, B-P's sister, was asked to take on the job of Chief Commissioner. A committee was formed and started off with a loan of £100 from B-P on 10 April 1910. The first employee, Miss Margaret Macdonald, was recruited to act as secretary, at the salary of £91 per annum. She dealt with enquiries, registered companies, and sent out kit and newsletters, all from one tiny room in Victoria Street. The committee met weekly to thrash out the details of Girl Guiding and create some overall standards. The red birettas seem soon to have disappeared; a longstanding debate was whether the official hat should be straw sailors or blue felt; when blue felt was chosen Miss Baden-Powell suggested those girls still wearing khaki hats could dye them blue with the help of a threepenny packet of dye (shades of *Terry, the Girl-Guide*, 1912).

The girls themselves were pretty unimpressed by some of the plans: 'The ideal of womanliness had no appeal for us at that age,' one girl is quoted as saying. Others simply refused to join, thinking it a great decline to go from being Wildcats or Kangaroos to Roses and Lilies, and continued as Scouts.

There was much opposition from society as a whole, and Society in particular, to the new movement. The very first mention of Guides in *The Times* comes in a report of the opening of a new High School for Girls by the Duke and Duchess of Devonshire, in September 1911. The Duke is quoted as praising the new gymnasium equipment, but adding that, as a strong opponent of the Girl Scout movement, he hoped that it would not induce the pupils to take part in 'demonstrations of force at Westminster or elsewhere', a non sequitur that illustrates the prevailing fear that Guides were out of the same stable as Suffragettes. Certainly, there was a general feeling that Guiding might lead girls into inappropriate behaviour, including unsuitable mingling with the opposite sex. One captain in Chelsea was reproved by headquarters for allowing her Guides to march to church in company with Boy Scouts. In her defence, she pleaded that the Scouts offered some protection as the district through which the girls marched was a rough one, and was allowed to continue, although the committee strongly disapproved.

There was certainly a lot of antagonism to Girl Guides from every level. One captain recounts: 'Of course we had all sorts of filth thrown at us, and I was generally invited to go to the bathroom immediately I reached home and have a clean up.' (*The Story of the Girl Guides*, Rose Kerr, 1932) Her Company, a Liverpool one, sounds tough enough to handle it, however. When girls started squabbling she made them put on boxing gloves and settle their differences in cold blood, an action, she reports, that proved very effective in stopping any tale bearing.

Disabled Guides, known as Extension, later Post, Guides, joined from the outset, and very soon special companies called Extension Companies were being formed for them. Commendably, from the very beginning children with learning difficulties were also seen as being capable of becoming Guides. The very first departure from the mainstream Guiding movement, however, was the Lone Guides. As its founder, Nesta Maude, recounts:

> A notice was put into the *Scout*, the weekly paper which all good Guides received, and in no time at all, letters were pouring in—thirty in the first week! I borrowed a typewriter and set to work. The letters were easy to cope with, but every would-be Guide had conscientiously worked on her Tenderfoot and Second Class assessment, and had sent the practical results of her labours by post.
>
> Union Jacks appeared in every form—sewn, painted and embroidered. Knots came tied in every variety of cord from the thinnest string to the thickest rope …

Most embarrassing of all, were the efforts of the girls who followed all too literally, the original Scout Assessment, 'be able to skin and cook a rabbit'! SO, I had rabbits boiled and rabbits roasted, and skins galore. Now since many of these grizzly relics came from Scotland and I lived in southern England, you can imagine my family's reaction.

The activities of the early Girl Guides tended to be very much dependent on the interests of their captain. Among other occupations early officers (the word Guider was not used until 1917) mention are spinning wool, keeping poultry, swimming lessons, harnessing ponies, tracking, and leaping ditches. Camping and first aid were fundamental to the spirit of Guiding, and drill was so popular that 'drill halls' were as common as Guide huts later became. The emphasis was very much on the outdoor life; when one Captain asked for suggestions of ways to raise funds for a drill hall, Agnes Baden-Powell replied with some asperity, 'But do they want a drill hall? I should much prefer to do my drilling in the open air, and would much rather have all my meetings out on a common.'

Folk dance was a popular activity, thanks largely to the instigation of Ernest Thompson Seton, Chief Scout of America, who felt it offered the emphasis on grace and beauty that he preferred should be a girl's ideal rather than strength and endurance. Rose Kerr tartly notes: 'Mr Cecil Sharp himself who hoped great things from the Guides … alas never saw them dancing as well as he wished.' Nevertheless, in 1929 a blind Ranger Company won the country dance competition at the London Singing and Country Dance Festival.

In 1912 the rousingly titled *The Handbook for Girl Guides, or How Girls Can Help Build the Empire* was published. (For some reason, title and subtitle appeared the other way round on the cover.) This was largely written by Agnes B-P, adapting her brother's *Scouting for Boys* to suit a female market. It made few compromises to the girls' female fragility. The book plunges straight into tips for camping in the wild, tracking and observation games that involve

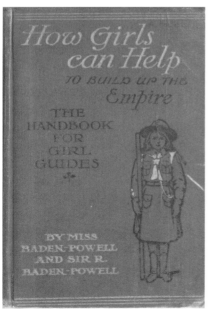

walking several miles, and other strenuous pursuits. It suggests girls learn how to tie up a burglar with eight inches of cord, fire a rifle, and do ju-jitsu. However, in the section for captains at the end of the book it does acknowledge that 'the less Girl Guides are seen marching in public the better'. Despite the mothers' concerns, it is clear that Guiding at this time offered girls an opportunity for adventure, comradeship and greater physical freedom, particularly in the countryside, and that many girls made the most of this chance. In less than three years, the movement had become a national institution. In 1914 Letts published the first Guide diary, production only ceasing in the mid-1980s.

From the point of view of the Guides, the First World War came at exactly the right moment. They were established on a more or less formal footing, but still needed to prove themselves to the public at large. There were 50,000 Guides all determined to do their bit for their country. Although Guides took on all sorts of social service, they were still hedged about with precautions; and care was taken to avoid them having any contact with soldiers. When Olave Baden-Powell wrote in the *Girl Guide Gazette* about useful war work Guides could undertake, she suggested sick visiting, making and serving soup, and knitting socks for the Boy Scouts. Needlework, cookery, and nursing must have seemed a poor sort of war work compared with the more active part being played by the Boy Scouts, but 'A Guide obeys orders', and the work was taken up and performed with goodwill. Guides also fitted out their meeting places as first aid stations, looked after children whose mothers had gone out to work, rolled bandages and collected sphagnum moss, which could be used as a dressing for wounds. Some captains started companies in the munitions factories and told with pride of taming 'rough, wild' girls. A few lucky Guides were employed by the War Office as messengers and typists, but their role was still very much seen as auxiliary and supportive.

Despite this, throughout the war the movement continued to develop and thrive. In 1914 Brownies, the branch for younger girls, was formed. It had also become clear that a branch of the movement would be welcomed for those girls too old to be Guides. This was formed in 1916 and initially called the Senior Guides, although in 1920 they were renamed Rangers, again a name suggested by Baden-Powell, the Chief Scout, who said he had hesitated between Rovers or Rangers for the boys. (Suggestions at a previous committee stage had included the rather sickening Eagerhearts. B-P's knack of finding the right name for things was a great asset to his movements.) Cadet companies, for older girls who were aiming to become captains and lieutenants, were also created in 1916. Sea Guides were added in 1920.

A council was formed as an advisory body, and nothing perhaps more reflects the nature of the society that was about to change forever than the fact that this council consisted mainly of the aristocracy: no doubt also tireless workers among the Guiding community, but one can't help feeling it was their ranks that got them their places: the Duchess of Norfolk, the Earl of Meath, Lord Charles Beresford, Viscountess Wolseley, Countess Roberts, Lady Swaythling. At the end of the list come the two women representing the changing community, those there solely for their achievements: Miss Gray, High Mistress of St Paul's School for Girls and Miss Faithfull, the Principal of Cheltenham Ladies' College. Guiding was certainly respectable now, and the wider community seemed to recognise that Guiding gave girls that extra quality. In a letter to *The Times* in 1917, a vicar praises the courage and steadfastness of the Guides attending a church service he was giving when an air raid suddenly broke out. 'As long as life lasts,' he writes, 'I shall remember with admiration and pride the perfect self-control and cheerfulness of those 80 daughters of England.'

In 1917 Agnes Baden-Powell was appointed President of the movement, under her brother's chairmanship. She was an energetic and, by all accounts, remarkable woman who was an accomplished balloonist, beekeeper, naturalist, musician, linguist and artist. She does not appear to have had great organisational skills, and lacked the thrusting charisma that both B-P and his young wife, Olave, possessed, but she undoubtedly inspired great affection among the early workers for Guiding.

She was however, unlucky in one aspect: B-P's wife was eager to get involved with the Guides as well, and Olave did not take to Agnes. In her autobiography, *Window on my Heart* (1973), Olave frankly accuses Agnes of being a terrible snob who was always snooping, and recounts how she and B-P used to laugh at the handbook Agnes helped to write, calling it the little blue muddle. Agnes in her turn had been outraged at Olave and B-P's wedding when she, the only member of the Baden-Powell family to attend, had not been invited back to Olave's

The Chief Guide visits Luton, 1947.

family home in Dorset after the ceremony but left to return to London by herself. On an equal battleground it is hard to know who would have won, but Olave had B-P's wholehearted backing, and the outcome was inevitable. In 1920 Agnes was given the honorary title of Vice-President, and advised not to take any further active part in Guiding. The official story was that she resigned the presidency in favour of Princess Mary, the daughter of George V and a supporter of the Guides. Agnes remained Vice-President until her death in 1945 but had no further direct organisational contact with Guiding.

In 1918 Olave was elected Chief Guide, and later that year she was presented with a gold version of the Silver Fish, the highest award a Guide could win, conferred by the Guide Association for exceptional services to Guiding. In 1918, B-P also finished the updated handbook *Girl Guiding* to replace *The Handbook for Girl Guides*.

In the 1920s Guiding overtook Scouting in terms of popularity. This may be partly accounted for by the different experiences of the young men and women who formed its leaders. Many young Scoutmasters had died, and others were perhaps disinclined to breed up another generation of ardent empire-loving cannon fodder. But it was different for the women. As Kitty Barne, a talented children's author and winner of the Carnegie medal who was married to Noel Streatfeild's cousin, says in *Here Come the Girl Guides*:

> One eligible man in seven had been killed, one in eleven disabled; the young widows, the girls whose hearts were forever buried 'in a Flanders field', service women who had learnt the pleasures of using their organising ability, and some

of the vast host of voluntary workers who had poured out the energy in a million incessant obscure efforts, all took a look at the Girl Guide Movement. Here was something to 'take up'—everyone was now going to take up something.

Moreover, a generation of girls had come out of the public schools taught to value achievement, but were now expected to yield up their hope of paid employment in favour of the returning heroes. It's perhaps no surprise that voluntary organisations which offered positions of command and executive ability benefited hugely from this wave of energy.

In 1920 the first Guiding international conference was held and heard reports from all over the world of how Guiding had developed, or was making its first tentative steps. In some countries, particularly those which had remained neutral during the War, uniforms were frowned on (Denmark); in others it had become a temperance movement (Serbia) or mainly an athletic one (Romania); Belgium had added an extra Law, that of respecting each other's opinion; in Holland religions mingled freely, but the different classes did not mix. The movement was spreading rapidly throughout the world, something which will be covered in more depth in 'Guiding around the Globe'.

The twenties and early thirties can be seen as the golden age of Guiding. There were still some decriers—in *The Honour of a Guide* (E M Channon, 1926), the elderly Miss Steele, when her niece asks to join the Guides, declares in horror: 'You cannot mean those village girls in most unsuitably short skirts, who play games and make a great deal of noise?' But apart from in the minds of a few elderly diehards, Guiding had entered the landscape of the respectable girl. Beatrix Potter, writing in 1928, summed up the feelings of a generation of post-Victorians who remembered their own stuffy childhoods when she said: 'I wish they had been invented when I was young. All I can do in old age is to lend them camps (and dry blankets) … it is a grand thing to enjoy playing and enjoy work which is what the Scouts & Guides learn to do.'

To be a Guide had become the rule rather than the exception, as a passage in Sybil B Owsley's *The School that was Different* (1932) illustrates. A young girl, Eustacia, has volunteered to do some hospital visiting and is met by a hospital almoner:

> 'I'll take you up to the ward,' she announced. 'It's a shame to ask you but one is always sure of a quick response from a Guide.'
> 'I'm not a Guide,' murmured Eustacia …
> 'Oh no, I forgot. Miss Glynn did tell me. Somehow I took it for granted that you would be a Guide. Which was quite absurd of me for there are lots of fine unselfish girls outside the movement. Tied to home … nursing invalid parents …'

Almost all the big publishing firms for children produced Guide stories. Rudyard Kipling published *Land and Sea Tales for Scouts and Guides* (1923). A Boy Scout helped Lord Peter Wimsey to find a body, and Miss Marple counted Guides among her regular occupations. A new skipping rhyme appeared on English playgrounds: 'I'm a little Girl Guide dressed in blue/These are the actions I must do/Salute to the Captain, bow to the Queen/And turn my back on the boy in green.'

In 1928 the World Association of Girl Guides and Girl Scouts (WAGGGS) was set up, and the basic principles of worldwide Guiding codified: that the members should make some commitment to 'the highest spiritual ideal' (carefully chosen words); to their duty to their country and to helpfulness to all. It was also established that Guiding must be voluntary, open to girls of every race, colour and creed, and non-political. The trefoil was adopted as its badge. To seal the occasion, Olave Baden-Powell was made World Chief Guide. By 1930 the movement reached its peak numbers, with one million members in Britain.

In 1937 the movement, whose membership had started to drop, was given an extra fillip when the young Princess Elizabeth and her sister Margaret Rose joined, and the 1st Buckingham Palace Guides were founded. Their Captain, V M Synge, describes the first meeting in her book *Royal Guides*, when fourteen girls in white gloves, accompanied by Nannies, Mamzelles and Fräuleins, presented themselves. The enrolment ceremony took place inside Buckingham Palace, where Miss Synge was in agonies of dread about a possible meeting between Guide staves and the cabinets of priceless porcelain. Synge tried as much as possible to make the Guiding experience a real one for the young princesses, and describes hiking, camp cooking and Scouting games played in Windsor Great Park. The future queen ended up as the Patrol Leader of the Swallows and gained the Interpreter, Swimmer, Dancer, Horsewoman, Cook, Child Nurse, and Needlewoman badges.

War, however, was imminent, and the membership declining, both in Britain and overseas. Guiding disappeared in Germany, Italy, Greece and Austria. Ever aware of changing times, WAGGGS made the next world gathering of Guides a peace parliament—a 'Pax Ting'—in Hungary in 1939. Guides came from thirty-two countries, the Polish ones with packed rucksacks, ready to hike back over the mountains if the borders should close. Three weeks after the gathering ended, war was declared.

The Second World War offered fresh opportunities to Guides. Membership had dropped to half a million, but those Guides threw themselves into the war effort. The restrictions of the last war were forgotten. Guides served at canteens, helped with evacuees, assisted in hospitals, grew vegetables, collected salvage, raised money to buy air ambulances, even gathered acorns and horse chestnuts to feed zoo animals (freeing up grain for human consumption). They set up camp kitchens to serve food to bomb victims, and by the end of the war were even helping change dressings and give out medicines in some hospitals. During the air raids, Guiders and Rangers drove ambulances, manned first aid posts and assisted the Home Guard. Some won the George Medal or the George Cross for exceptional bravery in carrying on their work during raids, or for rescuing the injured.

In 1941 Baden-Powell died, leaving, with typical foresight, a farewell letter for his Girl Guides. It is quite likely it had been written some years before, as its tone of restraint seems out of key with young women taking active roles in the war: '… you women are the chosen servants of God in two ways,' he urged; 'first, to carry on the race, to bring children into the world to replace the race of men and women who pass away; secondly, to bring happiness into the world by making happy homes, and by being yourselves good, cheery comrades for your husband and children.'

As early as 1941 the British International Commissioner Rose Kerr was thinking about the needs of the world once the war ended. She had the vision of a peace army of Guides who would move in to help relieve the suffering in countries ripped apart by war. Only the toughest Rangers and Guiders were selected to join the Guide International Service. Training included driving and maintaining lorries, basic medical skills, and camping in Welsh hills in midwinter. Questions asked of would-be GIS volunteers in Australia included: 'Could you scrub a hospital floor and wash dishes all day without any food? Can you eat whatever food is put on your plate? Can you stop a bad habit? Do you allow other people's bad habits to annoy you? Can you cut hair, handle a boat, delouse a head?' Teams went out to Greece, Hungary, Holland and Malaya, distributing food and supplies, and the service continued until 1952.

The younger Guides at home and overseas raised the money to finance these expeditions—a stunning £250,000 to start with, all of which, according to Guiding principles, had to be earned or given from their own pockets. 'Guides do not beg,' B-P always said sternly.

In the post-war years Guiding continued to be a mainstream part of British culture; three Girl Guides were introduced into the Rupert Bear stories in 1947 when one wrote to ask Alfred Bestall if he would put her and her two friends into a story; Pauline, Beryl and Janet featured in twenty-one stories in all. (There had previously been a Guide story in a *Rupert* annual in 1936.) The decline in popularity continued, however,

Wedding of Bury Park Brownies' Tawny Owl to the Akela of the Wolf Cubs.

perhaps partly because more women were now working outside the home. Moreover, where Guiding had once been seen as liberation, offering wider horizons and greater freedom, it was now developing an image of being the path of the conformist. In Antonia Forest's superb *Autumn Term* (1948) it is the conventional and rather staid Ann who sticks with Guiding, rather than the heroines Lawrie and Nick.

Guiding had lost its monopoly on the pleasures of organised freedom. In the 1930s Arthur Ransome had shown one did not have to be in a uniform-wearing single-sex organisation to enjoy camping, woodcraft, signalling and outdoor adventure. Other writers such as Malcolm Saville, M E Atkinson and Monica Edwards continued this theme. We learn in passing that Saville's David Morton is a Scout and Atkinson's Jane Lockett a Guide, but these are background details only; the implication is that the movements belong to the organised world of adults from which these youngsters escape into their own independent and adventurous lives. Monica Edwards, who started her writing a little later, in 1947, had been a Guider herself, but does not make either of her capable heroines into a Guide, and the only reference to the movement is that occasionally Tamzin's bed would have passed a Girl Guide test.

Guiding had perhaps started to become almost something of a joke among the post-war generation. It is often portrayed in this period as desperately earnest and rather galumphing. In *Our Hearts were Young and Gay*, written in 1946 although set earlier, two American adventuresses describe their co-travellers on a cruise ship, including '… two extremely hearty English girls with bright pink hands and a vocabulary which seldom exceeded the bounds of "I say!" and "Right-o". We dismissed them as a couple of Girl Guides in mufti …'

Within its ranks, however, the organisation concentrated on establishing the great worldwide movement on a yet firmer footing, with many energetic women working at the administration of what continued to be a voluntary movement. The end of the war with its restrictions on clothing and materials was taken as an opportunity to change the uniform, which had already undergone several mutations from the broad-brimmed hat days. In 1946 the old overall (sometimes called a dress) was replaced by a neat bright blue shirt-blouse and skirt, and a beret, later still replaced by a brimless 'air hostess' style hat. The Guide staff, beloved of the early Guides, had disappeared.

The Queen became the Patron of the Girl Guide movement with her sister taking over the Presidency when Princess Mary died in 1965. However, the disaffection with Guiding as an occupation, at least for older girls, was growing as something else was being discovered: teenagers. The Guiding movement has always evolved and responded to change, and in 1964 a committee was formed to suggest how Scouting and Guiding might become more up to date. In 1966, after careful consultation with Guides at every level, the 'Advance Party' of the Girl Guide Association voted to make some key changes. The ten Laws were reduced to seven (there are now only six) and greatly simplified. Those stern words beloved of the Edwardians— honour, duty, loyalty and purity—were excised from the Laws, replaced by the more contemporary equivalent virtues of honesty, helpfulness, reliability and respect. The Tenderfoot, Second and First Class badges were removed in favour of an eight point programme.

The movement has steadily embraced change over the years to keep it in step with modern times. As stated, there have been several redesigns of the uniform; and in 1987 a section for girls from 5–7 was introduced, called Rainbows. In 2002 the Guide Association chose the new operating name of Girlguiding UK. In 2007 the Scouts admitted girls for the first time, but this did not affect the continued single-sex status of the Guides. Today the average member is younger than in earlier days, but the Association is still the largest female-only youth organisation in the UK. 50% of British women have been involved at some point in their lives. 125,000 girls aged 10–14 are Guides, 20,000 Rangers (14–25) 250,000 Brownies (7–10), 80,000 Rainbows (5–7); and 100,000 volunteers help run the packs and companies.

As *The Sunday Times* commented in January 2009: 'For all the sophistication of the *Heat* generation, there's no escaping the fact that the old Baden-Powell formula seems remarkably resilient.' What Guiding offers may have changed; modern Guides are taught credit management and self-esteem alongside camping and first-aid skills; but the ideals of helping young women reach their full potential as fit, responsible and helpful members of their community still hold and continue to work their appeal on successive generations of girls. Ironically, in an age of health and safety directives, and a world where parents have once again, for different reasons, begun to worry about letting their daughters out alone, Guiding can offer girls the same freedoms they discovered in 1910: an organised but not over-protective way to have adventure, give service and live the outdoor life, just as B-P planned for them.

GIRL GUIDE FICTION: AN OVERVIEW
1912–1966

Hilary Clare

In the half-century after the founding of the Girl Guides, over two hundred stories for girls were written which, in whole or in part, treat with the movement. Books were provided for all ages, dealing with Brownies, Guides and Rangers, usually with an indication in their title of what the reader could expect. Sometimes Guiding was only part of a regular school story and therefore was not mentioned in the title (as, for instance, in Dorothea Moore's *Brenda of Beech House*), and conversely 'Guide' sometimes appears in the title but in fact bears little relationship to the plot (as with the same author's *Guide Gilly, Adventurer*).

This chapter will look at the development of the Guide and Ranger story (but not the Brownie books, which are necessarily for a younger readership), survey the major contributors to the genre, and plot its decline in the 1950s and 60s.

The first Guiding book, as is well known, was Dorothea Moore's *Terry, the Girl-Guide*, published by Nisbet in 1912. Dorothea Moore was a thoroughly professional author who researched her subjects and deliberately piled on adventure and dramatic moments to keep her schoolgirl audience's attention. Her books range from the school story pure and simple, so to speak, through historical romance to Ruritanian adventure, but when it came to Guiding there is no doubt that she knew her subject from the inside. Between 1918 and 1927 she served as a Guider in Eastbourne, and her practical knowledge underpins her writing. *Greta of the Guides* (1922) is dedicated to 'our first Patrol Leaders in the XIX Eastbourne' and includes a detailed account of the things needed to pass the Tenderfoot test. Greta admittedly ends by winning a Silver Cross for gallantry but she does not also become a First Class Guide and Patrol Leader, Moore keeping firmly within the possible if not the entirely probable. *Greta of the Guides* is, despite its name, effectively a school story on the theme of scholarship girl wins through, with Guides being a useful way of countering snobbery.

Guide Gilly, Adventurer (1922), as we have mentioned, has no official Guide input at all: Gilly is indeed a Guide, but the book is a Ruritanian adventure. No doubt Gilly's admirable handling of all her difficulties is due to Guide training, but one cannot help suspecting that her story was so titled because it first appeared (entitled *Guide Gilly, Adventuress*) in *The Guide*. *Brenda of Beech House* (1927), on the other hand, has considerable Guide input into what one might term a reversed Ruritanian school story: Brenda is a princess who is sent to an English school and finds her feet due to Guide involvement. As in *Greta of the Guides*, there is some good detail of actual Guiding, and in many ways it is a far more convincing story than Moore's famous—or infamous—*Judy, Patrol Leader* (1930).

That was one of Moore's last books (preceding *Sara to the Rescue*, 1932, whose heroine is also a Guide), and it is perhaps charitable to assume that it was written when she was in poor health; indeed, given the complexities of its publishing history it seems likely that it was originally written as three short stories which Collins (as they did with some Oxenham titles) then cobbled together as a book. Even so, that does not excuse Judy's over-the-top paragon capabilities and behaviour, which contrast rather unfavourably with those of some of her rather more realistic Guiding contemporaries.

Just how early Moore was involved in the movement is not known, possibly not by 1912, when Terry and her friends get their Guiding out of *The Handbook for Girl Guides* and are as amateur as the first Girl Scouts until Captain Evelyn, VC, takes them in hand. Just as unofficial are Aggie and her 'amateur patrol' in Brenda Girvin's *The Girl Scout* (subtitle *being the Adventures of Aggie Phillips and her Amateur Patrol*, 1913), another book by an established writer whom one may suspect of knowing a good idea when she saw one. Aggie and the other girls are in direct competition with the local Scouts (of whom Aggie's brother is one) and end up by retrieving some missing silver and vital blueprints; they are then firmly issued with Guide uniforms and equipment and brought sharply into line, 'members of that great body of Girl Guides which is being formed throughout the kingdom. Even as England has need of her men, so England has need of her women.' Emphasis is laid on the nursing skills girls will acquire: in these early years there was a nervous tendency on the part of the movement to stress the thoroughly womanly nature of Guides' pursuits, to allay parents' worries about their little ladies becoming thorough tomboys—ironically, since it was undoubtedly the excitements of tracking and camping and so on which were attracting the girls themselves in such numbers.

Girvin followed *The Girl Scout* with *Betty the Girl Guide* (1921) and *June the Girl Guide* (1926), which sound suspiciously like the same book re-titled (but are not); Guiding was for her only one among several plot devices, and apart from being an early exponent of Guiding fiction Girvin is not especially significant. Her career demonstrates the kind of altruistic nature which would lead her younger contemporaries to embrace Guiding: one of her interests was raising money for the League of Mercy via her magazine *The Jabberwock*.

The Girl Scout was uncannily prescient in stressing the need there was going to be for competent girls in the years to come, since it was published the year before the Great War. In the same year came A M Irvine's *Nora, the Girl Guide*, again a book from an established author seizing eagerly on potential good material. Nora is a shocker, rebellious and frivolous, but is redeemed spectacularly by Guiding. By the end of the book, and achieved in only the last third of it, Nora has become an exemplary Guide, saved life, been awarded the Bronze Cross, and finally, though without much detail, become a Silver Fish. The tone of her school has improved beyond recognition, and, as the headmistress concludes at the end of the book, 'I think I may say that if the day should ever dawn when all English schoolgirls become Girl Guides—it will be a happy day for England!'

Nora places so much emphasis on school life, albeit with Guiding as a dominant element, that we may suspect that A M Irvine herself had school rather than Guiding experience, and the dedication of the book ('To my friend M Upsher Smith who helped me to collect the material for this story') rather supports this—Matilda Upsher Smith is listed in the 1911 Census as an assistant in a school in Deal, where Irvine was then living. Irvine's Guides apparently belong to a single patrol (the Veronicas), rather than being a company with the several patrols which their numbers surely warrant, and there is no clear system of advancement beyond vague talk of a 'ladder'; *Nora* therefore belongs to a very early stage of the movement and

must very rapidly have seemed out of date; for this reason it is interesting as a portrait of a transient phase of the movement.

Irvine does not display any more knowledge in her other Guiding book, *Naida the Tenderfoot* (1919), which is largely concerned with the growth of responsibility and unselfishness in Naida herself, who is a thoroughly unpleasant piece of work in the beginning and whose mother has to be brought to the point of death before she can be fully redeemed: '… Naida the Tenderfoot … had, through a long and arduous training, come at last into possession of her own soul. It was worth more than if she had gained the whole world.'

A similarly religious note (Irvine was a clergy daughter, and it shows) is introduced into Constance Gregory's *The Castlestone House Company* (1918), where the heroine is only allowed to be confirmed when the accusations made against her have been shown to be false. The book is subtitled *a School Story of Girl Guides* and is very much of its period, with an infamous French Swiss (or is she really German Swiss?) Mademoiselle as the villain of the piece. It seems to be the author's only book, and was serialised in the *Girl Guides' Gazette*. Significantly, it was illustrated by Joyce Bruce, who had early been associated with the movement and whose own only book, *The Twins to the Rescue*, came out in 1923; it had previously been serialised in *The Guide* (sequel to the *Girl Guides' Gazette*), which explains why the twins of the title had to be Guides, although the book is really a holiday adventure story with no real Guide input at all. (Bruce wrote no other books, Guiding or otherwise, but has attained fame as the illustrator of Violet Needham.)

Moore, Girvin and Irvine were girls' writers who made good use of new material, Moore going on to become a Guider and, as we shall see, continuing to use the movement in her works. Constance Gregory was the first of what we may term the 'Guider writers'—writers who wrote as Guiders, initially perhaps to amuse their own companies but primarily to promote the movement. Almost all the early writers of fiction in *The Guide* seem to belong to this category, and by the mid 1920s several of the leading examples of this kind of author were well into their stride, H B Davidson and F O H Nash from 1923 and Mrs Osborn Hann from 1924. M Vera Armstrong, who as Vera Marshall edited *The Guide* between 1930 and 1934 (having been sub-editor 1928–30), was a slightly younger example, her only pre-1939 book being *The Quest of the Sleuth Patrol* (1931), but she later produced *Rival Camps* (1950) and *Maris of Glenside* (1953), as well as Brownie books.

The Guider writers' work is briskly competent, if not now particularly enthralling, and gives a fair, although naturally biased, view of Guiding in the 1920s and 30s. Davidson's work encompassed Brownies and Rangers as well as Guides and is mostly single books.

Hann most notably produced the 'Peg' series, taking working-class (in itself an innovation) Peg from being an 'ordinary' Guide through the various stages of lieutenant, captain, marriage and motherhood; also an innovation was her use of photographs of real Guides (presumably of her own South London Company) as illustrations. Nash had a series featuring Audrey, taking her up to Sea Ranger level, and several singletons. Davidson went out of production in 1940; Nash, with a break between 1936 and 1948, went on until 1952; Hann continued writing Guiding fiction until 1951. In 1934 she collaborated with Owsley, a friend from her schooldays, on *Three Guides Adventuring*, and, interestingly, was given credit by Owsley for her input into the latter's *M is for Mary* (1923): 'You girls who read this book have, of course, your own special school chums. I think it will make you doubly interested to know that it is to one of my school chums that you owe a great deal of *M is for Mary*. Some of it was thought out by her when she was a girl at school like you are. If you like Mary please give a vote of thanks to Dorothy Hann, the school friend of several years ago who created her.'

Owsley and Hann were both born in 1883 and both educated at Sydenham High School—early examples of the kind of girl who was to take up Guiding with enthusiasm as soon as it became available. Owsley and Hann, of course, did not have that option, but entered the movement as adults. Owsley's books tend to set their Guiding interest in the context of school and have good, realistic settings—unfortunately, perhaps, at the expense of her plots. Her Guides improve in character rather than engage in melodramatic life-saving—only two lives are saved in the course of her work, which betokens a rare self-restraint on the author's part. Her personal involvement with Guiding seems to have been to run a Brownie pack, and she contributed almost as many Brownie as Guide stories.

Hann is the only writer of the inter-war period who focuses exclusively on working-class Guides. Other writers introduce them, sometimes rather perfunctorily, to demonstrate that part of the Guide Law which states that 'A Guide is a friend to all and a sister to every other Guide', but their heroines are definitely middle class. Similarly Janet Aldis, whose one Guide book, *A Girl Guide Captain in India*, came out in 1924 (and, like Hann, has a photograph of a real Guide as an illustration), disappoints slightly by relating the story of a white Guide Company; Indian Guides in their white saris edged with blue or yellow are mentioned, but only in passing; the book, a first-person narrative in the form of a long letter to a friend (or perhaps a sister, since the book is dedicated to Aldis's own sister), appears to be fact very slightly dressed as fiction; it concludes with the Company's attendance at the Prince of Wales's review of Scouts and Guides in Madras on 16 January 1922.

By far the best of the writers who do introduce working-class girls into their cast of Guides is Winifred Darch, not only a prolific writer of school stories and a High School mistress but also a Guider. Had she written no more than her five Guide-based books (*Poppies and Prefects*, 1923; *Cecil of the Carnations*, 1924; *Gillian of the Guides*, 1925; *Cicely Bassett, Patrol Leader*, 1927; and *The Lower Fourth and Joan*, 1930) she would still deserve to be remembered as one of the best writers for girls of her period; as it is, the Guide books represent just over one fifth of her distinguished output. (This does not take into account her numerous short stories, some involving Guides, all published in Oxford annuals.)

Darch's Guide stories, by and large, fall into the general pattern of her work, which almost overwhelmingly looks at questions raised either explicitly or indirectly by the various tenets of the Guide Law, principally obedience and sisterhood. Her heroines are most typically older girls who are in positions of authority or influence within their schools but who, for one reason or another, lack the full backing of the powers-that-be, either because their own wild youth is against them or because the school powers themselves are, to say the least, misguided. (No pun is intended, but in fact the conversion to Guiding of the head or another mistress is often the result of the heroine's stalwart behaviour.)

Cecil of the Carnations, although the second of Darch's full-length Guide books to be published, began as a short story of the same name two years earlier in the Oxford *Golden Book for Girls* in 1921; the story deals with the central episode of the book, where Cecil, who has obeyed orders not to attend a long-anticipated party (because of the danger of infection), shields her slightly estranged friend Nina, who did go (or, at least, arrives at the party; in fact she leaves immediately) and who will suffer far more than Cecil from the consequences of being expelled. The book, in fact, turns on the question of whether a Guide's honour is to be trusted, with the clear rider that anyone who is not a Guide (like the false friend who is happy to drop both Cecil and Nina into trouble) is almost certainly dishonourable. The full-length version traces Cecil's development from a harum-scarum to a girl who comes to take both her Guiding and her school responsibilities seriously; Darch rightly saw the possibilities inherent in the short story and made the most of them.

Poppies and Prefects focuses even more on obedience, again within a school context but directly involving Guides, since Margaret Stevenson, whom we first meet as Patrol Leader of the Poppies, on holiday in Normandy, goes back to school the following term as Head Prefect with the task of pulling up school discipline, allowed to grow slack under her predecessors. Meriel, her chief antagonist, is an unsatisfactory member of her patrol, taking poorly to any kind of criticism or correction, and continues to defy Margaret, and indeed to undermine her, at school. Well worked into the plot is the difficulty the elder girls feel *vis-à-vis* some of the staff. As Margaret says to her sympathetic Guide Captain and maths mistress:

> '… lots of mistresses expect you one minute to act like a grown-up person and know exactly the right thing to do, and the next expect you to be like a small child and not use your reasoning powers at all. Miss Asbury [the headmistress] will always see our point of view, even if she won't always let us follow it—and you are like that, too, and let us explain things; but other people say—or if they don't say they look as if they thought—"You are a very impertinent child. How dare you have ideas of your own?"'

Margaret has a point, and plenty of right on her side, but she also has to learn tact and to handle people more gently than comes easily to her. It is made clear that it is Guiding which provides the stiffening and code of conduct which the school needs to function well as a community, and the obedience which Margaret can exact from her patrol is a significant factor in her reclaiming of the school to law and order.

The same theme is developed most memorably in *Cicely Bassett, Patrol Leader*, which involves one of Darch's favourite motifs, the headmistress with wrong ideas, which she was to use again in *Gillian of the Guides*, and with great comic effect in the non-Guiding *Alison Temple, Prefect*. Like *Poppies and Prefects*, *Cicely Bassett, Patrol Leader* opens with an extended section involving a holiday in Normandy. This time it is only Cicely who is having a fortnight in Rouen with her elder sister. In the same *pension* they encounter a group of girls dressed artistically in pale blue djibbahs and floppy hats; Cicely begins to make friends with

one of them, Vanna, and also observes the striking Sidonia, clear leader of the group, clandestinely partaking of a restaurant supper after the inadequate vegetarian fare provided at the instance of their headmistress. On the return to England, inevitably, the djibbah party turn out to be the school which Cicely's new headmistress has brought with her to incorporate into the High School. Miss Popham has Ideas about school discipline (as about many other things) and introduces a School Court to oversee discipline; she would also prefer the girls to join her own Society of Torchbearers (not unlike the Camp Fire, though carefully distinguished from it) and abandon Guides. The Guide Company, of which Cicely is Leader, has unfortunately lost its Guiders, and there seems little prospect, in view of Miss Popham's distaste, of finding replacements.

How Cicely maintains school discipline by careful wielding of her power as a patrol leader (thereby, incidentally, showing one of the mistresses the use of the movement and converting her into the new Captain), managing not to run counter to her new headmistress's decrees while still refusing to give way to Sidonia's devious attempts to oppose her, makes an excellent story, and if Miss Popham is a little exaggerated— well, that is what the plot demands, and Darch, like Cicely, is scrupulously fair about her.

Gillian of the Guides has another, much more low-key, headmistress with wrong ideas, in this case a relatively new head who decides to appoint her Head Prefect on academic achievement rather than character. Everyone has expected Gillian to get the position; in fact it goes to Ivy, who is not only shy but also a scholarship girl who is placed at a definite disadvantage by some of her snobbier middle-class peers. *Gillian of the Guides* is as much a book about a scholarship girl as it is about Guides, but of course the tenet of the Law which states that 'A Guide is … a sister to every other Guide' comes into prominence. Gillian herself loyally backs up Ivy, thereby coming into conflict with her erstwhile friend Phyllis—shown, of course, to be a poor Guide. The book deals well with a problem which must have been far more in evidence than Guide literature would suggest; only at the end, when Gillian deliberately sacrifices her own chance of an art scholarship to allow Ivy to gain *her* chance of an academic one, all so that Phyllis, suffering from a feverish cold, shall not be left alone in camp, is there a slightly overdone element of melodrama.

These four stories form a group spanning some six years at the beginning of Darch's writing career and probably also cover her Guiding period. (Loughton High School, where she taught for some twenty years, was one of the earliest schools to have a company, and Darch became involved out of necessity rather than personal inclination.) *The Lower Fourth and Joan* did not appear until 1930, and then takes a rather different slant. Joan is a much younger heroine than her predecessors, and for most of the book is for family reasons excluded from joining the Guides, which she very much wants to do. Three levels of Guiding—and indeed of school— are contrasted: Joan herself and her fellow fourth-formers, especially Joan's 'twin' Prudence

Waring and spoilt Chloris; Patrol Leader Tony, a prefect; and Patricia Waring, Prudence's elder sister, a former Head Prefect and star Guide, who returns to the school at short notice to take over from an inadequate mistress. The book is in fact quite as much about reforming the slack ways of the school as it is about bringing back the zest into Guiding. Interestingly, it represents what must have been a common problem of the period (and indeed was to remain one): Guides are no longer exciting. Gone is the early thrill of stalking and camping and doing what the boys were doing; instead, the school company of *The Lower Fourth and Joan* has spent too much time on signalling and company drill. Tony, one of the few left with 'real' Guide spirit, reminiscences about Patricia Waring's time as a patrol leader: 'She made you feel that Guides were really alive, not just a series of occupations and badges and observation games … nor the sort of horrible little pieces of perfection they are in so many stories—quite enough to put ordinary people's backs up.'

Joan, who tries hard to be as much of a Guide as she can, is certainly not a little piece of perfection; she does take part in her form's 'barring out' (a piece of rebellion neatly dealt with by Tony and the prefects), and she behaves fairly idiotically, if from the best of motives, when Prudence is suspected of causing a rick-yard fire. When she does, in the best traditions, Save Life, it is by raising the alarm and then by getting a rope to the right place, not by personally going down the cliff, and even Tony, though she acts fairly heroically, is not the last to leave the danger-point and is in fact responsible for her patrol's being in peril. The contrast with Moore's *Judy, Patrol Leader* could hardly be greater, and it is tempting to wonder whether Darch had that piece of perfection in mind, since the short stories on which *Judy, Patrol Leader* is based probably precede its publication in volume form in 1930.

By 1930 the Guide genre was well established, to the extent that non-Guide authors were jumping on the bandwagon. Ernest Protheroe, that indefatigable male writer of girls' school stories, had contributed several, writing both as the winsomely named Alys Chatwyn (*Two Schoolgirl Guides*, 1924) and as the more sober Phyllis Hanley (*Winning her Way, Girls' Grit* and *Bridget of the Guides*, 1924, 1926 and 1927). In 1932 another male author, Reginald Callendar, produced *Pamela, Guide and Captain, a story for Guides*. The Rev Mr Callendar (incumbent of Tidcombe and Hipperscombe with Fosbury, Wiltshire) at least had the excuse of writing for his wife and her Guide Company, but the book is poor for all that, and not even much about Guides, certainly not about Pamela as a Guide Captain.

A much better book written largely from the Guider's point of view (again about a Pamela) is Margaret Middleton's *The Guide Camp at Herons Bay* (1927). Middleton, who was herself a Guider, produced another four Guide stories (*The Guide Adventurers*, 1929; *The House of Golden Hind*, 1930; *Three Girls and a Car*, 1931 and *The Island Camp*, 1935), but *The Guide Camp at Herons Bay*, her first, has a particularly refreshing realism about it. For instance, on the second day of camp, Pamela, the young Guider, wakes early to the sound of rain. Suppressing an impulse to go back under the blankets, she looks out of her tent:

> It was barely dawn. The field and camp were outlined with drab harshness and everything looked unspeakably cold and wet. As Pamela sat on her bed pulling on a pair of gum-boots, she heard a sudden thud just outside and her tent shook violently. It was Leff, who had stubbed her bare toe against a tent peg in the half light and fallen against a guy-line. Pam crept out to find her standing on one foot and holding the other with both hands.

'"A Guide smiles and sings under all circumstances",' whispered Pam.

'I hate you!' muttered Leff, with intense sincerity in her voice.

'Nothing to what you will in a minute,' retorted Pamela. 'None of those wretched tents are trenched!'

We can feel no doubt at all that Margaret Middleton had been to camp, and enjoy her admission that even Guiders are human—something that all too many writers, with their super-competent young women in charge, seem reluctant to do.

In one of the cross-references with which Guide stories are interlaced, Middleton's dedication in *The Guide Adventurers* reads: 'To V M Methley this stepchild of her own is gratefully dedicated.' Violet Methley was a prolific rather than a talented writer for girls, but her output did include *The Bunyip Patrol, the Story of an Australian Girls' School* (1926), which has at least the merit of originality of setting. *The Windmill Guides* (1931), which seems originally to have been titled *The Windmill Patrol*, and *Mystery Camp* (1934), are much more run of the mill (no pun intended). Not much is known of Methley's life, but in the 1930s she was certainly in London, though living in Hendon, whereas Middleton was with her family in Ealing; it is not known whether Methley had Guiding experience or where her and Middleton's paths had crossed. Much later, in 1956, Methley's *Mystery Camp* and Middleton's *The Island Camp* joined Marjorie Taylor's *With the Speedwell Patrol* in Blackie's *Girl Guide Story Omnibus*.

Marjorie Taylor's three Guide stories, *With the Speedwell Patrol* (1938), *Prior's Island* (1939) and *The Highland School* (1940), all have the Scottish settings appropriate to her own background and Guiding experience. As with so many authors of the second rank, her plots rely heavily on coincidence and melodrama, but her writing has been described as 'balanced and compassionate' and the books as enjoyable. Presumably the Second World War took her away from writing, and it is possible that she may have emigrated to Australia after it, in company with the brother with whom she had been living.

Of the same period were Joan Herbert's school-cum-Guides books, *With Best Intentions* (1935), *The Trail of the Blue Shamrock* (1937), *The Three Halves* (1937), *One's a Pair* (1939) and *Jennifer Gay* (1944). Little is known about Joan Herbert, but she was London based and apparently closely involved with Guiding; she was presumably the Joan Herbert whom *The Guide* of 19 October 1939 reported as having joined the AFS (Fire Service), so that war service explains the cessation of her writing.

Guiding was introduced into the background by a number of writers not generally associated with the movement, but who were all professional writers interested in girls and used whatever material was to hand. E E Cowper's *Corporal Ida's Floating Camp* (1920) is her only Guide story as such, but she introduces Guides as characters in *The Mystery of Saffron Manor* (1921), *Wild Rose to the Rescue* (1922) and *Cross Winds Farm* (1927). Marjorie Royce produced *Eileen, the Lone Guide* (1924), and E M Channon *The Honour of a Guide* (1926). Despite its title this last is the story of a girl who wants to be a Guide but is prevented by her elderly great-aunt, who thinks the movement desperately unladylike; paradoxically Ethne is a talented needlewoman (usually a gift bestowed on the gentlest of girls). She determines to be a Guide at heart, even if she is not allowed to join her local Company, and this resolution sustains her through all her trials.

Nancy Hayes, whose writing career was cut short in her forties by her death from cancer, included four Guide stories in her output: *The Plucky Patrol* (1924), *Meg-All-Alone, a Girl*

Guide Story (1925), *The Caravan Patrol* (1926) and *The Guides at Calamity Hill* (1927), all competent if not especially memorable.

Christine Chaundler, another professional, produced at least three Guide stories: *Bunty of the Blackbirds* (1925), *Jill of the Guides* (1932) and *The Amateur Patrol* (1933). There is no evidence of her practical involvement with the movement, but in her handbook *The Children's Author: A Writer's Guide to the Juvenile Market* (1934) she remarks that 'Guide stories are popular' and lists *The Guide* among the periodicals accepting children's stories with a firm caution:

> Wants short stories … of adventure, school or Guide interest … Also uses serial stories, similar settings … Has opening for interesting, informative articles … on all subjects of interest to schoolgirls, and to girls just embarking upon their careers. It is, however, essential that these be written from practical experience.

Chaundler was certainly professional enough to take her own advice, and astute enough to tap into any popular interest. *Bunty of the Blackbirds* is a competent enough tale of the dud recruit who kyboshes her patrol's chance of winning the camp competition but nevertheless displays sterling worth; perhaps there is a thought too much emphasis on gaining marks, and a little too little on the sheer fun of Guiding, not to mention its real ethos, but the book was popular enough to be reprinted several times, Collins taking it over from its original publisher Nisbet and eventually putting it into their Children's Press imprint.

A Guide to the rescue
(*Bunty of the Blackbirds*)

Of the 'Big Five' school story writers (Brazil, Bruce, Brent-Dyer, Oxenham and Blyton), only Brent-Dyer seems to have had anything to do with Guiding, and only she and Oxenham contributed anything to the Guide genre. Oxenham, in fact, dealt with Guiding comparatively early, with *The Tuck-Shop Girl* in 1916—typically it had to be given the subtitle of *A School Story of Girl Guides*. Two years later, with *The School of Ups and Downs* (1918), she foregrounded the differing attractions of Guiding and Camp Fire, she herself being heavily involved in the Camp Fire movement and evidently finding Guiding, with its more structured approach and quasi-military discipline, definitely less appealing, as we shall see in 'Guides round the Camp Fire'. The same theme runs through *Patience Joan, Outsider* (1922), and in a sense she returned to it in *The Crisis in Camp Keema* (1928), where the heroine has to leave the Camp Fire (for the time being) and enter Guiding for the good of the school. After the early books Oxenham does not actually write much about Guiding as such, and it is clear that she had no inside experience of it. In 1933 and 1934 she produced two 'Jinty' sequels to *The Tuck-Shop Girl*, and thereafter she certainly mentions Guiding, in that her girls and young women are often said to be Guides (for instance, Joy Marchwood/Quellyn of the Abbey series becomes a Ranger captain), but she never again wrote anything which could remotely be described as a Guide story (*A Divided Patrol*, 1992, was of course a posthumous publication). For her, Guiding is only one way of occupying girls' time, not an alternative life ethic.

Brent-Dyer, on the other hand, was a Guider herself for a short time (Captain, 3rd South Shields Rangers, in 1926, and later of Hereford Rangers) and her Guiding stories more or less correspond to this period: *Judy, the Guide* came out in 1928, and there are a few Chalet School stories with Guiding input around the same date, notably *The Rivals of the Chalet School* in 1929 and *The Chalet Girls in Camp* in 1932. After that, even in wartime, she made little use of the movement, no doubt because she was no longer actively involved.

The major school story writer who did deal seriously with Guides was Ethel Talbot. No trace of her involvement with Guiding has yet been found, and from looking at the content of her books is seems quite possible that she was not an active Guider, but she clearly had a good idea of the movement and at least troubled to research the subject. Her *Peggy's Last Term*, published in 1920, is set during the First War (with the school being bombarded as the climax), and is thus among the first ten Guide stories; Peggy's determination to turn over a new leaf and become a 'good' Guide (as opposed to one who merely has a lot of badges) is the crux of the book, making it the earliest example of a girl getting back to the true spirit of the movement. As one of Peggy's friends remarks:

> 'Still, you've always been a jolly good Guide. *Could* have been, I mean, if you hadn't— Pardon, old thing, I mean you've got loads of badges and things, though our patrol did cut a pretty poor figure in the review.'

After this Talbot seems to have been more interested in Sea Rangers. *Jan at Island School* (1927), for instance, is dedicated to 'the Sea Guide Crew of the *Audacious*, North Berwick', and *Skipper and Co* (1929) 'to all Rangers, but specially Sea Rangers All' (apparently not a reference to her own book of that title). The books which feature them are more inclined to be adventure stories involving Sea Rangers than be about them as Rangers. This is true of several of her other books about Guides or Rangers: typically, a girl will, at the outset of a book, be described as a keen Ranger, but will then spend the rest of it meeting her troubles on her own and without a company. All too often, in a phrase which is characteristically Talbot, she is said to have her smile 'tied on behind'—presumably in the manner of a surgical mask.

Were it not for *Peggy's Last Term*, Talbot's books might be disappointing when viewed as Guide stories: in her later books Guiding provides an indefinite flavour rather than a major ingredient. But *Peggy* is an important Guide story and, with Talbot's many short Guide stories, puts the writer among the top authors of the genre.

By the 1930s just a hint of disillusionment with the movement was creeping into girls' books, possibly not as much as was actually felt, since most Guiding fiction was written by enthusiasts, who naturally tended to belittle the opposition. Margaret Masterman's *Gentlemen's Daughters* (1931) is not, strictly speaking, a school or even a girls' story: it was the author's first work, published when she was only twenty-one and still a Cambridge undergraduate. (She was to produce only two more novels, and then move on to philosophy.) *Gentlemen's Daughters* charts the progress of Joan's relationship with 'Jakie', an ugly but charismatic teacher somewhat in the Brodie model, whom she first (like nearly everyone else) adores and strives to please but gradually realises is completely selfish and self-centred. Guiding is only part of this, but is used with some detail as it is the first thing that shows up Jakie's obsessive desire to win, even at the cost of cheating. The fascinating thing is that it is possible that the school Masterman attended was also where the Guide writer E M R Burgess, then Miss Archibald, ran a company, at exactly the time Masterman was there (though as Burgess was also running one at the High School in the same time it is possible she was teaching there rather than at Masterman's). As Miss Jackson leaves to marry a civil servant, and Burgess apparently left on marrying a civil servant, one does wonder whether, in spite of the usual disclaimer at the beginning of *Gentlemen's Daughters*, Miss Jackson owed something to her. Was 'Jakie' a substitute for a real-life 'Archie'? The tone of the book is of course completely different from those written for girls, in that it admits the possibility that Guiders are fallible and some people—even 'good' Guides—offensive.

There is a shorter, though funnier, Guiding episode in Joan Coggin's novel *"And 'why' not Knowing"* (1929), when girls who have recently left Wycombe Abbey are talked into starting a Guide Company. Their startled first encounter with a Guiders' meeting, when the young and middle-aged enthusiastically take part in 'Kangaroo Tails', is splendidly comic, and the account of the (fairly disastrous) enrolment of their first Guides is, one feels, more true to life than the regulation moving experience of many Guide stories. When one realises that Joan Coggin was the real name of the school story writer Joanna Lloyd, author of some of the funniest passages in school literature, the humour of *"And 'why' not Knowing"* is scarcely surprising. She introduced Guides in a more orthodox fashion into *Betty of Turner House* (1935) and into the first of her 'Bramber Manor' series, *Catherine Goes to School* (1945). Joan Coggin had been a Girl Scout at Wycombe before Guides had even been invented (she was born in 1898), and went on being involved in the movement in adult life, but her dedication to it did not prevent her from seeing its funny side. Betty develops from a spoilt only child into a pleasant, reasonably competent person who has not shone at anything but has learned that the world does not revolve round her; Guiding is part of the process, and teaches her perseverance as well as practical skills—even if she does flavour the stew at camp with Jeyes fluid … Catherine, academically brilliant and practically hopeless, takes her Guiding seriously but, as usual, incompetently—the chapter describing how she is passed from one group to another as the Company prepares to take part in the competition for the County Shield ('I don't think you had better be in the Drill division, Catherine') is vintage Lloyd in her best deadpan vein. In the other Bramber books Lloyd does not feature Guiding at all, which is curious considering its importance in *Catherine Goes to School*, but in that book she has plenty of Guiding detail, including a long passage explaining the ideas behind it, and shows how the movement could unite girls from very different classes: it is the one thing the Bramber girls find in common when their visitors from the slums come to spend a day.

This sisterhood of all Guides was a message strongly proclaimed by Catherine Christian, perhaps the most quintessential Guide writer of them all. Again and again in her books Guiding brings together girls of different social stations; again and again, moreover, it is the 'working-class' girls who have something to teach the girls from 'good' backgrounds, who almost always turn out to be incompetent practically. Further discussion of Christian's work will be found in the chapter devoted to her, but she holds an important place in Guiding fiction not only for her own books but because she herself edited *The Guide* between 1939 and 1945. Her books became doubly important in the 1950s because several of them went on being available as

Blackie reprints, sometimes updated, at a time when other Guide fiction had largely disappeared. Nancy Breary's *It was Fun in the Fourth* (1948) has a Guiding element, but in the post-war years Guide fiction definitely became a niche market. Antonia Forest's *Autumn Term* (1948) is one of the very few examples of mainstream girls' fiction to include Guides. J M Page contributed the excellent *The Three Elizabeths* (1950) and *The Twins on Trial* (1951), and Mary K Harris *Henrietta of St. Hilary's* (1953), but these seem to be among the very last of the genre.

After 1950, in short, Guide books were Guide books and girls' books were girls' books and the two were no longer written by the same people. Some Guide authors ceased publishing during the Second World War, no doubt because of war service and occupations as much as paper shortage, and did not resume afterwards, but a few returned to the field. M Vera Armstrong continued, as, briefly, did Mrs Osborn Hann; Ivy Middleton, who had only started in 1937, began a new series to follow the (presumed) success of her earlier books about the Pimpernel Patrol. C R Mansell (*The Ragtail Patrol*, 1948, *The Littlest Guide* 1949, *Curlew Camp*, 1954 and *The Swallows See it Through*, 1955) began her writing career with Guide books to make use of her own experience, following the advice of the best handbooks for young authors. By the time of Ivy Middleton's last book, *The Poppies and Mandy* (1966), the cover is showing Guides in the new 'modern' uniform and the Guides are concerning themselves with raising funds to send a handicapped child (still, in 1966, 'spastic') to a special school.

But the writing was on the wall. The Guide market can never have been extensive—the movement did not provide 'rewards' in the way that Sunday Schools did—and by the mid-60s the genre was neither supported nor, perhaps, needed. *The Guide* itself ceased publishing in 1969, and though it had its successors their fiction distinctly lacked lustre. Blackie had in the 1950s reprinted some earlier Guide stories (notably Catherine Christian), even producing two Guide omnibus volumes, but did not continue the practice.

Thus the genre which had been launched with a bang with *Terry, the Girl-Guide* petered out with barely a whimper. In its heyday it had faithfully reproduced the excitement which the first couple of generations of Guides had enjoyed and had then, as Guiders and authors, tried to pass on to their more sophisticated juniors. Given a boost by the moral climate of the Second World War, it had a final burst of activity immediately afterwards—Forest's *Autumn Term*, of course, is distinguished by any standards—and then ground to an inevitable halt. 'Girls' books' as such were out of fashion; teenage problem novels were not going to deal with such questions as which kinds of wood were best for a camp fire or, indeed, how to remain pure in thought, word and deed. There was no way forward for it to develop, and insufficient audience for publishers to boost it. The Guide ethos was simply too much at odds with the popular climate of the late twentieth century for its fictional existence to survive. No author of the likes of Jan Mark or Jean Ure or Anne Fine (let alone Jacqueline Wilson) seems to have been sufficiently involved with the movement to consider writing about it. Guiding fiction as a genre in effect belongs to the thirty years between 1919 and 1949, and if there are very few books in it of pure literary merit, there are a great many which in their time served their generation well and now, in ours, serve to reveal their generation to us. Theirs was the generation which survived, and won, the Second World War, and it is ironic that the freedom they fought for resulted in their daughters and granddaughters largely rejecting the values which had enabled them to do it.

SERVICE

'The Girl Guides are a sisterhood of service; their whole aim and purpose is summed up in that phrase.'

The Oakhill Guide Company, Felicity Keith, 1933

Alongside the games and the woodcraft, the ideal of service was at the heart of Guiding, and many books exemplify this, often by making their Guides finer people than those around them. B-P's *Scouting for Boys* opens with the words: 'I suppose every boy wants to help his country in some way or other.' Many writers emphasise the point: 'The idea behind it is, of course, the aim behind the jolliness. We are making our world wider, you know, by learning to be of some kind of service to the world; and as there are Guides all over the world, we all feel linked up.' (*Ranger Rose*, Ethel Talbot, 1928)

Good deeds, whether the daily good turn or a protracted project, form the theme of much Guiding fiction. In Ivy Middleton's *Triumphant Pimpernels* (1939), the Guides visit an elderly lady weekly, collect Christmas parcels for poor families, assist daily in a small shop whose proprietor is nursing a sick sister, go carol singing to raise funds for charity, and crown their achievements by presenting the elderly lady with a wireless to relieve her lonely nights.

What constitutes a good turn can reflect the political and social sensibilities of the time or the author. In Brenda Girvin's *Schooldays* (1930), one Guide renders service by preventing an attempt to start a strike. In Sibyl B Owsley's *An Absent-Minded Schoolgirl* (1930), the Brownie pack which Guide Rosemary is assisting decides to send money to unemployed miners: 'There's lots of sad things about mines,' regretted Brown Owl, 'and one of the saddest of all at present is that there are many mines which do not pay.' None of these good turns sounds beyond the bounds of possibility for a team of teenage girls. Catherine Christian's girls, however, are often given tougher challenges: in at least three books they undertake to *build* or restore a house.

In Joanna Lloyd's *Catherine Goes to School* (1945), service is put to the public school girls, who are considering joining Guides, as part of the concept of *noblesse oblige*:

> 'Why are a few people in this world picked out to have easy pleasant gracious lives, while the majority scramble through as best they can? … Do you feel conscious of being better than the rest of the world? I hope you don't, because you are not. No, so far as we can see there is no particular reason for it. It is not your fault, either, though. You need not be ashamed of it, so long as you realise the enormous responsibility which it entails …

'The Girl Guides are a number of people banded together, who have promised to help other people at all times. I don't for a minute think that Guides have a monopoly of service, or that people who are not Guides cannot serve just as well, but I think it makes it easier to most of us ordinary people to belong to a big movement and to make a solemn promise, rather as the Knights of the Round Table used to do …'

With the desire to give service, of course, comes the need to train for it. The speaker continues:

'… the Third Law is: "A Guide is useful and helps others." Well, with the best will in the world, we can't be useful if we don't know how, so we learn to stop bleeding, to cook a dinner, darn stockings, wash clothes, mend an electric light fuse, clean and turn out a room, look after sick animals, and a thousand and one other things. But whatever we are learning to do it is all part of the great adventure and fitting us for our life-work, which is Service.'

The motto, Promise and the Laws embody the spirit of service. The Promise commits the Guide to do her best to serve God and her country, and keep the Laws. The Laws define what a Guide is: she is trustworthy, loyal, useful, a friend to all, courteous, kind to animals, obedient, cheerful, thrifty and pure. The Guiding ethos informs and underpins most Guiding fiction.

'You see—one doesn't bleat all the time about the Promise and the Laws, but they're always *there*, somehow, in the background, something to measure life up against, a standard to go by.'
The Marigolds Make Good, Catherine Christian, 1937

TERRY, THE (FIRST) GIRL GUIDE

Wendy Ingle

Dorothea Moore's *Terry, the Girl-Guide*, the first full-length book to feature the new Girl Guides, was published in 1912. I was therefore somewhat confused to discover that my copy had several references to the Great War. Did Moore have remarkable foresight, or was my bibliography of Guide fiction wrong?

Fortunately another copy came up on eBay very soon after I realised something was amiss. There on the title page, quite clearly, it proclaimed that it had indeed been published by James Nesbit and Co Limited in 1912. All the mysterious references to the Great War, and to developments in the Girl Guide movement, had disappeared. The obvious conclusion was that Dorothea Moore later rewrote the book. I have not been able to date the later edition, published in the Haversack Library, but internal evidence (which will be discussed as we come to it) shows it cannot have been rewritten before 1918.

Terry is one girl among five brothers, and her story begins as her brothers march away 'in all the businesslike glory of Scouts' uniform' to a fortnight's camp. Only once they are out of sight does she let her disappointment show. 'Oh, I wish I wasn't only a girl!' she says to herself.

Despite the fact that her brothers treat her as one of themselves, she accepts her lot as a girl, happy to admit to her father that 'I want to sew your buttons on, yours and the boys,' but feeling that alone is not enough. She wishes she could 'do something for one's country too'. A comment on Terry's general untidiness leads to Father reminiscing about Nurse Fleur-de-Lys; a story Terry has evidently heard before. He relates how he first saw Nurse Fleur-de-Lys on the battlefield:

> 'I shall never forget the look of her … She was a French girl, though she had trained at an English hospital [so that's all right, then!], and she had hair of the kind you only see in French girls, silky black, just touched with gorgeous copper in the sun. It was her hair I saw first, with a pitiless sun burning down upon it, and it was brushed and coiled as shipshape as could be under her nurse's cap. And her dress, with its red cross on the sleeve, and her apron, were both spotless, and she looked as cool and untroubled, kneeling there beside me with the Mauser bullets shrieking all around her, as though she were in her drawing-room at home. That was how Nurse Fleur-de-Lys looked, Terry, when she came to the help of young Arden, who had just discovered that the chap he had risked his life to save would bleed to death long before he could carry him into safety if something wasn't done soon.'

In the descriptions that follow we find the first difference in the two versions. In 1912 Terry knows that the retreat in which Father had been injured was 'far away in South Africa'. In the later version it is just 'where the fighting was', and Father is on 'the plain', rather than 'the veldt'. The 'pitiless sun' shines down unchanged.

This emphasis on the neatness of Nurse Fleur-de-Lys in the midst of a battle may seem

odd, but a similar insistence on grooming is found in *The Handbook for Girl Guides* (1912), with the author explaining that Guides have 'silky hair' and nails that 'shine like pink shells'.

Terry, wishing she could repay the French nurse for saving her father's life, writes in her pocket book:

> It is a Debt of Honner to do anything one can for Nurse Fleur-de-Lys or Mr Arden whenever one finds them.
> Sined. Terry Vaughan.

(Odd that she can spell debt, but not honour.)

Fortunately Terry's father has arranged to take her on holiday to Brittany, so that she will forget about missing her brothers. At the quaint hostel at which they stay is a mysterious young girl, known as La Pétite [*sic*]. Terry is told her 'mother died only a fortnight ago, and Mère Babette is looking after her till her people turn up'.

Major Vaughan plans to teach his daughter to swim while they are there, but before he can, on the first day, she witnesses two children in difficulty in the fast current. Terry stands helpless, knowing neither how to life-save nor how to render resuscitation. Father rescues La Pétite, but the other child, a young boy known as 'petit Pierre', is drowned. Terry feels 'as though she were a blot on England. Two people had been drowning before her eyes, and she had been able to do nothing—nothing except fetch father.'

La Pétite, inevitably, turns out to be Lys, the orphaned daughter of Lieutenant Arden and Nurse Fleur-de-Lys. The Vaughans sweep her up and carry her to England to go to school with Terry. Terry is in awe of the heroism Lys apparently showed in attempting to rescue Pierre before she herself got into trouble, but Lys goes red whenever her heroic rescue attempt is mentioned.

Lys is not the only new girl. In the next cubicle is the delightful character Penelope Calcot, whose father is a 'power in the press'. Penelope writes poetry. The first poem we are treated to is called 'Nashonall Decadence'.

> The splendidness of England,
> It was a splendid kind,
> But it will be Ainshunt History soon,
> If we don't mind.
> Young men and maidens, learn some sense,
> Oh! beware of nashonall decadence.

This might be only a quirky piece of character detail if it were not for the words of 'Pamphlet A', one of the two small publications which B-P wrote to help set up Girl Guides in 1910. The opening lines are:

REASONS FOR THE INSTITUTION OF GIRL GUIDES

Decadence is threatening the nation, both moral and physical; the proofs are only too plentiful. It is preventable if taken in time. Much of this decadence is due to ignorance or supineness of mothers who have never been taught themselves.

(The words appear in a slightly different form in the Girl Guide official history, but this is how the first pamphlet phrased it.) Decadence and degeneration of the race were powerful concerns at the turn of the century and among the reasons for the institution of Scouting and other youth training schemes.

Continuing Moore's theme of heroism, the school is thrown into paroxysms of hero worship when old girl Mary Mainwaring visits. After taking her degree at Oxford she had married a major and gone with him to India. Hearing that her husband was gravely ill in the frontier hill fortress he commanded, she had put together 'such medical comforts as were possible' and hurried there to nurse him. Finding a third of the garrison ill, Mary undertook to nurse them all, but then hillmen attacked.

When a relief column arrived at last they found 'the hospital, with one wall gone, beside which Mary had been kneeling in company with a Lee-Metford rifle, defending her sick'. Thus relieved, Mary put down her rifle and went back to making poultices.

Terry has the temerity to ask about Mary's heroism, but Mary tells her it was only the doing of 'everyday things'. 'It doesn't *make* a good nurse or sick-cook of you to be popped into a hill-fortress with people's lives paying the price of your mistakes: the making has to come first … I very much doubt if it is the opportunity that makes the heroine; it is the opportunity coming to people who are ready for it.' Once again Terry learns that preparedness is what is necessary if one is to be of use.

Terry ponders deeply on this lesson and at last proposes to the First Form: 'Girls can't be scouts, I suppose, but Hendrika says Gytha knows all about the Girl-Guides, because her sister is a captain in them. They get ready; they won't have to keep out of the way because they're no use if the big thing comes.'

So persuasive is Terry's oratory that the First goes at once to ask for the help of the Head Girl, formidable Gytha. She sends them away to prove their interest in serving the Empire.

Penelope's idea is to bring the 'power of the press' to bear, but since the Sixth will not accept the contribution of a first former in the school magazine she proposes they produce their own First Form paper, *Vox Populi*. As for editor, '… of course [she suggests] it would be better to choose those of you whose fathers happen to be editors, but anyone who doesn't mind the trouble will do.'

'The First Form did not seem to run, in general, to editorial fathers;' so Penelope finds herself in charge. Terry is deputed to write down what she had said to the First about becoming Guides.

This part of the book throws up some more textual differences; some of them useful for dating the Haversack edition. A list of those to be admired—'You want to be somebody awfully great—in the Sixth, or C B Fry, or the Kaiser, or a leading actress'—becomes 'in the Sixth, or

Armstrong, or the Chief Guide, or a leading actress.' C B Fry was a cricketer who captained England and Surrey, and an all-round sporting hero. He was at the height of his fame from 1907 to 1912. Armstrong is probably the legendary (and opposing) Australian cricket captain Warwick Armstrong. He led his team to eight straight Test victories, a record that stood for many decades. He thus (as my informant put it) eclipsed Fry in the popular consciousness of the era. Olave Baden-Powell became Chief Guide in 1918. While it is no surprise that the Kaiser ceases to be a heroic figure after 1914, perhaps it is surprising that he was one in 1910.

The original First Form newspaper has articles about women's suffrage, but, suffrage having been granted in 1918, Penelope's assertion that 'they should have the vote' has to become the much weaker 'they should be all professions' [sic].

While the Sixth, to their discredit, laugh at Penelope's efforts, Gytha is impressed enough to include the article about Guides in the Manor School magazine, with an introduction that states that 'intending applicants for the Girl-Guides might apply to her!' An interesting footnote here—in 1912 Gytha writes to the headquarters in Victoria Street; in the later version she has to write to Buckingham Palace Road, where headquarters still resides.

In 1912, they are able to form the single patrol of Daisies and be enrolled at once. In the later edition they have to form a patrol of 'prospective' Guides, and find themselves a captain. The make-it-up-as-you-go-along days of Guiding were giving way to more rules and regulations.

In 1912 Gytha presents Terry and her patrol with a copy of *The Handbook for Girl Guides*. This is the little blue book subtitled *How Girls Can Help Build the Empire*, written by Agnes Baden-Powell, based on *Scouting for Boys*, and published in 1912. In the later version the handbook is *Girl Guiding*, written by Baden-Powell, and first published in 1918. The price has risen in the few years between editions from one shilling to two shillings.

Moore gets herself in the greatest muddle when the eager First Form start to dye their clothes to provide a uniform. It changes from khaki to navy in the rewrite but since Moore seems to have attempted to revise without disturbing the pagination, the girls still have their discussion about what a dreadfully ugly colour khaki is before Terry reads out the uniform requirements. Having established that the girls will dye their own blouses and ties, Moore slips up and has them buy khaki Dolly-Dye in both versions.

This difficulty in expunging the khaki is redeemed by the sentiment with which Terry ends the session. '"And if we haven't got quite everything a proper Guide should have," she added, "the thing that counts is being it, not looking it."'

Terry and Co throw themselves into learning all there is in the handbook. They meet a one-armed hero, Captain Evelyn, VC, who not only teaches them but also provides a patrol meeting place in his home nearby. In the 1912 edition he tells them, 'I *do* happen to know something about tests—I was through Mafeking.' In the Haversack version this becomes: 'I was a Scoutmaster before the War.'

In a frantic climax to the story, Evelyn's home is attacked by strikers, who think he is harbouring a hated mill owner, and is set on fire. Terry, recalling that he keeps a box of gunpowder in his workroom, rushes in to save the box. Clutching her Guide badge in her hand, and singing 'God Save the King', she fights her way out through smoke and flames. Penelope, on a high place, is able to send Morse smoke signals for help to the newer Guides in the school. And Lys, a poor athlete in Terry's eyes, nevertheless runs with a message. This emergency does not find them unprepared—Terry is brave and determined, Penelope is a doughty signaller, cheering herself with 'Theirs not to reason why' as she works, and Lys is ready to put a twisted ankle and her own urgent business aside, boosted as she is by Terry's unwavering belief in her heroism. Thus the Daisy Patrol saves not only Captain Evelyn's home, but also his mysterious visitor—not the mill owner but an unnamed royal personage. The near-collapse of part of his home reveals a lost fortune, too.

All of the textual differences noted so far seem minimal—too trivial, one would think, for a rewrite. But in the final chapter great swathes of text have been changed. In 1912 this final chapter is 'The Little Bronze Cross'. On the last day of term the Manor Guides represent three-quarters of the school, and are to be reviewed by 'The Hero'—a figure who is never named or described in the book. 'Everyone,' we are told, 'was wildly anxious to pass their tests and arrive at the dignity of being First Class Guides', so that 'a goodly number of First Class badges shone conspicuously upon left arms' when the day comes. '[T]he original Lone Patrol which made its way against the stream wore proudly displayed the "Order of the Silver Fish".' This was the highest award a Guide could achieve, originally awarded for winning every proficiency badge except Sailor and Signaller,

Terry braves the fire in the workroom

'which are extra' ['Pamphlet A']. Considering the amount of signalling those early Guides practised, the omission of the Signaller badge seems odd. The fish symbolised one who was willing to swim against the tide, which the Lone Patrol had certainly had to do.

At the end of the review in the 1912 edition Lys and Penelope are called up to stand before the Hero, and each is presented with 'a little gilt wreath on a white ribbon', the Badge of Merit, an early Guide award. But Terry's reward is to be greater. The Hero tells the assembled school: '"Terry Vaughan rose to receive that royal visitor Opportunity … It has been decided to award her the Bronze Cross for saving life at great risk to her own." … "The Bronze Cross—the greatest honour a Girl Guide could have."' Presenting the award, the Hero tells Terry: 'Go on as you have begun.'

The differences in the Haversack edition are considerable, and this I believe is particularly why the story was rewritten. Guiding had been established eight years or more, and it had evolved its programme of training and reward and had its second handbook published. No longer can half the school attain First Class in such short order. By the time of this second edition the fifty girls are merely ready to be enrolled. The great Gytha is only a patrol leader, albeit 'exceedingly efficient', not a captain, and Gytha's older sister has been drafted in as Captain. Moore, by now a Guide leader herself in real life, describes the enrolment in stirring terms as 'girl after girl' marches forward to make her 'threefold pledge' and to be told in a 'ringing proclamation' that she is 'now a member of the sisterhood of the Guides'.

The Badge of Merit has disappeared in the later edition; Penelope and Lys are merely honoured by a handshake from a commissioner—and Terry wins the 'Nurse Cavell Badge for special pluck and calmness in danger' instead of the Bronze Cross awarded to her in 1912. The Nurse Cavell badge, named after the British nurse who was shot for helping Allied soldiers escape, was introduced by the Guide Association in 1918, and only used until 1928.

Not one of the girls in the Haversack edition holds the Silver Fish. The new version makes a better story because if Terry and her friends could achieve all that so quickly one has to ask what then would fill the remainder of their time as Guides? The first real Silver Fish were awarded to PL Nesta G Maude (who went on to found the Lone Guides) and PL Rotha B Lintorn Orman in November 1911. By the end of 1913 there were still only eleven holders of the award. Conditions for its presentation were changed in 1917, so it became an award for those who had given exceptional service to the Guiding movement, and in the Haversack *Terry* all mention of it is gone.

Gone too, in the Haversack edition, is The Hero. In 1912 the chapter begins: 'It was the last day of term, and it was a memorable day. For a great soldier, whose name the Manor School had long venerated with a distant worship, was actually coming down to review the Manor Guides, which stood now for three-quarters of the School.' Stiff as the plot is with heroes, The Hero is not Captain Evelyn, VC (who, one might feel, is hero enough), nor his mysterious royal visitor, returned to witness the enrolment of the Guides. I cannot help but deduce that The Hero is meant to represent Baden-Powell himself. In 1912 he was a national hero, famed for the defence of Mafeking, and also for the foundation of Scouting. One wonders why Moore dropped him from the later edition where a commissioner is the grand personage reviewing the school.

By 1918 Moore was herself a Guide officer and would have seen it as important to reflect the changes in organisation. *Terry* was, after all, also a propaganda tool. Agnes Baden-Powell herself wrote a foreword (although one early edition credits the introduction to Lady Baden-Powell on the title page, which must have considerably annoyed Agnes); 'Here,' Agnes wrote, 'is a book giving the key to all the mysteries of the Girl-Guides' pursuits, and I expect this delightful *Terry, the Girl-Guide* will have a great vogue.'

For all the curious changes brought up by comparing Moore's two versions of *Terry, the Girl-Guide*, one thing remains constant throughout: the message of the need for preparedness. It is illustrated by its absence, when petit Pierre is drowned, and in its presence, both in the example of Mary Mainwaring, and in the climactic deeds of Terry and her patrol.

I thoroughly enjoyed becoming acquainted with the gallant Terry and her friends. Their determination to Be Prepared for service to their country surely reflects the ardour of the real pioneering Guides. Penelope sums the sentiment up in another of her inimitable verses, inspired this time by the school's heroine Mary Mainwaring:

> 'Ye maidens of the Manor School, with loving hearts and true,
>   Come listen to a story which shall be told to you;
>   Come make a circle round me, and mark my tale with care,
>   A tale of what a woman dared, and what we ought to dare.'!

FRIENDS AND SISTERS TO ALL?
Social Class in Guide Stories

Helen Vincent

One of the most striking elements of the Girl Guide movement was that it offered—indeed insisted on—interaction between the classes, as witnessed by the Fourth Guide Law. In its best-known form it simply stated: 'A Guide is a friend to all and a sister to every other Guide', but its earliest version was more explicit: 'A Guide is a friend to all and a sister to every other Guide, no matter to what social class the other belongs.'

In the early twentieth century, this was still a radical idea. Previously, organisations for girls had been regarded as the domain of the lower orders, with their elders and betters serving as leaders rather than participants, and this was reflected in fiction. There was a clear divide between books aimed at the young ladies who taught Sunday Schools, and books for the children who attended them. In Edwardian England the largest society for girls was the Girls' Friendly Society, with over one and a half million 'associates', established in 1875 within the Church of England. Charlotte M Yonge, leading author of Victorian books for girls, had featured this organisation prominently in her later novels such as *The Long Vacation* (1895), where membership of the GFS is a clear indication of upright moral character in a working-class girl. In Yonge's novels, the middle-aged spinster Miss Jane Bohun, younger daughter of a baronet, is presented as an admirable if bossy woman who is a very active leader in her local GFS—but there is never any thought that Miss Bohun's nieces, the protagonists of these books, should join such an organisation and mix with their social inferiors.

Guiding was different. Its early enthusiasts insisted on doing things in exactly the same way as Boy Scouts, including the adoption of the Laws originally penned by Baden-Powell:

> A scout is a friend to all, and a brother to every other scout, no matter to what social class the other belongs. If a scout meets another scout, even though a stranger to him, he must speak to him, and help him in any way that he can, either to carry out the duty he is then doing, or by giving him food, or, as far as possible, anything that he may be in want of. A scout must never be a SNOB. A snob is one who looks down upon another because he is poorer, or who is poor and resents another because he is rich. A scout accepts the other man as he finds him, and makes the best of him—'Kim,' the boy scout, was called by the Indians 'Little friend of all the world,' and that is the name which every scout should earn for himself.
>
> *Scouting for Boys*, 1908

These ideas were incorporated directly into the Guide movement—and into books about Guides. Women who wrote about Guide companies began to use the theme of Guides as 'friends to all' to tell new kinds of stories. Some were determined to showcase Guiding's ability to bridge the gaps between the social classes, while for others the idea of being a 'little friend of all the world' offered romantic possibilities to the storyteller. In the process of telling

from *Nora, the Girl Guide*

these stories, Guide authors brought working-class heroines centre stage for the first time in fiction which had previously been very much the domain of middle-class young ladies as both the subjects and readers of the books. But the way class appears in these stories can also show the cracks between the ideal of the Fourth Law and an author's own bias towards a belief that some classes were, indeed, superior to others.

The revolutionary impact of the idea that Guiding meant an end to class divisions can be seen in one of the earliest novels to feature the movement, *Nora, the Girl Guide; or, from Tenderfoot to Silver Fish*, by A M Irvine, published in 1913. This book marks the first appearance of a plot which was to be used in Guide school stories for years to come: a schoolful of slack, snobbish girls who think nothing of lying their way out of trouble are transformed by the Guide sense of honour into keen, upright, honest young women of whom their school and country can be proud.

The whole of Chapter XII of *Nora*, 'Guide Law', is devoted to a scene in which the charismatic local Captain answers the girls' various objections to the ideas of the Guide movement. One such objection is to the Fourth Law, precisely because of its egalitarianism, but Miss Baldwin offers an eloquent defence of the principle very much along Baden-Powell's lines:

> Don't you almost think that anyone, whether a duke's daughter or a sweep's, who kept these rules, would be worth having for a sister? It's too late in the day for us to pretend now that because we happened to be born in one family instead of in another, we are a different sort of animal entirely! No, no, we're all the same flesh and blood, and have no more right to despise those who are poorer than those who are richer. That does not mean that we have the same social obligations, for that is nonsense. But we have all one common humanity, and the best and noblest people in the world are those who recognise it, and live up to it!

While this quite overcomes the girls in this particular discussion ('Fanny dropped her eyes. She could not withstand sentiments like that!'), the issue of class comes up again when the conversation turns to practical Guide activities. Another girl objects to having to learn 'making beds and lighting fires' because, as Miss Baldwin ironically notes, they 'can't be of any mortal use to ladies'. But here she gives an interestingly different justification of such tasks:

> There are such things in the world—thank God!—as women in high positions who do not feel degraded by such simple little services for their fellows, and

there are vast numbers of ladies—as you call them—who think it is their duty to know how things ought to be done, by experience, *in order that they may be able to direct others*, besides being able to fill any post in emergency. [My italics]

In real life, independent school Guide companies saw themselves as producing these kinds of leaders: the *Jubilee Book of the Clifton High School* (1927), for instance, describes how this school's Guides went on to become leaders of other companies serving girls from less fortunate areas of the city. This idea that Guiding could train young ladies to become leaders would be repeated by other authors as well, as will be seen.

However, in *Nora*, Guiding does not reinforce social distinctions but breaks them down: when she is told again that 'no Girl Guide must ever be a snob', Nora replies that 'we're all snobs, every one of us', because the boarders look down on the day girls, who come from mere shopkeeping families as opposed to the more exclusive circles of the boarders. While Nora herself soon sees the light and becomes a Guide, accepting the Guide insistence on equality and hence, ultimately, unifying the day girls and boarders together, her villainous rival Averill refuses for a long time to become a Guide precisely because it would involve consorting with those social inferiors, the shopkeeping day girls.

Dorothea Moore's *Greta of the Guides* (1922), dedicated to 'our first patrol leaders in the XIX Eastbourne', has as its heroine a girl Averill would despise: a working-class girl who wins a scholarship at a large public school, where she encounters Guiding for the first time. Greta's various mishaps at this school come from her fish-out-of-water status. How will she manage at school to learn the social graces of the upper classes and yet retain an honourable affection for her humble origins?

This is one of the few school stories published in book form, as opposed to a magazine story, where the scholarship heroine is not from impoverished gentility but is really working class. It seems at first glance as if Moore here is on the side of our humble heroine, but on closer examination she is doing something rather different. Greta herself, anxious about her social status, is a snob. She has already turned down the chance to join her home company of Guides because 'the Lanes—such little pigs!—were in, and Mother wouldn't let me if that kind was to be my associates'. Here Greta shows us how much she has to learn—not just social interaction, but also better grammar.

The girl to whom she makes this comment, Betty Curwen, is baffled by it, and it is Betty who emerges as the real heroine of the book. She befriends Greta, bravely saves at least two lives (this *is* a Dorothea Moore story, after all), and is the person who brings Greta to an understanding of what Guiding really means. Betty readily accepts Greta's background, and tactfully tries to help her adjust to life at school. But Betty is also Lady Betty Curwen, younger daughter of the Marquis of Cunover, and in her we see the power of Guiding to produce a young leader of the Empire. Betty is not praised for her brave self sacrifices—she is expected to be quietly capable, like the long line of her heroic ancestors. And her kindly impulse to befriend Greta can easily be seen as *noblesse oblige*, particularly when Betty is seen in the setting of her ancestral home with her benevolent parents over the half-term weekend. The whole family share Betty's friendly acceptance of Greta, and all respond with nothing but polite kindness when they discover that Greta's sister happens to be their housemaid. Cynical housemaid Evie has a different take on Guides—'Well, I daresay it's very nice for them that has time … Lady Betty hasn't got her living to make, you remember that … Lady Betty, when she grows up she'll go to dances and races, and Hurlingham, and all that. She won't have time to go on with Guides, you'll see.' But Betty's grown-up sister Katherine proves Evie wrong: she spends her time working as Captain of a local company rather than living the life of a Bright Young Thing.

Greta of the Guides

Betty and Greta's friendship can be read both as a positive depiction of social equality and as an example of how Guiding can provide young ladies like Lady Betty with a way of leading their humbler sisters, just as men like those in the Curwen family lead their troops in the service of the Empire (we hear for instance of the war service of Betty's brother and father). Moore never explores the contradiction between these two ideas. Greta may be working class, but Moore shows her family as the loyal servants of their local gentry, living in a cottage tied to the Big House. Greta's parents never question the superiority of the ruling class, nor does Greta, and nor, ultimately, does Moore.

Other books also reflect this idea about Guiding providing a platform for those of superior social status to lead. Elsie J Oxenham's books show organisations like Guides and Camp Fire allowing girls of different classes to come together on equal terms—but in *The Abbey Girls Play Up* (1930), when Joy and Jen discuss whether Joy should become a Guide leader, Jen points out that Lady Joy Marchwood, doyenne of Abinger Hall, is certain to 'become District Commissioner. You know you'd be asked at the earliest possible moment.' This is not because of Joy's leadership qualities or expert Guide skills, but because her title and prominent status as a member of the local gentry would make her the natural choice for the role. Perhaps a trace of the same attitude may be seen in a post-war book by Mrs A C Osborn Hann, *Five in a Family* (1951). The 'five' of the title are the children of the local manor house, and though their mother, unlike the Marchioness of Cunover, doesn't play lady of the manor but concentrates on running her own house without domestic help, eldest daughter Pat is still the competent born Patrol Leader.

For those authors who did not want to wrestle with the thorny question of social class and the sisterhood of Guides, fictional school companies offered a way to write about Guiding without having to negotiate questions of class. In this context, the idea of 'friend and sister to all' was most often worked out in a plot about how joining the Guide Company enabled a troublesome or unhappy pupil to fit in to the school ethos, as in Nancy Breary's *It Was Fun in the Fourth* (1948).

For others, the 'sister to all' idea was expressed in somewhat romantic encounters with the humble poor, particularly Gypsies, who could generally be relied on not to join the school company and complicate matters. Ethel Talbot borrows Kipling, as quoted by Baden-Powell, to provide the chapter heading 'Little Friend of All the World' for an incident on the theme of the Fourth Law in *Betty at St. Benedick's* (1924). The school company's Guide Cup is stolen, and Betty's patrol go on a tracking mission to see if they can recover it. Some of Betty's friends think that the local Gypsies have stolen the cup, but they are mistaken. 'It was evident that these were a party of proud and respectable working-people.' It is Betty who saves her friends from getting into trouble for their mistake, because before she came to school and joined the Guides, she had helped one of the Gypsy mothers and her baby. Thus she is able to apologise to the Gypsies on behalf of her friends:

> 'I wouldn't, and not one of us would, even think you'd taken our Cup. We're Guides, and we're friends of all the world, you see—at least we'd like to be—and if we've done anything unGuidy, we're very sorry.'

As Patrol Leader Sybil says, 'Betty was "Guidy", as you called it, then—even before she knew us, or joined the Daisies.' Talbot's interest, however, is really in her schoolgirl heroine and not in the 'world' she is so eager to befriend, and this incident is there to show that in spite of Betty's many other mistakes she has the true Guide spirit and deserves to belong to the school company.

Perhaps the most interesting way the concept of 'sister to all' was worked out in a fictional school Guide company was in Elinor M Brent-Dyer's Chalet School books. In *The Chalet School and Jo* (1931), a group of mischievous juniors find runaway Biddy O'Ryan and decide to 'adopt' her. Of course their exploit is discovered, and then their elders must address the question of what will happen to Biddy. Will she go to the local children's home? How could the school possibly support her? Head Girl Jo dismisses both the idea that Biddy would be an appropriate companion for her adopted sister Robin, and the 'toshy' suggestion that she would devotedly serve Robin as a lady's maid (and here Biddy's 'brogue', said to be the main objection, obviously stands for all the social differences between the middle-class schoolgirls and the daughter of a maid and a chauffeur). In the end it is Frieda, one of the Austrian girls, who suggests that the school take care of Biddy—but 'Let us do it as Guides!'

While it's the Chalet School ethos of being an international family as much as the Guide notion of being 'friends to all' which leads to Biddy being 'adopted' by the school rather than being sent to an orphanage, it's perhaps the Guide notion of being sisters 'no matter what social class' which allows Biddy, once adopted, to be swiftly treated as a schoolgirl on the same footing as everyone else. She ends her career completely assimilated by both Brent-Dyer and the Chalet School into the inner circle of characters, first becoming a popular teacher and then receiving the final seal of authorial approbation when she marries a doctor.

For a more realistic portrayal of what Guiding could offer the normal working-class girl, we must turn to Mrs A C Osborn Hann, whose stories deal with the 'ordinary life of an ordinary girl', as she says in the dedication to *Smiler, a Girl Guide* (1925). Dedicated to the Guides on whom her stories are based, and surviving in copies often presented to actual Guides, Mrs Hann's books focus on 'ordinary' girls who range from the daughters of clerks to those who would today be classed as socially excluded. Smiler, for instance (real name Gwendolen Alicia, perhaps noteworthy to Malory Towers fans), first appears in a scene where she returns to Walworth after a camping trip to discover that, not for the first time, her alcoholic father is so

The real-life Peg   Podge (*Captain Peg*)

violent that her mother won't let her enter their rooms. Left to her own devices, Smiler heads for the local rectory where she knows she will get a friendly welcome, and spends the night camping in its grounds.

Mrs Hann's most notable Guide books are based around the fictional world she first wrote about in *Peg's Patrol* (1924), telling stories about a group of Guides in the slums of 1920s South London, where she herself was vicar's wife and Captain of a Guide Company. At a time when most books for girls were written by, for and about the middle class, her books stand out for their difference. Eve Garnett's *The Family from One End Street* (1937) has been claimed as a milestone in the realistic depiction of the lives of 'ordinary' boys and girls in children's fiction: Mrs Hann predates Garnett by over a decade with her stories of working- and lower-middle-class Guides, never caricaturing their speech in the cockney dialect so often found in books of this period. She provides a naturalistic, unpatronising depiction of girls who have to spend a large proportion of their time helping with the housework in tiny houses or rented rooms in grubby run-down slums, with no modern conveniences. Her heroines have to leave school as soon as they turn fourteen, visit the Labour Exchange and head straight for the nearest factory floor. Hann's central heroine, Peg, works in a bottle factory; in *The Pluck of the Coward* (1926) it is friendly Guide Emma who helps Hope tackle bullying co-workers at a nut factory; and the long commute almost causes Smiler to lose her job in a large West End store. Compared to contemporary books for girls where fourteen-year-olds are carefree Middles with no greater anxiety than whether or not they get caught during their midnight feast, the Peg books give a window on to a dramatically different world which reflected the lives of thousands of working teenage girls in the inter-war years.

The roots of Mrs Hann's books in Victorian stories about poor orphans and melodramatic slum scenes are evident. For instance, Rhoda, in *Rhoda the Rebel* (1925), is the daughter of a burglar who trains her to break into people's houses and steal for him. In a scene straight out of *Oliver Twist*, she is caught red-handed by the vicar who had offered a shelter to Smiler, the first step on her road not to finding a rich benefactor but to redemption when she joins the Guides. But Mrs Hann's pragmatic heroines have more in common with the twenty-first century girls created by Jacqueline Wilson than with Victorian moppets. Timid Hope, in *The Pluck of the Coward*, spends most of the book suffering nervous agonies over one crisis after another, but through Guiding learns to be brave rather than go to pieces. But she will still have to return to the job, the workplace bullies, and the unhappy home she has left behind.

When Peg's patrol goes camping, in the book of the same name, they meet 'what St Martin's Guides would have called a "posh school company"'. Peg forms a friendship with the Honourable Viola, daughter of Lord Lenox. Where Lady Betty Curwen had been the natural leader in her friendship with Greta, Peg is as capable and as natural a leader as Viola, encouraging her own girls to compete against Viola's in a cricket match while well aware of their lack of training compared to the posh schoolgirls. As her friendship with Viola develops over several books, she robustly insists on their equality as Guides while dealing with the differences in their social status, as when Viola invites Peg's patrol camping: 'The only thing you've got to remember … is that Viola's a Guide, and so are you! I bet you she doesn't once make you feel she's any higher or better than you are. What about the Fourth Guide Law …?' (*Rhoda the Rebel*) As an adult, when she moves to the country Peg surprises her village relations by forming friendships with the vicar's wife and doctor's daughter, and explains that it is Guiding that makes these friendships possible.

In portraying the lives of 'ordinary girls' on their own terms, Mrs Hann introduces something to British children's literature which had previously been lacking. It would not have been possible for her to do this without the Fourth Guide Law and the idea that a Guide is 'friend to all, regardless of her social class'. Guiding was never intended to cause a social revolution, but once writers started to put the Guide principle of disregarding social class into their books, they created a space in girls' stories where traditional assumptions about class were challenged and working- and lower-middle-class girls were given a central place of their own and, sometimes, allowed to speak for themselves.

SISTERHOOD

'Belonging to a family of a million certainly tends to broaden one's outlook.'

The Marigolds Make Good, Catherine Christian, 1937

The Fourth Law is probably the one most frequently cited in Guiding fiction. As Puck in Joanna Lloyd's *Betty of Turner House* (1935) puts it: 'It … does away with different classes and all that bilge.' In Josephine Elder's short story 'Sisters—skin and all' (*Guiding Stories*, undated), Alice, an inner city slum dweller, has befriended another Ranger who is a junior doctor. They find each other at camp, where 'you could only tell by their voices which girl belonged to which group'. Guiding links them together, and after Alice tracks the other's stolen car she is rescued from her cardboard box factory to become Erica's chauffeuse and handywoman.

Some writers show how sisterhood only goes so far. May Wynne, whose writings often deal with snobbery, even has a Guider in *The Girls of the Pansy Patrol* (1931) who disapproves of the social mix of a visiting company so only invites certain patrols to her house: '… they would not be wanting the whole Company up there, as some of the girls seemed to be of such different class.' But this is very much the exception. The general assumption is that Guides embrace the message of sisterhood. When the very poor company in Mrs A C Osborn Hann's *Peg's Patrol* (1924) can't raise the money to go camping, they decide to ask for help from their sister Guides: 'Let's get Captain to write an article in *The Guide*—not a begging letter, of course, but just telling other Guides our difficulties here—and see if they would like to put the fourth Guide Law into practice.' Naturally, the money floods in.

Many Guides are shown as having almost a mystical sense of connection with all other Guides. In *Jill, Lone Guide* (Ethel Talbot 1927), Jill sustains herself through difficult times by holding in her mind the great sisterhood of which she is a part: 'the company of Invisible Guides seemed to troop round her in just the same cheery comrady way as when they had helped her with her worries and extra chores. Only this time they were glorying in her happiness, as Jill knew.'

GUIDES ROUND THE CAMP FIRE
Guiding in the Books of Elsie J Oxenham

Adrianne Fitzpatrick

Elsie Jeanette Oxenham was a prolific writer of girls' stories, publishing around ninety books during her lifetime. Approximately fifteen or sixteen of the fifty-five books written between 1916 and 1936 included Guiding, sometimes as the main theme of a book and sometimes as an incidental but often significant feature. However, she has never been viewed as a mainstream Guide author, and this is probably because of a fundamental paradox in her attitude. EJO, as her readers call her, had another passion: Camp Fire, a movement similar in many ways to the Guides, almost identical in its values, but very different in surface appearance and emphasis. There is no doubt that in her heart she was drawn to the Camp Fire way of doing things; yet at the same time, she recognised the fundamental value of Guides and its place in society.

When EJO wrote her first Guide book—*The Tuck-Shop Girl* (1916)—both Scouts and Guides were still in their infancy, as was Camp Fire. Robert Baden-Powell, the founder of Scouting, had decided that girls should not be in the same organisation as the boys, and the Girl Guides had been founded in the UK in 1910. The Boy Scout movement of America was also established in 1910, and Dr Luther Gulick, a well known and respected youth reformer, and his wife, Charlotte, who had an interest in child psychology, established a summer camp for the girls the same year. In 1911 Dr Gulick and some of his associates got together to discuss ways of creating an organisation for girls along the same lines as the Boy Scouts. They wanted a movement similar to the Girl Guides but with more emphasis on creativity and the individual. As a result the Camp Fire Girls of America was incorporated as a national organisation in 1912. The British Camp Fire Girls followed officially in 1921, although it had been active in Britain for some years. Girl Scouts of the USA, the sister organisation of the Boy Scouts, was incorporated in 1915. Thus in America, Camp Fire as well as Girl Scouts (Guides) sprang from the Scouting movement. The two also co-existed in Britain for some years, though Guides predominated from the start.

Elsie Oxenham became a Camp Fire girl. She was the keen Guardian of Camp Watéwin, the Camp of those who Conquer, which she ran in Ealing from 1916 to 1922 with girls from local families, her church, and her folk-dance classes. On moving to Worthing, she tried to set up another Camp Fire, but found that Girl Guides was more popular. This conflict between the two organisations is a recurring theme in her books, as we shall see.

One might speculate as to why EJO wrote books about Guides at all: did her publishers specifically request it? Did she see the popularity of the movement—and perhaps of other Guiding books being published around that time? Had she seen Guides on parade—at her church perhaps?—or giving displays? Whatever her motivation, Guides play a significant role in her fiction, appearing to varying degrees in at least twenty percent of her stories, and we start here with an overview of these, moving on later to a more detailed analysis of EJO's response to the movement.

Five of the Guide-related books (one series of four, and one other) make no mention of the

Camp Fire movement, and we shall look at these first of all. It is noticeable that even here she has a tendency to present an alternative to Guiding, so that the girls are obliged to make a choice.

In *The Tuck-Shop Girl*, the first of the Jinty books, published in 1916, the conflict is between Guides and Gardening, the school's other major preoccupation. 1916 was the year in which EJO started her own Camp Fire, but she may have been unfamiliar with the movement at the time she was actually writing the book, and thus she chose gardening as the foil to Guides, rather than Camp Fire, as she was to do in later books. Barbara is the Head Gardener, who sacrifices her chosen pursuit and returns to Guides when one of the patrols loses its leader.

> Barbara took off her pinafore and big hat, and laid them on the grass with her gardening-gloves, then faced the other two. '... I shall miss the gardening dreadfully. I really think I enjoyed it more than the other; but I can do this job, and there seems nobody else, and it has to be done ... I have my badges, and I was corporal for a year, and I'm seventeen. I'm qualified, you see ... The other things [gardening competitions] aren't necessary, and this is.'

Highlander Jinty, new to the school, is desperately keen to be a Guide, and a good Guide, but constantly gets into trouble through 'neffer thinking' and brings shame to her patrol and trouble to the whole school. In this book Guiding is seen as a character-building activity, most suitable for a girl like Jinty, but it isn't presented as the best or preferred option for everybody. When another new girl, Drusilla, arrives, the question—'Shall you have a garden, or would you rather be a Guide?'—is very casually presented, with neither expectation nor censure, regardless of the answer.

In *The Reformation of Jinty* (1933) Jinty meets 'the Poet' when she trespasses on his garden to try to take a photograph of him. The Poet lectures her on behaviour unbecoming for a Guide but is impressed by her quick contrition and allows her to take the photograph after all:

> 'Because you were going to confess, even at the cost of your badge, and because I don't believe you had realised what you were doing,' he explained. 'But you must remember, you know. It is not on yourself alone that you bring discredit, now that you are a Guide. You must not disgrace your uniform ... Your ideals are high, you must try to live up to them, or you have no right to wear your badge ... You must always remember that the honour of the Guides is in your hands.'

A friendship develops between the two and Jinty learns of his granddaughter Molly, a keen Guide who died trying to save another Guide from drowning. The Poet had made fun of Guides while Molly was alive, and, bitterly regretting his attitude after she was gone, had vowed to learn more of the organisation.

When Jinty's two young cousins, Sheila and Morag, arrive at the school, she is expected to set them a good example, much to the amusement of all the other girls, but having to do so helps her to learn to think. With Jinty as the Guides' representative, the Poet reassesses his view of the organisation, and decides to leave his home to them as a rest-home and conference centre, on condition that Jinty is on the management committee once she turns twenty-one.

When Betty, Patrol Leader of the Thistles, fails to return to school in *Jinty's Patrol* (1934), Jinty is unanimously appointed to the position by her patrol members. ('"Mad, quite mad!" said the school.') Jinty wants to go all out to make the Thistles the best patrol, to justify their choice of her as leader, while the other members of the school look forward to ensuing disaster. They aren't disappointed!

For the first few weeks the girls stay out of trouble—'Captain loves us at inspection, and she says our drill's very smart,' says Sheila—but Jinty isn't satisfied: they are 'trying so hard not to do things' that they 'aren't bothering to *do* things'. It's time to be on the lookout for good deeds! Jinty's patrol goes out at dead of night to correct the spelling and punctuation on the signboard of a nearby café, rival to that run by the Tuck-Shop Girl. Sheila, the Patrol Second, insists it would be a 'ripping good deed': 'It's enough to put anybody off the place. No one would go into a wretched little hole with "Tea's" over the door! It looks so low-class!' When a new sign—The Bungerlow Tea Rooms—appears, the girls convince themselves that fixing the sign would be a good deed worthy of Guides, but their Headmistress, returning at two in the morning from a good deed of her own, takes a different view. The Guides are obliged to pay compensation, and are denied the pleasure of the first night in camp, the highlight of the term. However, the adults and other Guides secretly approve of their enterprise and rally round to help pay the debt, and the Poet, who is to officiate at the opening of the camp, 'discovers' he must attend an event in London on the first night and won't be able to perform his duties until all the girls are present. During the Guide camp, Jinty is unwittingly instrumental in helping another girl overcome a deep-seated fear of—tents!

The fourth and final book in the Jinty series, *A Divided Patrol*, was posthumously published in 1992 after the manuscript was unearthed by Elspeth Dunkerley, Elsie's niece. There is no way of knowing when this book was written, but stylistically it has the same feel as the earlier books, so it seems likely that EJO wrote it around about the same time as the others in the series but for whatever reason it was never accepted by a publisher. In this continuation of the series, the school's Guide Company is attempting to raise funds for the local Animals' Hospital, and each of the patrols must also

Disaster in camp in *Jinty's Patrol*

conduct its own fundraising activity. Although the whole Company will hold a rummage sale at the end of term, Jinty decides that her patrol should hold a small jumble sale with seeds and plants, photo-plates and other items.

Ann, one of the younger girls, joined Guides nine months earlier and hasn't yet earned her Second Class badge, though according to Sheila, one of Jinty's cousins and Patrol Second, she ought to have had it ages ago, but it seems their Captain 'isn't quite sure yet if Ann really has the proper Guide feeling'.

A split develops between the younger members of the Thistle Patrol, including Sheila, and the older members, most of whom are 'young' as Guides. The younger girls have a secret which they keep from the other members of the patrol, but their mischief impinges on their attendance at a patrol meeting. The conflict comes to a head during the patrol's jumble sale and Jinty decides she must resign as leader. 'It isn't really Sheila, it's me. It means I've been a bad leader.' Her Guide Captain refuses to accept Jinty's resignation without the agreement of her patrol, so Jinty returns to the waiting girls. The younger members of the patrol, convinced that Jinty has reported Sheila and requested her removal as Second, are defiant, but when Jinty explains that she has asked to go up to the Rangers, the whole patrol protests. Sheila rushes off to the Captain to explain, and her companions in crime follow in quick succession. Sheila finally realises the trouble she has brought to the patrol and willingly gives up her stripe. Apart from Morag, who remains defiant in spite of everything, the girls repent and look forward to a new era with Kirsteen as Second.

In *Deb at School* (1929), the first in the Deb sequence of books, the choice is not between two different organisations but between the right and the wrong kind of friend. Deb Lely is sent to boarding school for the first time, by her aunt/guardian, at the age of fifteen. She is young for her age and has no experience of girls of her own age and class. She is a girl of wild enthusiasms, and is several times warned not to go overboard in friendship with the wrong type of girl.

On the way to school she meets Rosemary, a prefect of the right type and a Guide, and is impressed by her. On arrival, however, she is put in the care of Guide-hating Chloe, whom she has heard some younger girls praising extravagantly. Chloe is head of her dormitory, and proves to be a self-seeking type who bribes the girls with flattery and chocolates. She makes Deb her protégée, and convinces her that it is 'sporting' to break rules and tell lies on her idol's behalf and take the blame for her misdemeanours. Guiding is mentioned only a few times in the course of the book, but always strategically, so that it comes to epitomise the right kind of girl.

> '… I'd rather like to be a Guide some day.'
> 'My dear, you'd hate it! It's drill and work all day; as if we didn't get enough of both! You have to swot everlastingly for badges to satisfy Rosemary's crowd. I'd advise you to go in for something more thrilling. You'd be wasted in the Guides. You have original ideas,' Chloe explained. 'The Guides are all right for girls who can only obey orders. But you can think of things, new and thrilling things. Besides, you haven't time for all that stuff.'

And later, when Deb has begun to see through Chloe, she declares her intention of joining the Guides:

Jinty to the rescue in *The Reformation of Jinty*

Girl Guides and Camp Fire Girls work in unison in *Patience Joan, Outsider*

Chloe came striding down on them in her most queenly manner. 'I forbid it. We've no use for Guides in South Dorm. Deb must find some other way to amuse herself.'

…

'Forbid it as much as you like,' Deb said cheerfully. 'I don't care. I shall be a Guide if Rosemary will have me. I'm certain that's not one of the things the head of a dorm has a right to forbid.'

In the end, encouraged by Deb, Chloe manages to own up to her deceitful behaviour and deserve Deb's friendship. EJO successfully avoids the obvious: Chloe does *not* become a Guide, as far as we know!

All the rest of EJO's books with any mention of Guides also include Camp Fire, and that generally in far more detail, since she was able to write about it from the inside. It was in 1917, a year after starting her own Camp Fire, that she published *A School Camp-Fire*, and the following year she combined the two movements for the first time in *The School of Ups and Downs* (1918). Here we encounter what was to become a favourite theme of hers: Guides and Camp Fire, both excellent in themselves, appeal to and suit different types of girl. The story concerns two sisters, Libby and Tibby, one of whom is attracted to Camp Fire and the other to Guides. They have always done everything together up till now, and Libby views this divergence of interest as a threat to their relationship.

Could she give up the Camp Fire? *Could* she? Her heart would always be there; she knew that well. Could she be a half-hearted Guide for Tibby's sake? … Could she bear to be separated for all her school life in all her interests from her sister?

She wrestles with her dilemma, and seriously contemplates sacrificing her own wishes so that they can continue to be together. But Rowena, a Camp Fire girl whose own younger sister is a Guide, puts her right.

'You don't think I ought to try to be a Guide?'

'You simply couldn't; it would be wrong—wicked! … You can't go against your whole nature … For you to squeeze yourself into a Guide's uniform would be like dressing yourself in clothes several sizes too small … I don't mean that we're bigger than Guides … But the Guides don't fit *you* … You'll find what you want in the Camp Fire; you've got the nature that needs it. The Guides would leave one whole side of you starved, as they would me. But they will suit Tibby, as they do Sammy.'

This book has a sequel, *Patience Joan, Outsider* (1922), in which Patience Joan turns up at the school with an attitude of antagonism towards both Guides and Camp Fire.

'The Camp Fire's sentimental. You dress up, and hang beads all round you, and say pretty-pretty bits of poetry, and make up fancy stuff about fire, and imagine all sorts of ideas that don't exist at all, and have romantic names and mottoes and things. And it's silly to pretend you're Indian maidens. It may be all right in

America, but there's no sense in it here. The Camp Fire's just right for a mooney sloppy kind of girl …'

'The Guides are military! … They drill, and they copy soldiers and scouts, and do things to orders and bugles, and all that sort of rot; and go out marching in uniform to make people look at them; and have flags and parades and inspections, just as if they were boys being trained for soldiers.'

Patty-John, as she becomes known, makes some very forthright comments, which could have been offensive, but secretly the girls had already thought the same about whichever group they were not in, and so she meets with widespread if reluctant support. She is eventually convinced of the value of both organisations: she opts for Camp Fire, and her cousin Mercy chooses Guides.

The 'Torment' books (heroine Tormentil Grant) are primarily Camp Fire books, but Guiding plays a significant part in this series, which is fundamentally about the unwillingness of the Torment to invite newcomers into her circle of friends. Tormentil is the only girl pupil at a boys' school, and has two girl friends, Tony and Marsaili, who live nearby but do not attend the school. In *The School Torment* (1920), having made a place for herself in the school, she has to learn to share her friends among the boys with Tony.

She, Tony and Marsaili have set up an 'unofficial' Camp Fire, which cannot apply for a charter because they have no Guardian. At the beginning of *The Testing of the Torment* (1925) a new girl, Pen, comes to the school under the care of her stepfather, and is excluded both by the boys (who say one girl is quite enough) and by Tormentil, who does not want to invite her to Camp Fire. Pen occupies herself by becoming the unofficial leader of a band of Wolf Cubs whose Akela has left. In the course of the book, she wins acceptance and is finally invited into the unofficial Camp Fire.

At the start of *The Camp Fire Torment* (1926), Marsaili has turned eighteen and is old enough to become the Camp Fire Guardian. However, to be regularised the group must have six girls, so three more are needed. Twins from the vicarage are readily recruited, and the girls decide after a considerable inner struggle on the part of the Torment to make up their numbers with a girl she has always avoided, having taken a dislike to her on no grounds at all. But when they call on Veronica (Ronny) and are ushered into the house, to their horror they find her wearing Guide uniform. To make things worse, Ronny is a Lone Guide, as there is no local company, and regrets the isolation, though she likes and admires her Guide Captain and attends occasional meetings at some distance. And she would have loved to join a Camp Fire, but is adamant that she is bound in honour to the Guides and that it is not possible to do both.

'I'm afraid you can't have me. Thank you very much, but I'm a Guide.' Veronica spoke steadily, but her voice was curiously without expression, almost as though she were allowing herself to show no feeling lest she should show too much. Then suddenly her self-control gave way. 'Why didn't you ask me before?' she cried vehemently. 'How I'd have loved it! Now it's too late. Why have you come now? I've only been a Guide for six months. I've read about the Camp Fire, and I'd have loved to belong. But I was lonely; I haven't any friends … I was aching to belong to something with other girls in it. Then I heard about the

Lone Guides, and it was better, heaps better, than nothing. So I joined, and my captain's been awfully decent to me; she's a dear, but it's not like belonging to a real company, or being in a Camp like yours. Oh, why didn't you come in time?'

By the end of the book, all the girls have learnt important lessons about sharing and negotiating, and Ronny has been given permission by her Guider to join the Camp Fire as well, while continuing to work as a Lone Guide, taking badges and tests by post.

'She says I can still go on as a Lone Guide, and still do my Guide work by letters, as I've always had to do, and yet belong to your Camp and come to your meetings. That is, if you don't mind. She knows about the Camp Fire, and she says its aims and promises are all the same as in the Guides, only the Guides are stronger on some points and the Camp Fire on others. But there's nothing in either to make it impossible to do both; nothing that opposes or contradicts.'

In *Ven at Gregory's* (1925), EJO develops for the first time a situation where girls who are already keen Camp Fire members move over to Guides for the good of the community. The local Guides have become slack, and the new Commissioner appeals to the Headmistress for girls with personality and education to join and become Patrol Leaders. In this book EJO gives an eyewitness description of the dedication of a new Guide flag, and her heroines are able to recognise some similarities between the movements.

'It's really rather like the Camp Fire, you know … the Brownie book is full of symbols. You have the Wise Brown Owl, and her Tawny assistant—not quite so wise or brown as she is!—and the Dancing Ring, and the Pow-wow; and the kiddies are Elves or Pixies or Imps or Sprites. The whole thing is a sort of play-picture, with meanings behind.'

In fact in this book, Elsie Oxenham shows most clearly her appreciation of Guiding as a national force: Camp Fire though they are, Ven and her friends recognise Guides as something much bigger than they had supposed, and acknowledge that those who benefit from it will change society for the better, as a part of the war on deprivation and ignorance. 'It may seem a little thing to be a leader of Guides or Brownies, but it surely means that when to-day's girls are women, they will have knowledge and ideals which their mothers haven't had, and so could never teach them. They'll want more than their mothers wanted; and the Boy Scouts will want more; and we shall have a new and better country.'

It is, however a real and deep sacrifice on the part of the girls concerned: '… to ask me to become a Guide, and to call it my Camp Fire service, is a blow I never expected. I'm still staggering under it …' But all ends well when the girls find that not only can they remain Camp Fire girls, attending occasional meetings in school holidays, but they may even be rewarded with Camp Fire honour beads for their service to the Guides!

An even greater sacrifice is required in *The Crisis in Camp Keema* (1928). Miss Moore, the Camp Fire Guardian, is leaving the school, and it is hoped that the new gym mistress will take her place. However, Miss Curtis is a Guide, and indeed a Guider, and she decides to start a school Guide company. She appeals to the members of Camp Fire to join the Guides for the sake of a united school and to promote a strong Guide spirit. Maribel Ritchie, the Head Girl of the school and Torch-Bearer of the Camp, feels she has no option but to go along with this.

> Maribel looked up, despair in her eyes. 'But, Miss Curtis, don't you *see*? The school will be split in two. Everyone will be Guides or Camp Fire, and we shall be rivals, whether it's right or not. We shall never do anything if we're all pulling against one another. It will ruin the feeling in the school!'
> 'The remedy's in your hands, my dear girl … The matter is very largely in your hands, Maribel. As head-girl, your example will carry great weight …'
> 'And give up the Camp Fire to be a Guide?' Maribel asked despairingly. 'Miss Curtis, how *can* I? I *am* Camp Fire!'

And Miss Curtis responds:

> 'You'll think first of the good of the school, Maribel … I *am* a Guide, and I believe in the Guides. The organisation is national, and is recognised everywhere. As Camp Fire Girls you no doubt felt you were pioneers in a new movement; but there is surely equal inspiration in enlisting in so large and proved a body as the Guides. You will have friends wherever you go if you are wearing the trefoil badge. And there is nothing whatever in the Guide Law and Promises, or in your Camp Fire Law and Promises, which makes it impossible for you to keep both …'

As a result a split occurs between Maribel and her closest friend Phyllis. A feud develops between the few Camp Fire diehards and the rest of the school, although that finally ends when Maribel's new friend Rosalind gives Phyllis the dressing-down she deserves.

This story is carried on in *Peggy and the Brotherhood* (1936), in which Peggy and her elder sister Marian move to a new neighbourhood and meet up by chance with the small group of residual Camp Fire girls led by Phyllis, who ask Marian if she will become their Guardian. These girls have a strong sense of grievance against the Guides who have 'bagged everything'. Peggy starts at their school, 'Miss Ransome's school', where Sharly, the Head's niece, is also a new girl. Peggy naturally joins Camp Keema, and Sharly, attracted to Maribel, wants to join the Guides. After much soul-searching they realise that they have got it wrong: Peggy switches to the Guides, and Sharly to Camp Fire. EJO again draws the moral that each movement has different strengths, which are more suited to particular girls.

> 'You mean different things are better for different people!' Peggy cried. 'You don't mean that Camp Fire's better than Guides for everybody?'
> 'Not for a second. But for me it takes in things the Guides seem to leave out …'
> Peggy sighed. 'I'm one who would find more in the Guides.'

The Camp Mystery, though published earlier, in 1932, and parts of it in short story form as early as 1927, continues this sequence as a sub-plot. Maribel, Rosalind and Phyll all make an appearance in this story, but it cannot be said that either Guides or Camp Fire plays a major role, although the cover illustration might lead one to expect a Guide story. An international gang of criminals is attempting to steal a note-book containing sensitive business information, and insinuates a child, Cecily, into a school camp. The Guides, staying nearby, befriend her, although interestingly they are up a mountain when the main action takes place down below. They do, however, have the vital note-book with them! Overcome by the kindness she is shown, Cecily throws in her lot with the Guides, and is adopted by them.

It is at this stage that Guiding enters EJO's most celebrated series, the Abbey books. Up until this point there have been only a few passing mentions of the movement, but now it becomes a significant, albeit minor, strand.

Church Parade in *Peggy and the Brotherhood*

In *The Abbey Girls Play Up* (1930), Cecily has moved to England with Maribel and Rosalind as her guardians on behalf of the Guides. She attends a country dance class run by Joan Raymond, and thus is drawn into the Abbey circle. Maribel and Rosalind go to Joan for advice, and Joan, discovering that Cecily is musical, recommends her to Joy Marchwood's music school.

A group of girls from the village are at a loose end, and Maidlin di Ravarati, Joy's ward, wants to do something to help them. She considers Girl Guides—the village Company needs another lieutenant before any more girls can be admitted—and asks Rosalind and Maribel, as Guiders, for advice. Maidlin ultimately chooses Camp Fire over Guides, and the discussions preceding her choice shed considerable light on the differences EJO perceived between the two movements.

> 'Are you going to be a Guide?' [Rosalind asked.]
> 'I don't know. I hate the very thought of it. But I think perhaps—'
> 'Then you couldn't possibly be one!' Rosalind cried …
> 'Maidie's sure it isn't in her line, and I agree with her,' said Joy. 'But she feels it's up to her to do something with certain girls in the village …'
> …
> 'She's been reading up about Guides, but she hates the very thought of them,' Rosalind explained to Maribel.
> 'I didn't say that. I think they're splendid—for girls like you. I said I hated the thought of being one myself.'
> '… But you can't be one if you feel like that, you know.'
> 'Why do you hate it so much?' Maribel looked down at her. 'And if you do, why are you considering the idea at all?'
> 'It's so energetic and—and smart, and everything it ought to be. I'm not like that.'

Mary Devine, who doesn't believe Maidlin should become a Guide, says it wouldn't suit her at all. For Maidlin is 'just the opposite of everything a Guide should be'. Mary explains to Rosalind and Maribel that 'there's no room in Guiding for the things she's strong in. It would cramp her in everything she cares about. She'd have to develop other sides, and it might be good for her, but she'd find it a very great effort.'

Rosalind suggests Maidlin start a Camp Fire and introduces Maribel as 'Kataga, "the Stormy Waves", Torch-Bearer in Camp Keema, the Camp that faces the Wind'; and Maribel explains that she was in Camp Fire before she joined the Guides.

> 'I gave up Camp Fire to be a Guide, not because I preferred it but because it was better for our school. I was head girl, and we had a new mistress who wanted to start Guides. It was better I should work with her. It nearly broke our hearts at the time, and I quite meant to go back to Camp Fire as soon as I left school. But when that time came I couldn't bear to give up my Guides. I still have my gown and honours, and some day I may take up Camp Fire again.'

And with the encouragement of the two Guiders, Maidlin gains the confidence and courage to begin a Camp Fire for the girls of the village.

Joy, however, balances this by taking up Guiding, in response to a suggestion which originates with Rosalind and Maribel, but is forcefully presented to her by Jen.

> 'Margaret will certainly ask why her mummy doesn't do things as other people's mothers do … By the time they're ready to be Guides, you'd certainly have become District Commissioner. You know you'd be asked at the earliest possible moment.'

Later, when Joy has had time to think it over, she says:

> 'Until I'm used to it, can't I do it only at home here in the village? I don't want to go to big county rallies and things. It's just for our own girls you'd want me, isn't it?'

After some discussion, she chooses to become the Ranger Captain, and we catch glimpses of her in this role in *The Abbey Girls on Trial* (1931) and again briefly in *Joy's New Adventure* (1935).

> As they talked together, Joy came out on to the terrace again, and Audrey and Elspeth sat up with exclamations of surprise, for she looked very smart in the uniform of a Guide Captain, with the red tie which showed that her girls were Rangers.
>
> 'Gracious!' Audrey murmured. 'The last thing I'd have expected her to do! What surprising people you are!'
>
> 'Stars! Is she a Girl Guide?' Elspeth whispered.
>
> …
>
> 'Captain the Lady Marchwood!' Rosamund remarked, as Joy disappeared into

the Abbey. 'That's the shortest way to the village. Doesn't she look *it*? She's a splendid Captain; the whole Company worships her, and she's adored by her Rangers.'

'It's splendid of her to do it, but rather surprising,' Audrey ventured.

Rosamund laughed. 'Like to know what screwed her up to it? She hated the idea at first, though she loves Guiding now. She wants to be District Commissioner by the time Elizabeth and Margaret are ready to be Brownies, so that they can all be Guides together.'

The Abbey Girls on Trial

It seems clear that Elsie Oxenham had little personal experience of Guides, and when contrasted with her detailed descriptions of the inner workings of Camp Fire, her accounts of Guide activities appear purely external. Her only eye-witness accounts of Guide events deal with church parades, and the dedication of a new Colour (*Peggy and the Brotherhood*, *Ven at Gregory's*). Yet some common themes emerge from the various mentions in her works—aspects of Guiding which seem to have stood out for her as epitomising the movement.

The most important of these seems to have been the concept of honour. The first Guide Law states 'A Guide's honour is to be trusted', and this, together with loyalty and obedience, seems to have made a particular impression on EJO.

In *The School of Ups and Downs*, when the Camp Fire Guardian has helped would-be Guide Tibby to find a way out of a dilemma caused by her own dishonourable behaviour, she says to her, 'And after it is over you must join the Guides, and be very careful to remember that a Guide's honour can be trusted. You will have to be very careful on that point … It would hurt them all terribly if you disgraced them.'

The same virtue is highlighted by the Poet, on the occasion of his first meeting with Jinty (dressed in full Guide uniform):

The Poet and Jinty

'One might be forgiven … for taking you for a Guide. But that, of course, is impossible!'

'I am a Guide!' Jinty faced him with the courage of righteous indignation. 'I've got my Second-Class Badge!'

'Impossible!' he assured her. 'A Guide never creeps about as if she were ashamed, doing dishonourable deeds and keeping out of sight. What about the honour of the Guides?'

The Reformation of Jinty

And in the short story 'Freda Joins the Guides' (1931), it is the honourable behaviour of a couple of Guides which transforms the attitude of Freda's father, who had previously forbidden her to have anything to do with the movement. He overhears her suggesting an underhand course of action. Guide Gina's refusal wins him over, and he tells Freda to join the Guides, saying, 'See that you are a good Guide. I can't have a girl of mine left behind in a matter of honour.' (See *Peggy and the Brotherhood*, GGBP edition.)

In this story, Gina makes it clear that she is a Guide all the time, whether or not she is in uniform. References in the Jinty books, however, suggest that for EJO, uniform and honour were almost inextricably linked:

> 'I never thought about being in uniform!' Jinty pleaded. 'No, it wasn't proper for a Guide. It wasn't playing up. They've told me why it matters more what you do when you're in uniform … I'll have to go and tell them … Maybe they'll take my badge away; they said they would, if I did mad things.'
>
> *Reformation of Jinty*

> 'It was nothing to do with Guides,' [Sheila pleaded].
> 'You're in uniform. When you're in uniform, you're a Guide.'
> …
> 'We didn't do anything so very awful, Jinty.'
> 'But you were in uniform,' Jinty retorted. 'I want you to remember that when you're in uniform you're Guides, and you're on your honour to behave like Guides.'
>
> *A Divided Patrol*

Uniform is an important factor in Elsie Oxenham's view of Guides. Her Camp Fire girls are often initially attracted by the gowns and beads; it might almost seem that, fascinated herself with the trappings and symbolism of the Camp Fire movement, she then projected that feeling on to would-be Guides. This may be seen in its crudest form in *The School of Ups and Downs*: Libby wants to see Rowena 'dressed up', while Tibby wants to see 'uniforms'; and then, a few pages later, Tib wants to see the uniforms again, and Lib wants to see the Indian dresses and the beads. And rather quaintly, in *Peggy and the Brotherhood*, Peggy herself at her enrolment wonders if 'Sharly's as keen on her gown as I am on my uniform!'

EJO seems to have been particularly struck by the white lanyard and patrol leader's stripes which stood out in contrast to the dark blue uniforms, to the point where she uses them as a kind of shorthand: 'I want my whistle and stripes,' says Ven (*Ven at Gregory's*). And the same phrase is used almost in self-mockery by Rosalind in *The Camp Mystery*:

> Astrid eyed the uniform curiously, the stripes, belt, whistle. '… Did you wear these things at home, Rosalind?'
> 'Rather! My dear, you'd never believe how imposing I looked!'

Oxenham was equally well able to take a derisive view of her own movement where it suited the story, as is shown by some remarks from Phil in *Ven at Gregory's*, defending herself against having to become a Guide as a piece of community service:

'By going about in a blue felt hat, and a white cord with a whistle, and some bits of ribbon? … I'd like to see one of your Camp Fire people give up her swanky gown for a blue uniform! Or come out of your nice cosy easy-going Camp to drill and be a Guide!'

Elsie Oxenham was among those who viewed Guiding as a somewhat militaristic organisation, and she frequently emphasises this in books where she is drawing a contrast with the Camp Fire movement. In *The School of Ups and Downs*, Tibby would love to join the Guides, who 'were marching beautifully, keeping step'; whereas we are told that the Camp Fire preferred to avoid the military atmosphere altogether. And in *Peggy and the Brotherhood*, the description of the church parade marks the point where Peggy begins to realise that Guides rather than Camp Fire will suit her. She says to Sharly, 'But weren't you thrilled when the flags came in? Weren't you dying to have your uniform and salute as the Guides do, and stand at attention when you see the Colours?'

In *Joy's New Adventure*, too, a contrast is drawn, this time between the romantic world of the Abbey and the different side of Joy's character which emerges when she performs her Guiding duties.

[Gail] drove to the village with Joy one evening, to watch the Ranger meeting, and marvelled at the change in Joy when she wore uniform and inspected and drilled her girls.

Joy's New Adventure

Here Joy is shown as being very much in charge, and if there is a stereotype to be found, it is in EJO's portrayal of Guiders, who come off very badly alongside the sympathetic Guardians of her Camp Fires!

Miss Fenton [the Guide-mistress] was tall and businesslike, brisk and smart in manner. Miss Betts [the Camp Fire Guardian], or Betty, as the girls called her, was little and fair-haired, with a pleasant expression …

Patience Joan, Outsider

And in *The School of Ups and Downs*, Tibby says of Miss Fenton, 'She's awfully bossy. I think some of the girls are a bit afraid of her; I know I should be!'

Maidlin's view of Guiders is equally forthright:

'I should hate it!' Maidlin exclaimed. 'Uniform and drill and saluting, and being boss! I've never ordered anybody about and I'm sure I never could.'

The Abbey Girls Play Up

And perhaps most telling of all is this response to Rosamund's self-analysis, not even in a Guide context:

> '… I'm not original or artistic; I like to do things and hustle round and boss.'
>   'It sounds like Guiding,' Audrey said laughing. 'Aren't you a Guide Captain too?'
>
> The Abbey Girls on Trial

But it is not only the leaders who are so vividly contrasted. While EJO fully recognises the shared ethos of the two movements, she consistently portrays their outward manifestations as strongly polarised. It is romance versus practicality.

The Guides in *The School of Ups and Downs* are shown in 'their blue uniforms … drilling smartly' or 'making bandages or poultices, or finding out new ways to build camp ovens, or doing carpentry, like boys'. They would not, we are told, waste time on handcrafts! Camp Fire girls, on the other hand, may be found doing 'embroidery, and beadwork, and designing, and stencilling, and modelling, and fancy arts of all kinds … You can make lovely chains, and bags, and trimmings for hats and evening frocks.' Camp Fire 'has more poetry and romance about it. But the Guides have some fine points about them too.'—However, what these are is not stated! In reality, of course, Guide proficiency badges—Artist, Basket worker, Embroiderer, Needlewoman, Knitter, Lace-maker, Milliner and Toymaker—covered all of these Camp Fire activities; and certainly by the time she wrote *The Camp Mystery* and *The Abbey Girls in Town* (1925), EJO was aware that country dancing formed part of Guide activities.

We are given one pointer as to what EJO felt to be missing from Guides: Libby reflects that '"Seek Beauty" seemed to be the only [Camp Fire law] not covered by the Law of the Guides, and this first conclusion was only strengthened, the more she came to know of both'. (*School of Ups and Downs*)

In *Ven at Gregory's*, however, published seven years later, the author has a deeper understanding of Guides and its meaning:

> 'It's a bigger thing than I thought,' Barbara said gravely. 'It's not just drilling girls and teaching them signalling and tying knots, and saluting one another when you meet. It has big inner meanings, just as Camp Fire has. I never saw the deeper side of the Guides before; I just looked at the outside. The uniform, and salutes, all are symbols of something; I didn't understand, and so I hadn't judged the Guides fairly. There's more in it than I thought.'

And another three years after this, she was able to put the following sentiments into the mouth of a prominent character:

> '[Camp Fire is] not my style at all! It always strikes me as unpractical and sentimental. I'd be a Guide if we had them in the school; the Guides are some use in the world! They're national, and recognised; they're often asked to take part officially in things in the town. I'd be proud to wear uniform; Maribel and Phyllis hate the very idea of it, but I'd like it. We wear school uniform; and they wear a Camp Fire uniform! But they see red if anyone suggests a Guide company in the

school, and say they hate uniform for girls. They won't admit they aren't logical … I could never throw myself into Camp Fire … I don't want to sit round candles and say poetry, and do action-songs and dances, and wear a long frock with fringe and beads to get in my way! No, thanks! But I'd like a neat, smart uniform, with badges on my sleeve.'

Rosalind laughed. 'But does the dress matter so much? Isn't it the inner feeling that counts?'

'But the uniform is an expression of that feeling! … The Guides are smart and neat in themselves, and ready for anything; prepared for emergencies, and they look it. A Camp Fire gown's all right to wear for sitting beside a fire and saying poetry, and it's quite the thing for acting about in and trying to look pretty in. But for real use—no, thanks!'

The Crisis in Camp Keema

Elsie J Oxenham worked very hard to be fair to Guides, though her heart remained with the Camp Fire. No doubt she was disappointed that Camp Fire did not endure in the UK, but she generously recognised the worth of the other movement, and she knew that in the essentials there was very little difference between the two. As Miss Curtis the Guide Captain puts it in *The Crisis in Camp Keema*:

'Camp Fire and Guides have the same objects, with perhaps a slightly different emphasis on definite points. They should be allies, not rivals; they should be friends, and help one another at every point.'

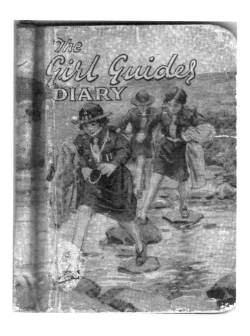

Always Be Prepared!

RESCUES

'Did you know you would be able to save him?' asked some one
curiously afterwards.

'No,' she said, and Captain's eyes twinkled as she overheard the
words, 'I just didn't stop to think I mightn't—that's all.'

'Soaking Camp', E L Haverfield, *Collins' Schoolgirls' Annual*,
undated

Scouting for Boys tells many stories of rescues, and fictional Guides are always
prepared to respond to an emergency. They rescue people from mine shafts, cliffs,
quarries, wells, mad dogs, ditched planes, burning and buried houses, as well as
throwing many coats over people on fire. A common theme shows the duffer
Guide rising to the challenge of a rescue. In Chaundler's *Jill of the Guides* (1932),
Jill's brothers send her a false Morse message saying her school is on fire. She
rushes to evacuate everyone before realising it is only a gardener's bonfire. Jill's
PL tells her crushingly that she did the wrong thing: 'Before you said a word to
anybody you should have gone and looked at your fire, seen … if you couldn't
have put it out yourself.' (This is *not* according to B-P: in the Guiding handbook
of the time, the first rule he gives in case of fire is to warn anyone inside the
building.) After a series of botched Guiding moments, Jill redeems herself when
she and some Patrol Leaders, in a splendid display of rope-work, knots and sheer
courage, rescue her brothers from a bog that is sucking them down.

The Guiding motto, Be Prepared, means more than anything else that a Guide
should be ready to act in an emergency, both because she will have the right
knowledge of how to deal with it, and because she will keep calm. Many fictional
Guide meetings show Guides practising the skills that will enable them to keep
their heads in a rescue attempt: 'While they were all placidly seated in their
Patrol Corners, the news was suddenly shouted that the far end of the gymnasium
was on fire; the patrol up there were trapped on the top story [*sic*] of a blazing
building … and it was up to the other Patrols to go to the rescue at once.' (*The
Highland School*, Marjorie Taylor, 1940) Some Guides have to wait a long time
for their chance: 'I have been a Guide for six years,' Deborah remarked 'but this
is the first time I have ever put a loop on a lifeline in real earnest.' (Margaret
Middleton, *The Guide Adventurers*, 1929)

Mary K Harris gently mocks the idea of the dramatic rescue in the late Guide
story *Henrietta of St. Hilary's* (1953):

She went about hopefully prepared for anything. Her hope was so
great that she was sure one day it would be fulfilled—the mad dog
would materialise, the ferocious bull, the burning house, and she
would be there, on the spot, to do all the rescuing that was necessary.

> She kept a bandage in her pocket … and rescued herself from an
> imaginary fire by dropping out of a first-floor window. It was only
> such a pity that so far nothing had happened to justify all this frenzy
> of preparedness.

The Guiding manuals support the idea that the Guide should leap in to carry out a rescue. They include instructions on how to drag an unconscious person out of a burning house in such a way as to keep the rescuer's head out of the smoke, and how to rescue and resuscitate someone who is drowning. The assumption, carried out at least in fiction, is that a Guide is *better* than the average adult in a crisis. 'You can't expect everyone to keep their heads like them Girl Guides,' a man says in Nancy M Hayes' *The Plucky Patrol* (1924). In this book the Guides are caught up in floods and undertake a series of life-threatening rescues:

> Time after time Margery and Eleanor had practised life-saving
> in the river … but she had never expected to encounter conditions
> so terrible as those she faced now, swept relentlessly onward by the
> foaming stream.

In Violet Methley's *Mystery Camp* (1934), the girls deal with flooding in a far loftier manner: they have taught themselves to walk on stilts and stalk about the countryside dry shod giving assistance to stranded and damp villagers. 'Stilts must be frightfully healthy,' cries one of the Guides; 'everyone ought to be taught to walk on them as soon as they can stand.'

Rescues are often a means of effecting a rapprochement between Guides and someone previously antagonistic to them. In 'Captain's Roll of Honour' by Beryl C Lawley (*The Great Book for Girls*, undated), the previously crusty Squire, deeply moved after Guides have rescued his grandson, declares: '… to my dying day I shall never think or speak of Guides without deep and heart-felt respect.'

The highest award that could be given to a Guide was the Bronze Cross, for saving life at extraordinary risk to one's own, and these are fairly liberally scattered throughout the pages of Guiding fiction. Below this came the Silver Cross and the Medal of Merit. 'It's too bad!' Grizel mourns in Elinor M Brent-Dyer's *Jo of the Chalet School* after Joey has saved Robin's life. 'If only our Guide company had been formed, Joey would have been a Guide, and then she might have had the Silver Cross for saving life at the risk of her own.'

The formula for responding to the praise that follows a rescue is well established. First comes the modest disclaimer: 'It was nothing … anyone would have done the same.' (*Chris Temple, Patrol Leader*, Ivy F E Middleton 1964); followed by the deflection of any tribute away from the personal and towards the Guides: '"I'd be a pretty poor Guide if I hadn't learnt by this time how to put out fire," she announced crushingly.' (*Hilary Leads the Way*, Irene Mossop 1933).

ETHEL TALBOT AND THE GREAT SISTERHOOD

Tig Thomas

Of all the girls' story writers, it is Ethel Talbot who seems to be the most schoolgirlish: her writing is disorganised at times, breathless, a little gushy, slightly superstitious but good hearted and absolutely straight. Her Guiding books are bursting with enthusiasm for the movement, and tend to idealise the established Guide; although new members—who may sometimes be the heroine—have to learn what it means to be Guidey through and through. She covers a wide range of Guiding themes including Guides in and out of school, Lone Guides, Brownies, Rangers and, especially, Sea Rangers, or, as they were called before 1927, Sea Guides. Her Guide companies are competent and true blue, to the extent that there is sometimes little sense of the different personality strengths that can be brought to Guiding.

This blade-straight quality, however, often sits uneasily alongside her other big interest, the mystical elements of British folklore. In at least three stories her heroines have to repeat 'Guides don't believe in Ghosts!' while investigating eerie occurrences, and her books are sometimes weakened by the queasy mix of straightforward Guiding and what would now be called new age thinking. *Jan at Island School* (1927, a Ranger story which gives the impression of having been written on mescaline) contains references to Drake's drum, mermaids, Lyonnesse, King Arthur, ghosts, and the strange legends of the island. Talbot was also patently thrilled by the romance of the Gypsy, towards whom her Guides are always courteous and respectful. It is, however, noteworthy that the sisterhood of Guides only extends so far: in *The Peppercorn Patrol* (1929), the middle-class patrol takes two small Gypsy children into its ranks, but to the end of the book the Gypsies address the other members of the patrol as 'Miss'.

Recording in the Log Book ('The Singing Spook')

Talbot is at her best in her more prosaic stories when she forgoes the otherworldly motif. She does not underplay the difficulties of being a Guide, whether physical or moral. The camping chapters of *Peggy's Last Term* (1920, her second book and first Guiding story) certainly suggest she has experienced at least one Guide

Back-breaking work in *Peggy's Last Term*

camp and knows exactly how painful, tiring and time consuming it can be to gather bracken for beds or build a camp kitchen: 'Gypsy fires aren't the least scrap of good—not for water for thirty-five people. If I hadn't done a Camp kitchen when I was working for the Pioneer badge, I don't know what I would have done.' She has an interest in badge work, and often includes it in her stories.

The difficulties involved in trying to be a perfect Guide in a community of fallible people is a subject that Talbot returns to several times. She is also particularly strong when writing about the clash between the demands of outward success and inner integrity that can often overwhelm the Guide (interestingly, this theme was taken up in greater depth by Antonia Forest and is discussed in the final chapter of this book, 'Kicked Out').

Her best Guiding book, *Peggy's Last Term*, articulates this problem very clearly. Peggy returns to school in disgrace having learnt that she is not to be allowed to remain at the school after this final term. She has fooled around too much. Her stern aunt presents it as expulsion, and Peggy tears off her Guide badge and thrusts it into her pocket, feeling she has failed at everything, but her headmistress, who is also her Guide Captain, reinstates her and makes her Patrol Leader: 'I still trust you on your honour, Peggy, to keep the law of the Guides.' Peggy, finding herself 'rebadged', fingers the trefoil lovingly and thinks 'dear old Guides'.

Peggy determines to stop her patrol rotting about and works at making them into real Guides—interestingly, her patrol has won lots of badges, but Peggy recognises that as simply a form of pot-hunting and not what truly makes a Guide. A Patrol Cup to be awarded to the all-round best patrol offers a tangible reward to work towards. At first, in their frantic keenness to win, the other patrol members so muddle their poor Tenderfoot that she wrecks the rival patrols' gardens in order that theirs should win. The headmistress identifies the wider error:

> 'We may all be letter-perfect Guides, but we must be Guides at heart too … The law must be a real part of our lives. We must be rooted and grounded in it if the results are to be worth while … the new Guides—the Tenderfeet—must be trained not only in the actual finger-practice and lip-service, but also in the spirit that underlies the movement—the spirit of loyalty, honour and friendship to all the world.'

One patrol member criticises Peggy for continuing to coach members of other patrols at tennis when there are now fifty games points to be won towards the Patrol Cup. Talbot does not need to point the moral out any further than Peggy's fierce: 'I've always done it, haven't I?' Another girl suggests they spend all their spare time at camp working to gain points for the nature section of the cup; Peggy inarticulately points out that camp is an opportunity to become prepared on a very real level for more serious things.

> 'I've been thinking. It's wartime and this Camp's a Guide *chance* … we've got to rig ourselves up as useful Guides all round. Suppose now we *did*, all of us, spend the whole camping-time in tracking and snapping … and suppose we won the Cup. Well, even *that* wouldn't be everything, if something came along that we *couldn't* do on account of how we used the time.'

Lying in her tent on the first night of camp, she determines: 'I'll be a true Guide, or none at all.' Her Captain supports her view: camp is presented not as a treat but as a means of preparing for the possibility of invasion. 'After listening to or reading the stories of privations to women and children refugees in Serbia … the thought must have entered the minds of each of you: "How should *I* have behaved at such a time? Should I have been helpful or just a drone?"'

When Peggy catches her arch rival (who is in her patrol) cheating in an attempt to win the nature points for the cup, she is coldly official: 'Maisie had insulted her. But she was not dealing with personalities just now; at present she was acting as the head of her patrol.' She tells Maisie that she will not tell anyone, and Maisie gushes out her sense of relief that there will be no disgrace. Peggy is immediately able to see the utter weakness of Maisie's approach to Guiding and bitterly challenges her statement: 'as to "no disgrace!"' In her own mind, Peggy works out what really matters: 'I'm only just beginning to understand … that to keep *honourable* is the thing, and that I'd rather be dead without it; and that what other people think doesn't matter.'

When Peggy's own crisis occurs—in the best traditions of the school story she is falsely accused of the crime Maisie committed—she has established a secure sense of what is really important and prepares herself to endure the judgment of the Court of Honour with a calm mind: 'It can't really matter, because my honour's all right; it can't hurt the patrol really because of that.' *Peggy's Last Term* is a deeply thoughtful book, with challenging things to say about the difference between external and internal honour and an interesting twist on the usual ending.

Talbot's second Guiding book, *Betty at St. Benedick's* (1924), pitched at a younger age level, contains elements of the same conflicts but is slight in comparison. Betty is the thirty-third girl to arrive at a school where there are four patrols of eight. Unable, therefore, to be a full Guide she is adopted as the mascot of the Daisies who treat her with a disturbing patronage: 'We like little new girls to have nice dreams.' The rather twee storyline ('May Guides believe in fairies?') is overchoked with romanticism, but demonstrates Talbot's versatility.

Talbot never again quite reached the heights of *Peggy's Last Term* but many of her subsequent Guiding books make interesting comments on what it means to be a Guide. In *Jill, Lone Guide* (1927), the heroine, cast out on the world by her own sense of what is right (she leaves home, virtually penniless, so her brother can stop feeling he has to care for her, and marry the girl he loves), works, first as a cook then in a boarding house. Throughout the book she is comforted by the thought of the community of Guides which she feels surrounds her, to the extent that she faces a night on a stone step with equanimity, choosing to sing 'Taps' to herself. (Sue Sims and Hilary Clare suggest in their *Encyclopedia of Girls' School Stories* that Talbot, a lapsed member of the Plymouth Brethren, created girls who make a religion of their school; the same point might be made about her Guide books.)

Jill, Lone Guide depends far too much on a range of coincidences, but it has some careful insights into the importance of distinguishing between those faults that are unattractive but venial, and ones that are serious character flaws. The likeable heroine, whose sense of being a Guide is always kept well to the fore, is able to see beyond the bad temper of a fellow traveller and the irritability of her employer to appreciate their sterling qualities within, but is unforgiving and outspoken about her fellow-servant's deep selfishness.

The theme of Guiding giving one the sympathy and understanding of people who initially appear very different and, perhaps, unlikeable, is one to which Talbot returns. *The Peppercorn Patrol* avoids a too easy solution to the problem the Guides encounter of a nervous hostess who has a deep antipathy to Guides. They do not change her mind by gloriously saving her life. Instead they give her sympathy, and gently alter their own ways to make her feel more comfortable, giving up, for example, working at bookbinding and leathercraft in favour of the Embroiderer's and Needlewoman's badges with which she can give them assistance, and which they can do indoors with her. By the end of the book, their thoughtful response has worked a slow transformation: 'I've had such surprises, my dears, from the beginning about you Guides

… that I'd be surprised at nothing now except perhaps—if I found a Guide who wasn't right-down calculated to lift one clear out of the doleful dumps.' *Pioneer Pat* (1937), one of Talbot's last books, is a reworking of the themes of *Jill, Lone Guide*, this time showing Ranger Pat taking on the running of a bookshop to make her living. Once more, Talbot's heroine has the ready empathy to grasp the essential goodness behind a series of initially disconcerting people.

From her output, one imagines that Talbot leapt at the creation of Sea Guides in 1920 with a joyous 'Bags I'. Sadly, her Sea Guide/Ranger stories are among her weakest; *Skipper and Co* (1929), *Sea Rangers All* (1935) and the other Ranger books are rather predictable villain-defeating stories featuring a characterless group of girls. Their ducky little caps, with their white slip covers worn in the summer, never fail to get a mention, nor the habit of calling their headquarters their ship. Her last Guiding book, *Rangers and Strangers* (1938), a collection of short stories of which only the title story is about Guiding, is very much mixture-as-before and represents a perfunctory piece of work.

Ethel Talbot is often used as an example of the mediocre writer—she is even referred to as 'Awful Ethel'—but she has her champions. Several of her Guiding stories have a thoughtfulness about the meaning of being a Guide that offers a valuable contribution to the genre, and *Peggy's Last Term* should be on anyone's list of top Guiding books.

GUIDING AROUND THE GLOBE

Judy Harris

As Girl Guiding began to gain prominence in the UK, expatriates throughout the British Empire could not help but take notice of the new movement. Wives of government officials returned from 'home leave' with tales of Guiding, and before long girls around the world were enthusiastically joining fledgling Guide companies.

Commonwealth countries such as Canada and South Africa were quick to introduce the movement, both setting up Guides in 1910. Girls in the Falkland Islands were earning Tenderfoot badges as early as 1912, and New Zealand and India were included in Miss Agnes Baden-Powell's New Year's greeting list for 1913. Assisted in many cases by missionaries, Guiding also spread to countries such as Papua New Guinea, where the first Company began in 1927 in Papua, near Port Moresby. In non-Commonwealth countries too, the movement was often introduced by British expatriates. In Argentina, for example, the first Girl Guide companies were established in British schools as early as 1915, although the country's own association, the *Asociación Guías Argentinas*, was not started until many years later, in 1953.

Meanwhile, Scouting was rapidly spreading across Europe, followed by Guiding and, as with the British Empire, the European countries often then introduced Guiding to other countries under their rule. The Netherlands, for example, brought Guiding and Scouting to Aruba (1941) and Surinam (1947)—and so Guiding continued to spread throughout the world.

SOUTH AFRICA

B-P always had a special fondness for the Guides and Scouts of South Africa, the country where he first developed his Scouting skills. Guiding started in Johannesburg in 1910, but spread countrywide very quickly. Many companies were small and in remote areas. In *The Story of a Million Girls* (Rose Kerr, 1936), Miss Worters, an early Commissioner in the Transkei, describes an isolated village where one devoted woman fulfilled the duties of Captain, Vice-Captain, Brown Owl and Tawny Owl in one, and wore all four of her warrant badges—two in her hat and two in her tie. In another story, she recalls a remote village 'where only ten children of both sexes were to be found ... I suggested that Brownies and Cubs might, with discretion, be worked together. Shortly afterwards I had a letter telling me that the plan was not working as "the Cubs did not want to wear the Brownie uniform".' South African Guiding experienced some

Girl Guides in Kenya learn to tie knots

tensions, which are discussed below, but it has also had many memorable moments. Guiding in South Africa has continued to develop, and with the end of apartheid in 1994, further barriers to unity and progress were removed. The South African Guides have gained particular recognition for their work in areas such as the fight against HIV/AIDS and poverty.

AUSTRALIA

Although Guiding quickly spread around Australia, it was (at any rate initially) seen as an activity for the more upper-class members of society. A newspaper advertisement in 1911, seeking new members for one of Victoria's early Girl Guide groups, stated that: 'The troop will be kept strictly select and only girls of good character and respectability will be allowed to join.'

Lone Guides were particularly quick to gain popularity in Australia. With many girls living in remote towns or on isolated stations (in some cases, many days' travel from the nearest Girl Guide unit), it was necessary for Guiding to be delivered by correspondence course. After the Federal Council of the Girl Guides of Australia was formed in 1926, changes began to be made to adapt Guiding to Australia. For example, it was agreed that the Southern Cross should be substituted for the Pole Star in the syllabus for the Astronomer badge, English Patrol badges such as Forget-me-Nots were joined by emblems such as the Rosella, and the Domestic Service badge now required girls to show how to keep flies out of the house. In Ethel Talbot's *The Peppercorn Patrol* (1929) an Australian Guide visiting England comments that their tests are much the same except: 'We have to know how to treat snake-bites, while you have to know how to rescue folk under ice.'

Guiding in Australia continued to go from strength to strength, and by the mid 1970s Australia had definitively asserted its own identity, having assumed responsibility for its own leader training and, for the first time, begun producing its own handbooks.

The uniforms also began to change in the period from the late 1970s to the early 1980s, as I myself recall. Whilst a friend of mine wore a brown dress, yellow tie and brown felt beret in 1983, my Brownie uniform just one year later comprised a brown tunic, yellow polo top and broad-brimmed brown hat. Obviously, the authorities had finally realised that berets offered insufficient protection for active Brownies running around in the Australian sun! It was around this time, too, that the Brownie Six emblems changed, with Elves, Pixies and Gnomes making way for Australian bushland 'fairies' such as Moora Mooras, Woorails and Lalagullis.

NEW ZEALAND

Whilst girls in Australia were discovering the joys of Guiding, their sisters across the Tasman Sea were also showing a strong interest in the new youth movement. Initially, the girls followed their brothers in forming troops of 'Peace Scouts', with Patrol emblems including the Morepork, Pigeon and Kiwi. In 1923, however, the organisation became the Girl Guide Association of New Zealand and was formally recognised as a member organisation of the World Association.

With New Zealand experiencing a cooler climate than Australia, the New Zealand Girl Guides found it easier to follow the English Girl Guides in uniform style and programme. Joan Lees, who was enrolled as a Girl Guide in Invercargill in February 1937, recalls her earliest experiences as a Guide.

Invercargill, the most southerly city in New Zealand, can get very cold. Winter and summer, our uniform was the same: navy-blue woollen frock with long sleeves and patch pockets. A brown leather buckled belt encircled our waist, and a jade-green triangular tie was folded and knotted underneath our collar at the back with a reef knot.

My favourite Guiding memory is a floating camp fire on the Kina Peninsula. It was a warm evening just at sundown. We had prepared a raft and built on it an enormous camp fire … As the opening words were spoken we lit the fire and pushed the raft out into the tide. It was magical to sit on the beach singing, with the fire crackling and the flames reflected in the calm water.

The New Zealand Girl Guides read British Guiding fiction, with Leigh of the Christchurch Church Corner Trefoil Guild recalling Ethel Talbot's *Ranger Rose* (1928) as one of her favourite books. They also followed the fortunes of the Founders closely; Ngarene (also from the Christchurch Church Corner Trefoil Guild) recalls all Brownies and Guides being asked to donate a penny towards B-P's car, and Joan Lees remembers taking her Girl Guides to Christchurch on the occasion of Lady Baden-Powell's visit to New Zealand in 1967. Joan was particularly impressed by Lady Baden-Powell's memory—she recognised Joan from a meeting at Hampton Court five years earlier!

THE UNITED STATES OF AMERICA

Returning in 1912 to her native Georgia, Juliette Low, a charismatic woman who had been a Guide Captain in the United Kingdom, called her cousin on the telephone with the famous words: 'Come right over! I've got something for the girls of Savannah, and all of America, and all the world, and we're going to start it tonight!' She formed two companies of eighteen Guides, and within two years there were 60,000 girls in the movement. Initially the US movement used the name Guides, but it was not long before the name changed to Girl Scouts; the term Girl Guides was felt too similar to the Indian guides in the western States, and Scouts were already well-recognised through the Scouting movement. The uniform was also changed from navy to khaki, khaki being seen as more appropriate for the clay soils of Georgia. The name Girl Scouts was much disapproved of by the Baden-Powells and the British Guide leaders, who tried many times to persuade the Americans to accept the name Guide. The American Girl Scout Vice-President, Helen Storrow, was blandly diplomatic but unbudging in her replies, agreeing that uniformity was desirable and wondering if the Guides would consider changing their name to Scouts!

Girl Scouting quickly became part of the United States mainstream culture. The First Lady has held the office of Honorary President of the Girl Scouts since the 1920s when Mrs Hoover was active in the movement. The movement has changed in many ways from B-P's model but the emphasis on Scouting principles stays strong. The American Girl Scout organisation today numbers 3.7 million members and is the largest member of WAGGGS (World Association of Girl Guides and Girl Scouts).

STRIVING FOR UNITY

From the early days of Guiding and Scouting, a number of countries faced the problem of accommodating different races and religions within the one organisation. B-P had always held to the philosophy of one world, one movement, and tried hard, often working against the

An Anglo-Indian Girl Scout before the days of Guiding proudly wears her hat even on a family picnic

social mores of the day, to resolve issues of segregation. However, he found himself facing intractable customs and even laws.

In South Africa and in the southern United States there was great opposition to the idea of a mixed movement, South Africa did not admit mixed troops until the end of the apartheid era, and the US movement did not become fully desegregated until the 1950s, although there were Afro-American companies as early as 1917, and American Indian companies in 1921. Similarly, the first Guide Company in India was formed in 1911 in Jubbulpore but was for British and other white girls only. In 1916, the Viceroy vetoed the idea of allowing Indians to become Scouts and Guides, but alternative movements sprang up, some led by the Fabian socialist and founder of Theosophy, Mrs Annie Besant, and in 1921 Sir Robert Baden-Powell arrived in India to induct these various organisations into the official Scout and Guide movement.

Race was not the only thing that divided different nations: the first International Conference, held in the UK in 1920, received Russian delegates from both Bolshevik and counter-Bolshevik companies. Further, in many parts of the world there were separate organisations for different denominations and beliefs: the *Guides* in France were for the Catholics, the *Eclaireuses* for Protestant and secular movements.

Elsewhere, separate movements were created on the basis of language. In Canada, where Guides had started in 1911, the Girl Guides of Quebec formed an affiliated French-speaking organisation, giving their age groups French names, such as *Jeannettes* for the Brownies.

Despite the many instances of segregation, a united sisterhood of Guiding gradually became a reality. Indeed, there were some surprisingly early triumphs: the All-Malayan camp of 1930 was attended by Japanese, Malays, Eurasian, British, Australian, Chinese, Indian and Ceylonese Guides. Of course, the acceptance of members from different religions necessitated adaptations to the uniforms and accepted ways of working. Some Indian Guides wore saris, whilst Moslem companies designed their own uniform based on the salwar kameez.

However, some movements faced cultural difficulties that could not be overcome by simple means such as the adoption of a different uniform. In 1920, at the first International Conference, delegates from Persia, whose girls wore the chador, spoke of their hope of borrowing a walled garden so that their girls might go camping with no risk of being seen by any men.

Challenges were also faced in reconciling the objectives of Guiding, including the aim of fostering girls' independence, with the social requirements of other cultures. Miss Priyanthi Hemamali Rajapaksa joined the Sri Lankan Guiding movement in 1969, and soon after progressed to the Rangers. She recalls: 'One day I was asked by the senior Guide Captain to bring my mother to the meeting. The Guide Captain told my mother that I would have to leave Guiding if I continued to be chaperoned to meetings by the maid. She said that as a Ranger, I should be able to travel by myself. My mother got the shock of her life, as I am the eldest in the family and I had not previously gone anywhere alone. The Guide Captain made arrangements for me to travel home with another Ranger after the meetings. That was a major change in my life.'

Although the Promise and the Laws are important aspects of Guiding worldwide, the movement is sufficiently flexible to allow countries to amend the Promise and Laws to suit their cultural and social ideals. For example, whilst girls in countries such as Egypt, Venezuela and Zambia still have a Guide Law requiring them to be thrifty, girls in some wealthier (but time-poor) countries such as Australia are required instead to 'make good use of [their] time'! In Ireland, Guides belonging to the Catholic Guides of Ireland (as opposed to the Irish Girl Guides) follow a Law that 'A Guide does all Things for the Glory of God', whereas in Belgium from very early on they had the option to promise to serve a high ideal rather than God. Meanwhile in Tonga, where Guiding was introduced by Queen Salote in 1952, Girl Guides specifically promise 'to serve the King of Tonga', and the Japanese Promise contains a reference to Buddha as well as God.

GUIDING FICTION WORLDWIDE

Given the way in which Guiding spread so quickly around the world, and given the diversity of cultures and countries represented in the movement, it is surprising that aside from a number of Girl Scout stories emanating from the United States, very little Guiding/Scouting fiction appears to have been published outside England.

There are many possible reasons for this. Perhaps, particularly in Commonwealth countries, the Guiding fiction market was already saturated by imported English Guiding fiction; perhaps publishers in other countries felt that Guiding was not sufficiently prominent to result in a viable print run of Guiding stories; or perhaps, particularly in poorer countries, very few story-books were published at all.

In the case of Britain's colonies, the lack of 'local' Guiding fiction is possibly unsurprising. With their population still relatively small and, at least in the early years, unable to afford the luxury of story-books, colonial authors would likely have wanted to write books that would appeal to English readers, thus justifying a larger (and more profitable) print run. Books about Girl Guides, even set against an 'exotic' backdrop such as the Australian bush, offered little novelty to British girls. Tales of the stereotypical 'wild' Australian bush heroine, such as Norah Linton of Mary Grant Bruce's *Billabong* series, or Judy Woolcot of Ethel Turner's *Seven Little Australians*, would have been seen as far more exciting and interesting. Admittedly, Pixie and Molly, heroines of Mary Wright's *Sugar & Spice*, set in a small Australian town in the 1920s, do join the local Girl Guides. Although the girls follow the English system of proficiency badges and First Class and Second Class Guides, wear navy uniforms and learn traditional skills such as first aid, the patrols have Australian names: Kookaburras, Lorikeets and Waratahs. As the book was actually written in the late 1980s, however, it is difficult to know how accurately this reflects the usual activities and patrol names of the Australian Guides in the 1920s.

Other countries were sometimes featured in English Guiding story-books, but this was usually in the context of English Guides; the stories rarely featured girls belonging to the

Frontispiece from *A Girl Guide Captain in India*

Guiding organisations of those other countries. Writing about local Guides in foreign countries would have been quite difficult for British authors who had no personal experience of Guiding in the relevant country. Elinor M Brent-Dyer's Chalet School girls, for example, are active and enthusiastic Guides during the Tyrol days, but their companies are clearly run along English lines (hardly surprising, given that it was an English school with Guiders trained in England), and the girls never encounter Austrian *Pfadfinderinnen*, despite the fact that Guiding was established in Austria prior to the First World War. Similarly, E E Ohlson's Pippa meets no fellow *Pfadfinderinnen* in Switzerland, and Winifred Darch's Poppy Patrol encounters no *Eclaireuses* in Normandy, France.

There are several notable exceptions, however, to the reluctance of British authors to write about Guiding overseas. The *Girl's Own Paper* published a book by Mary Lean in 1934 titled *Joan of Glen Garland, a Canadian Girl Guide Story*. In Sibyl B Owsley's *Nicolette Goes Guiding* (1934), Nicolette, an English Guide, enjoys adventures with the local *Guides* in Monaco. Owsley describes the Guide meetings and activities, and reproduces songs in detail, suggesting that she may herself have encountered French Guides (whether in Monaco or France) at some stage. Violet Methley even has a Guiding story set in Australia—*The Bunyip Patrol* (1926). Janet Aldis describes in great detail a Guide Company in colonial India in her book *A Girl Guide Captain in India* (1922). Although the Company is run on British lines, there are concessions to the Indian climate and culture, such as khaki uniforms and sun hats, and servants to carry the provisions of the (British) Girl Guides on their hiking expedition. Indeed, the reliance on domestic servants by the British families in India appears to have been the cause for some exasperation amongst well-trained Guide captains, with Aldis's captain lamenting that her Girl Guides have 'no more idea of washing up than a crow has of making ice-cream'!

As noted earlier, the general exception to Britain's monopoly on Guiding fiction was the collection of Girl Scouting series emanating from the United States of America. Perhaps a lack of interest in the US in the school story genre left room for the emergence of several popular series dealing with Girl Scouts. Aside from the stories of the globe-trotting *Rugged Dozen* discussed below, various series of Girl Scout stories were published, including those by Margaret Vandercook (*The Girl Scouts of Beechwood Hill* etc, starting in 1921), Lillian E Roy (*The Girl Scouts at Dandelion Camp* etc, 1921), Lilian Garis (*The Girl Scout Pioneer* etc, 1920), Edith Lavell (*The Girl Scouts at Miss Allen's School* etc, 1920—the cover of this shows the Girl Scouts performing a dance in their middy blouses and daring bloomers rather than skirts) and Katherine Keene Galt (*The Girl Scouts Rally* etc, 1921). The books provide reasonably detailed accounts of the adventures of small troops of Girl Scouts. All of these authors were writing in the 1920s; it appears that in the United States, the heyday of Girl Scouting fiction ended much sooner than in England.

THE WORLD CENTRES

Given the number of books featuring adventures in the Swiss Alps, it is somewhat surprising that authors did not make more use of Our Chalet, one of the four 'World Centres', where Guiding and Scouting members from around the world can gather to experience new cultures, activities and international friendship. (The others are Pax Lodge, London, opened in 1991 but preceded by Our Ark and Olave House; Our Cabaña, Mexico, opened in 1957, and Sangam, India, opened in 1966.) One can only assume that no writer ever visited it. It is certainly a shame that Elinor M Brent-Dyer never had the chance to visit Our Chalet. Keen Guides, the Chalet girls would undoubtedly have enjoyed the chance to attend the opening in 1932, or to spend a weekend there as a treat to celebrate Madame's birthday in the later Tyrol years.

A book which does refer to the World Centres is *The Rugged Dozen Abroad* (1960). Based in part on the European adventures of Ms Dudley's own Girl Scout troop in the 1950s, the book follows the fortunes of an American Girl Scout troop touring England (where Our Ark is mentioned), Scotland, Holland, Germany, Italy, France and Switzerland—where they attend a World Camp and also visit Our Chalet. The surroundings of Our Chalet are described briefly—the pine woods, the snow-capped mountains and the World flag flying from the tall flagpole. However, the description of the girls' arrival is clear evidence of personal experience.

> She would never forget the long trek from the bus stop up the steep slopes toward the chalet and their first view of the building, looking so new and inviting and yet built in 1932. The Guider-in-Charge, Miss Pen Wood-Hill, had met them at the door and bade them welcome, a tall, slim, erect Englishwoman who, even in this short time, had made herself felt.

Those who have visited Our Chalet can easily identify with the 'long trek', and no doubt those who visited during Miss Pen Wood-Hill's time as Guider-in-Charge (1952–1968) would be able to relate to her description.

Other little details are clear evidence of personal experience; the fresh, crusty bread, large attic dormitory and international camp fires continue to be enjoyed by girls today, just as the Rugged Dozen enjoyed them in the early 1950s. Similarly, the references to placing guests in patrols named after local mountains, colour coding the rooms and allocating bathroom tickets would bring back many memories for those who visited Our Chalet at the time when these customs were practised.

ONWARDS AND UPWARDS

From the first girls who spoke out at the Crystal Palace Rally, Guiding has developed into the largest organisation for girls and women worldwide; 10 million members in 145 countries, girls and women of all cultures, religions and colours, are now united to build a better world. From building schools in Kenya to ski-ing world-famous Alpine pistes with companions from every corner of the globe, Guiding continues to offer girls and women around the world amazing adventures every day. Perhaps a new golden era of Girl Guiding and Girl Scouting fiction may yet emerge—authors would certainly not be short of exciting storylines!

Pitching camp

KIT

'All self-respecting Patrols have oddments,' Lois Sanger says firmly when she starts her new patrol in *Autumn Term* (Antonia Forest, 1948). And so they do. In *The Swallows See it Through* (C R Mansell, 1955) a Guide looks round the hut, thinking: 'Someone … must have provided those things—whipped the ropes, cut out and stitched morse flags, embroidered and framed patrol emblems, sawn and sandpapered the log seats.'

Guides from the golden age of Guiding fiction love to load themselves up. Bean bags, first-aid kit, knives (of course), string, collapsible drinking cups and lengths of cord. Ethel Talbot has a particular interest in all the paraphernalia: in her 1929 story *The Peppercorn Patrol*, three sisters are sent to stay at a remote house. Eager Guides, they are determined to work for various tests while there and take with them Kodaks, a portable gramophone, billy-cans, raffia bundles, book-binding tools, nature note-books, some signalling flags, other Guide impedimenta and a small Union Jack. A large part of the story simply consists of their quest to find a room in which to keep all their kit.

One very important item of equipment in the early days was the staff, or 'staves' in the plural at that era, and one can imagine how much the girls enjoyed wielding them. 'We never moved without our poles!' one captain is quoted in Rose Kerr's *The Story of the Girl Guides* as saying. 'Ready for any emergency—making a stretcher or fording a river.' I have yet to find a story, however, which features tracking irons, mentioned as a piece of Guiding kit in the 1946 Guiding manual *Be Prepared*. These were strapped to a Guide's feet and left the track of an animal for others to follow. Did blacksmiths up and down the land make them for their local companies, one wonders?

If one counts uniform as kit, then the most fundamental piece of kit of all is the Guide badge; it announces the wearer as a member of the great sisterhood, and a common motif in Guiding stories is the feeling of relief encountered when the Guide badge is spotted and a fellow Guide recognised. Most girls go on wearing their badge even when they leave active Guiding. For many, the badge had tremendous symbolic value. In *The Great Test*, Catherine Christian's account of Guiding in the Second World War, she tells of a Guide in a German concentration camp who kept her badge safe throughout all searches by hiding it in her mouth. The badge symbolises the Guide's honour and represents her right to be a Guide: 'You are certainly not worthy of wearing this trefoil until you have wiped this stain from your honour.' (*Pamela Ventures Abroad*, Pauline Hope, 1934)

If the badge is the individual piece of kit that is most sacred, the colours—the company flag or the flag of their country—represent the same for the company as a whole and have intense symbolic value. Colours are always carried, raised or struck with ceremony by a colour party consisting of one person to carry the flag and one Guide either side 'in case of attack or accident', as B-P excitingly puts it. The deep patriotism of Guides is expressed in the way they revere their colours, and the handling of the colours is one of the most militaristic elements of Guiding. For example, colours must never be left unguarded, so when a camp goes off on an expedition, the colours are struck. They are also struck at dusk and always with reverence:

> Perhaps in all Pamela's carefully planned afternoon nothing left such a deep impression on the parents as that sudden glimpse of what, to the camp, was everyday routine.
>
> They saw the almost wildly hilarious Guides, who had been racing about the field a moment before, spin suddenly round to face the flagstaff, spring to attention and stand silent and rigid as statues … The little ceremony was over in two or three minutes and work and play went on as before, but the knowledge of it remained in the hearts of the older onlookers.
>
> *The Guide Camp at Herons Bay*, Margaret Middleton, 1927

A GUIDE'S HONOUR

Wendy Ingle

The concept of honour was at the heart of Guiding right from the start. It is in the First Law and embedded in the Guide Promise. And honour runs like a shining thread through much of the early fiction.

Generations of women learned and repeated their part in the Guide enrolment ritual, where the Captain asked the new recruit: 'Do you know what your honour means?' The girl repeated, 'My honour means that I can be trusted to be truthful and honest.' She was then asked, 'Do you promise on your honour to do your best to do your duty to God and the Queen, to help other people and to keep the Guide Law?' The Promise, with honour at its core, appeared first in *Home Notes* on 8 September 1910, where Agnes Baden-Powell, in 'Some Extracts from the B-P Guide Law', stressed: 'A Guide's honour is to be trusted: If a Guide says "On my honour it is so," that means it *is* so just as if she had taken the most solemn oath.'

'The Girl Scouts' is a story by Evelyn Yates, published in the *Girls' Reader*, 'The Bright Saturday Story Paper', from 17 July 1909. It is said to be the first story of Girl Scouts. In the story two nieces are wished on the Bishop of Hawlsbury by his brother. The Bishop's wife envisages 'two sweet darling little girls'. What they get is two young women of sixteen and fourteen, attired in Scout uniform, complete with staves and axes.

The girls proceed to organise a patrol in the village and administer the Promise to Meg, the 'wholly incorrigible' orphan whom they transform into an obedient Scout. Their oath is quite distinctive: 'I swear to be loyal to God and the King! To help other people at all times. And to obey the Scout law.' There is no mention of honour, but the effect on Meg is as powerful as if there had been:

> '… lor', miss, you've done it now! You've made me swear on to be'ave proper and decent like I should! An' I'll do it, too! I'll do it for you! Meg Lotts may be a wrong 'un, but she won't break no oath she's took for you!'

With the concept of Guide's honour so well embedded in popular culture it is perhaps surprising that there are only three Guiding books with honour in their titles:

The Honour of the Company, Jane Agnes Staunton Batty, 1922
The Honour of a Guide, Ethel Mary Channon, 1926
The Guide's Honour, May Wynne, 1929

A Guide's Honour frontispiece

I have also found a short play—*A Guide's Honour*, a dramatic sketch for Girl Guides by Florence Una Norris. This is undated, but listed as new in the 1923/4 catalogue of the publisher, Abel Heywood & Son, Ltd, of Manchester.

The play looks at the concept of Guide's honour through the eyes of the Scout brother of one of the Guides. His sister, Joan, is to be tested on her Laws next week, so she has been saying them over to herself. She begins to repeat again, 'A Guide's Honour is to be trusted.' And Ted responds: 'A lot girls know about honour, or anything else.'

Joan is then left alone in the Guide shed with a new recruit called Edith and a piece of fine needlework which has been brought in for a Needlework badge. When Ted calls Joan away, Edith leans across the needlework to look at some nature pictures, and upsets a bottle of ink over it.

Edith is in no hurry to own up to the disaster. We are obviously to understand that as she has not yet absorbed the Guide ethos she is ready to lie to protect herself. And so the blame falls on Joan.

This leads to a dichotomy which crops up time and again in Guide fiction.

Joan is asked by her Patrol Leader: 'Joan, on your honour as a Guide, do you know anything about this?

JOAN (desperately)—I—I—I can't answer you, Margaret!

She knows that as she did not do it the culprit has to be Edith (in fact Edith has owned up, to Joan, in an aside). One does not tell tales, and neither does one lie to a PL, so Joan is trapped. She dissolves into tears.

Nonplussed, Margaret sends Joan off to wash her face and sets the others to working. She sits down with Edith, ironically to teach the Laws.

MARGARET (to EDITH, who looks frightened)—Now, Edith, the first Guide law is one of the most important ones. It says, 'A Guide's honour is to be trusted.' That means that whatever happens a Guide is always trustworthy, honourable and truthful. When a Guide says a thing, you know that it is true. Now say that law.

EDITH (slowly)—A Guide's—honour—is …

As Edith bursts into tears, Ted returns to complain that 'plucky' Joan is crying and he believes she is covering for someone. Edith owns up. She is unanimously given a second chance, and all bridges are mended.

Ted sums it up by saying: 'Whatever other girls are like, I'm prepared to admit now that Girl Guides have got some grit!'

One theme that recurs frequently in early Guiding fiction is the idea that Guides hold themselves to a higher standard of honour than the general run of girls. Indeed, surprising as it may seem, if you read only Guide stories you might believe that schoolgirls' honour consisted only in sportily breaking school rules and refusing to tell tales on their schoolfellows. A book which uses the perceived difference between Guide honour and schoolgirl honour is A M Irvine's *Nora, the Girl Guide* (1913). The eponymous Nora is the chief rebel at the school and sworn opponent of Brenda, new girl and Second Class Guide. Brenda's enthusiasm for introducing Guides to the school is seen as a threat to Nora's supremacy.

One of Nora's clique leaves a hateful note in Brenda's desk, which a mistress demands to see. Brenda throws it into the fire to prevent her anonymous tormentor from getting into the trouble she would quite rightly be in. She is interrogated about the paper, but:

> … to this question she could give no answer without implying that the blame lay at another door. By this time the Abbotswell idea of school honour—that to shield a companion at any cost was the bounden duty of all schoolgirls—was well absorbed by Brenda Gale [so she has learned schoolgirl honour]. But she could not do that at the expense of truth [Guide honour]. Therefore the only way out of this difficulty lay in silence.

Her silence leads the headmistress to lock her into a small dressing room, on a diet of dry bread and milk.

Provided with paper and ink to write her confession, she does 'the first deceitful thing that had ever occurred to Brenda Gale'. She writes to her mother, and asks the maid to post the letter. This—in the world Brenda inhabits—is a great crime: '… it was intolerable to think that she had stooped to a surreptitious act.' This brings into the story another concept connected with a Guide's honour, that of the trefoil, the Promise badge, as her 'life': 'Then she suddenly thought of her Guide badge—her "Life"—and with a burst of tears tore it off. She could not wear that badge of honour with this sin upon her conscience!'

Agnes Baden-Powell explains the concept: 'If a Guide were to break her honour by telling a lie, or by not carrying out an order exactly, when trusted on her honour to do so, she would cease to be a Guide, and she may be required to hand over her Guide badge, and never be allowed to wear it again—she loses her life.'

Brenda is mortified that she has been so dishonourable and begs to see the Headmistress and confess.

Meanwhile Nora has been realising that Brenda is not only imprisoned for shielding the true culprit, but is also gaining respect, even fame, from the rest of the school for her way of taking the punishment.

'Brenda is not the sort of girl, and besides, she's—well, yes, I'll say it—she's a Girl Guide … It is quite impossible to imagine such a thing—that is, when a girl is a Girl Guide.'

Nora sets out to solve the mystery of who actually committed the crime—saying, typically, 'I don't see why she should absorb all the honour in the school merely because she's a Guide …'

Nora is eventually converted by Brenda's example, and goes on to become the school's chief recruiter and first Silver Fish in no time at all.

Nora, the Girl Guide throws into relief the huge gulf that Guide writers suggest could exist between the concept of Guide's honour and that of schoolgirl honour, and suggests Guide's honour exists on a higher plane than schoolgirl honour and might replace it. Nora exclaims when the idea is first proposed, 'This idiotic idea would put an end to all fun, and turn the lot of us into canting hypocrites.' She believes that 'to shield a companion at any cost was the bounden duty of all schoolgirls'.

The idea that being a Guide necessitated a higher ideal of honour is often illuminated by actual anti-Guide clubs formed in the fictional schools. In Darch's *Poppies and Prefects* (1923) there is a group calling itself the anti-Guide league. Its prime mover is Meriel, who thoroughly dislikes the heroine, Margaret, who is not only a patrol leader but also the new Head Girl of the school. One of Meriel's chief objections to Guides had been the good turn which a Guide is on her honour to perform. 'I did think it was a good thing—I won't deny that. But I hated to be forced to do a good turn every day.'

May Wynne's 1929 *The Guide's Honour* is another tale full of the conflict between Guide honour and the schoolgirl code. The third complication thrown into the mix is family pride—the honour of the parent!

Evebell Scrayne, shy and quiet, is a Second Class Guide and a new girl at Bisford House school. She is pleased to be welcomed into the school Company, 4th East Linsley, where at their first meeting camp is spoken of. It transpires that they always camp at Sattlesbury-on-Sea, at which information Evebell goes white.

Another Guide, Nina, has been unkind (and unGuidelike) enough to say, 'We don't want any freaks in the 4th Linsley … I'm rather sorry Captain is recruiting. We were quite a happy family before.' She is the only one who is observant enough to connect the name of Sattlesbury with Evebell's reaction. Nina suggests, very unpleasantly, that Evebell might be a blot on the Company's good name: 'We couldn't take a Guide down to camp with a dishonoured name, could we?' Honour means different things to different people and produces strong responses. A true Guide would, of course, remember that every Guide is a sister and accept Evebell, whatever the truth about her family.

Evebell's family encourage her to camp, even though Sattlesbury is where they used to live, and where her brother was unjustly accused of a crime. They hope that while she is there she will find evidence to clear him. It becomes clear that if poor Evebell is not to be sacrificed for the Company's honour she is to be sorely tried for her family's. The burden placed on her forces her to break rules constantly.

Eve is alone in camp when she hears a cry for help from the shore, 'raised in sobbing notes of fear'. Local notable Mr Wratheley's small grandson has got himself stranded on a rock 'completely surrounded by foaming waters'. With no thought beyond 'Be Prepared' Eve rushes to his aid, and holds him safe while the nursemaid runs for help. One wonders why the nursemaid could not have rushed into the sea for him, but then, she's not a Guide. As they are finally rescued, Eve overbalances in the sea and the next she knows she is waking up 'in the dear old Vicarage'.

Finally, the Company is proud of her; life-saving is an honourable Guide accomplishment!

And grumpy Mr Wratheley's conscience is stirred sufficiently for him to admit that it was his son, Ronald, who signed the fraudulent cheque, as he has confessed on his recent death bed. Having redeemed her family's honour, Eve is able to take her rightful place in the Company. Nina absents herself from Evebell's triumphant return to camp, but she has so misguided a concept of Guide's honour that perhaps she is beyond redemption.

May Wynne rewrote this story almost exactly as *Girls of the Pansy Patrol* in 1931, with Jessamy playing Evebell's part.

Batty's *Honour of the Company* looks at honour in both the small things and the profound. Her heroine, Joan, is 'not strong' and is sent to the vicarage to share lessons with the daughter of the house, Bessie. There Joan learns about Guides, and is eventually permitted to join them, due to the intervention of a local bigwig, Lady Falconer, whose own daughter Dorothy is a member of the Company when she is home from school.

Frontispiece from *The Honour of a Guide*

Dorothy, Joan and Bessie become friends, but it is quiet Joan who frequently has to prompt Dorothy's conscience. 'The idea of Guide's honour had taken firm hold upon Joan's mind, and she had been surprised to find that on many points Dorothy was not nearly so particular as she was.' Dorothy forgets small debts, and is over generous when marking her own tests, such as Kim's Game results.

When they think that Dorothy has entered a blouse for her needlework test which she had not sewn herself, Joan and Bessie steal the parcel from the examiner's table. Needless to say this is the wrong parcel, Joan's quiet disappointment having made Dorothy confess and retrieve the parcel herself.

> 'I used to think she [Joan] was so fussy,' she added [to her Captain].
> 'Do you think so now?' asked Miss Warner. Dorothy lifted eyes that were still honest.
> 'No, I think I'm not a proper Guide, Miss Warner. Are you going to turn me out?'

Dorothy is not turned out, and soon the whole Company is off to camp ten miles from home. Miss Warner, in a talk to her girls, emphasises that honour emanates from 'Christ—the Captain of the Company, and all the rest of us are to work under him and find out what he wants us to do'. Guide stories rarely point out the religious ideals underlying the concept of the Guide's Promise this clearly.

When the camp is disturbed by a night-time air raid, and bombs fall close by, the Guides are steadfast in their refusal to panic. Death, Captain reminds them, is nothing to fear, because if killed they would go to the Captain of the Company. So they brew cocoa and take their bedding downstairs where they will be marginally safer. Joan feels they have upheld the honour of the Company well that night. They can justly take pride in being brave and not becoming a burden by panicking. The early Guide handbooks emphasised the need for girls to be ready to face the hazards of war (as reflected in the story of Mary Mainwaring in *Terry, the Girl-Guide*).

Honour as linked to notions of chivalry and of the knights of old was present from the beginning in Guiding. It featured especially in *Scouting for Boys*, and teaching about chivalry was in the programme of B-P's experimental camp on Brownsea Island in 1907. But it is seldom made so explicit as in *Seven Wild Swans* (1936) by Catherine Christian, writing as Patience Gilmour.

Rangers are expected to take their Promise into the wider world, and the Wild Swans—a group of Rangers—consider themselves akin to the knights of the Round Table, treating all members equally and valuing each other's different strengths, skills and jobs. They progress from incident to incident, looking for real good to do, and often adding to their number through these good turns.

The Seven Wild Swans barely mention honour, but are amongst the most honourable heroines I have encountered. The plot revolves around two of the Rangers giving up the chance to win an important air race, in order to fly a blinded child to a doctor who might save his sight, even though winning the race would enable them to save an orphanage from being closed and keep two of their number in their jobs there. Luckily the surgeon, Dr Craigie, has recently had a generous bequest which he does not really need. He has been looking for a good cause and is pleased to invest in the orphanage, thus ensuring that it will remain open and two of the Wild Swans will keep their jobs.

In the last book with honour in its title, Channon's *The Honour of a Guide*, orphaned Ethne learns Guide honour through the friendly contact she has along the way with Guiders and Guides. So thoroughly does she imbibe the spirit of Guiding that she patiently bears her great-aunt's refusal to let her join any movement so unsuitable for a girl! On the aunt's death, she has to be persuaded that it will not be dishonourable to go against the old lady's wishes and become a Guide.

The concept of a Guide's honour is not always easy to define, as its various aspects portrayed in these early tales show. However, it appears time and again throughout the heyday of Guide fiction, until it is so much a part of the Girl Guide spirit that it barely needs mentioning. Many Guide stories bring us girls who have shown in their lives the honour at the heart of the Guide Promise, or, as Patience Gilmour has it in her dedication to *Seven Wild Swans*: 'all those, who, following the Clover Leaf [the Guide Trefoil], have found the star'.

CATHERINE CHRISTIAN: A WRITER IN SEARCH OF A QUEST

Hilary Clare

Catherine Christian was perhaps the most influential writer of Guide fiction of all, not because she was remarkably prolific (though with six Guide stories, seven Ranger stories and two for Guiders her output was not negligible) but because she was, for the six years of the Second World War, editor of *The Guide* and closely involved with *The Guider*. Crucial also is the fact that several of her books were reprinted by Blackie in the post-war period, thereby extending her audience to include a new generation at a time when Guiding books had significantly declined in number. Very few of her books have no Guiding context, and they are not among her best work.

She was born in Chelsea on 22 July 1901 as Mamie Mühlenkamp, the only child of Christian and Catherine Mühlenkamp. Her paternal grandfather had been born in Germany but came to England as a young man, married an English girl, and prospered as a shirt manufacturer; the family firm eventually had a shop in New Bond Street. Christian joined his father in the business, and eventually moved his family to Croydon, where he died in 1935. His wife was

Cherries in Search of a Captain
frontispiece

the daughter of a jeweller and trained as a teacher, as did two of her sisters. The author's background was therefore comfortably middle class, with an inheritance of hard work and craftsmanship, both of which figure prominently in her writing.

She was educated at Croydon High School (like 'Josephine Elder', her senior by some five years) and became a journalist; in 1934 she listed her 'special subjects' in the *Author's and Writer's Who's Who* as history and child psychology; she is known to have been a violinist and to have been interested in (coloured) light therapy. During this early adult period of her life she appears to have lived at home, presumably working freelance though between 1931 and 1934 she recorded that she had been assistant editor of *The New Merry-go-Round*, a publication which has not been traced but which sounds like a children's periodical.

Although we have no definite information on this point, it is inconceivable that she was not herself a Girl Guide, quite possibly from very early in the movement; she would certainly have known slightly older contemporaries who could have been among the very earliest Girl Scouts. From 1919 (when she turned eighteen) to 1921 she was

Lieutenant of the 1st Purley Company; from 1921 to 1923 Lieutenant of the 35A Croydon Company, and between 1923 and 1925 Captain of the 9th and 9A Croydon Companies. In 1927 she was briefly Tawny Owl of the 9th Croydon Pack, and in 1928–29 Captain of the 6th Surrey Lones. All this was useful background for her Guide books, and indeed her first Guide story, *Greenie and the Pink 'Un* (1928), is dedicated to the 9th Croydon, St Michael's, Guides and Brownies, showing that like many other Guide writers of the period she was inspired by contact with real-life young members of the movement.

None of her books was published under her real name. *Greenie and the Pink 'Un* appeared under the pseudonym Catherine Christian (the name clearly derived from her parents' first names), perhaps because she hoped to write 'real' books as Mamie Mühlenkamp (though her only non-Guiding adult contemporary novel, *Syringa Street*, 1930, was published as Christian), perhaps because of the negative connotations of a German name, which cannot have made life easy for a girl who was a teenager during the First World War. Whether she ever formally changed her name to Catherine Mary Christian is not clear, but she was certainly known as such by the end of her life and, as we shall see, probably much earlier. For most of her Ranger books (and for one little book of rather undistinguished verse, *Bells and Roses*, 1936) she adopted the name Patience Gilmour; her Ranger story *Diana Takes a Chance*, which was published in book form in 1940 as by Catherine Christian, had originally been serialised in *The Guide* in 1939 as *London Venture* by Patience Gilmour.

This use of a different writing name in *The Guide* may have been due to the fact that by then she was editing that periodical, her appointment (as 'Miss Christian', suggesting that by then she was using her writing name for general purposes) having been approved on 6 December 1938. In the same period the editor of the companion paper, *The Guider*, was Margaret ('Peg') Tennyson, five years younger, who was to become Christian's great friend and who wrote (mostly Guide stories) under the name Carol Forrest. They shared a flat in Battersea and after this was destroyed in the Blitz, moved out of London, first to a Gypsy caravan at Blacklands Farm, West Hoathley, Sussex (a Guide centre) and then to Woldringham, Surrey. Here Christian was again attached to a Guide company (as Lieutenant of the 1st Woldringham, 1942–46), and, judging by her contributions to *The Guide*, was also moving around the country participating in various aspects of war work. She and Tennyson became involved with the Guide International Service and with the exiled Polish Chief Guide, Madame Olga Malkowska, whom they helped with a home for war orphans at Hawson Court near Buckfastleigh, Devon; they ran a smallholding and Christian was for a time curator of the Salcombe National Trust Museum. Tennyson died in 1972, and Christian, of lung cancer, on 12 November 1985. She asked that her ashes be scattered on Dartmoor beneath Cave-Penny Cross, reflecting her long love of the area and of the wild. An acute appreciation of the natural world runs through all her work.

Christian's Guiding books fall conveniently into three groups, the first being those centring on Guides. The earliest was *Greenie and the Pink 'Un* (1928) in which the 'Greenie' of the title is fourteen-year-old Avril Delawny, who runs away from her guardian aunt and uncle, steals a Guide uniform while the owner is bathing, and goes through various vicissitudes before the inevitably happy ending. She is befriended by a Boy Scout (who nicknames her 'Greenie' because of her obvious lack of knowledge of Guiding and indeed of real life), and who introduces her to the ideals of the movement. The book is interesting because it is clearly aimed as much at girls outside Guiding as those inside it; Avril does not become a 'real' Guide until the end of the story, having seen and repented the error of her ways (and saved a Brownie, the 'Pink 'Un' of the title, from a road accident). The plot is implausible but Avril and Bob are not, and there is plenty of realistic detail.

There is a not dissimilar idea in one of the later Guide stories, *A Schoolgirl from Hollywood* (1939), in which Mary Ellen, who has been thoroughly spoilt as a child film-star, comes to an English school and works her way to redemption via the Guides.

Christian's three central and important Guide stories, *Cherries in Search of a Captain* (1931), *The Marigolds Make Good* (1937) and *The 'Kingfishers' See it Through* (1942), share a theme, that of a patrol which has lost its company or captain and which decides to make do without one. The Cherries are befriended by Major John Sylvester ('Little John'), who teaches them woodcraft, provides them with a base and (ultimately) with a captain in the person of the apparently scatty 'Miss Henderson', who turns

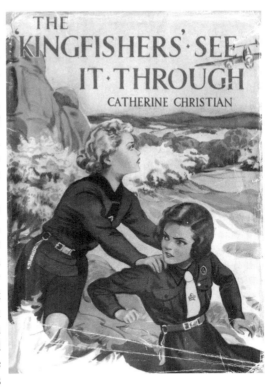

out to be a favourite author with her eccentricities explained by illness and family trouble. This is in the well-worn tradition of *Terry, the Girl-Guide*, but Christian makes it her own by her emphasis on the importance of getting back to the basics of Guiding. As Cherry, the leader of the patrol, explains to Little John: 'We mean to go back to beginnings and be like the girls who first did Guiding by themselves, years and years ago, before the war. We want to skin rabbits, and build brushwood huts, and do extra special good turns without being found out, and—oh, stacks and stacks of things.' Typically Christian, too, is the fact that the most efficient member of the patrol is not middle-class Cherry or Petronella (her Second) but working-class Lottie, who has learnt country lore from her ex-gamekeeper father, housecraft from her mother, and who has to leave school (at fourteen) and go into service as Miss Henderson's maid to help the family finances. The sisterhood of all Guides was always something Christian was keen to emphasise, and on the whole she manages it without condescension.

The Marigolds Make Good, six years later, again concerns a patrol which decides to stick together, this time when their Company is disbanded for slackness. They too resolve to get back to basics, and although the ostensible plot of the book deals with providing a new home for an old Gypsy, its real theme is the regeneration of the Guiding spirit among the girls. It is one of Christian's most appealing works, with distinctive characters, a not too improbable setting, and a fine climax in the County Rally where the Marigolds prove their worth in spite of being involved in a road smash on the way. Its popularity is attested by the fact that Blackie reprinted it three times in the 1950s.

The 'Kingfishers' See it Through, on the other hand, is so much of its time that it is easy to see why it was not reissued. Once more the book opens with a patrol in distress because their Company is closing down, and deciding to go it alone. The narrator, Sylvie, who has been a not very enthusiastic Guide for two years, joins with Paddy, the newest recruit, to write letters from Paddy's (invented) grown-up cousin 'Lorn', to help them along; the situation becomes incredibly complicated when a real Lorn turns up in the village. (Bizarrely, Sylvie reflects that 'probably a great many people are called Lorn'.) Alongside the Kingfishers we meet the Blue Tit Patrol (renamed the 'London Prides'), evacuees who fiercely resent the middle-class exclusiveness of the old Company and who also decide to do their own thing. Of course the two groups gradually come together, and end by uncovering a spy plot involving carrier pigeons. In the resurrection of the Company which follows, Sylvie becomes leader of a new patrol with girls from both groups, to be named the Carrier Pigeons. She is again the narrator of the sequel, *The Seventh Magpie* (1946), which was edited, not to its advantage, and reissued as *Sally Joins the Patrol* (1948 and 1966). This welded together the two themes of reforming an unsatisfactory character (Sally) with rehousing and assisting someone in need (a shell-shocked ex-airman artist who is struggling to come to terms with the loss of his right hand), but it also has as a subsidiary theme the familiar one of regenerating a slack patrol, and contains some strong propaganda on behalf of the Guide International Service.

The School at Emery's End (1944) focuses on two sisters who have expected to join a school 'run on Guide and Scout lines entirely', but who instead find that they have inherited an orphanage and heroically set out to run it themselves, of course assisted by their Guide principles and training. (A good Guide foundation had also been the cause of success of the heroine of *The Pharaoh's Secret*, 1940, which is really a fantasy involving the Lords of Shadow and the Brothers of Light and rather too much emphasis for modern taste on the Great White Brotherhood.)

An equal number of Christian's books, written both as Catherine Christian and as Patience Gilmour, focus, either largely or in part, on Rangers. Her earliest contribution to this genre, as Catherine Christian, was *The Luck of the Scallop Shell* (1929), with a sequel serialised in *The Guide* in 1929, which did not achieve book publication. It concerns a group of grown-up girls who were once 'the Poplar Patrol of the 1A Colston Cadets, and even before that, in the dim and far off past when Guides wore khaki hats and carried broomsticks, the Poppy Patrol of the 1st Colston Guides'. The narrator describes what they are all now doing, and their resolve to continue as 'the Pilgrim Patrol', but after this promising beginning the story becomes a Ruritanian adventure and rather loses its Guiding flavour. However, Christian returned to the idea of a group of older girls with her much more successful series *Three's a Company, a Story for Lone Guides* (1935), *Seven Wild Swans, a Story for Rangers* (1936), *The Quest of the Wild Swans* (1941) and *The Cygnets Sail Out* (1943). The first of the series involves only three of the girls: orphaned Laurie, who has got stranded in the South of France, invalid Ann, and stalwart, rather older, Dorothy, who comes to nurse Ann and is instrumental in rescuing Laurie; together the two younger girls find themselves through a return to Guiding principles. *Seven Wild Swans*, perhaps the best of this attractive group, follows the three into adult life and introduces other characters at the same stage, focusing on their Ranger involvement. *The Quest of the Wild Swans* merely takes them a little further on the same road (despite its 1941 publication date it does not deal with them in wartime), but *The Cygnets Sail Out* both introduces new characters and shows us how the original set are affected by the war. It ends with a strong commitment to the work of the Guides after the war, something which Christian had imbibed from Madame Malkowska and to which she was personally committed.

Just before the war (1938) she had published *Bringing up Nancy Nasturtium*, which featured a Ranger and her Brownie cousin; like the Wild Swans series, which it somewhat prefigures, it brings Rangers and Rovers together; like the Guide books it involves the loss of a captain and of a headquarters; like so many of Christian's books it describes the restoration of a building. It also brings in the question which was clearly felt by others as well as Christian: what is a Ranger? She supplies the answer:

> 'A really, truly, *grown-up* Guide … A Guide who has taken her Guiding into a wider world by growing bigger and wiser and wider-minded in herself; a Guide who still keeps exactly the same promise and law, but with more depth of meaning, more scope of vision, more real understanding of life, and herself, and the Law.'

This is quintessential Christian and shows what she thought 'real' Guiding was about. Similarly *Diana Takes a Chance* (1940), set in just pre-war London, shows how Guide ideals, finally put into practice, reform a rather spoilt and hitherto lackadaisical Ranger when she is abruptly left in charge of young step-siblings.

The idea of the Guide Law underpinning a positive attitude to new things runs strongly through Christian's two books for Guiders—*Harriet, the Return of Rip van Winkle* (1941) and its sequel, *Harriet Takes the Field* (1942, following serialisation in *The Guider* between June 1939 and December 1940). These books were of course intended for adults, and reflect not just what was going on in the Guiding world but also what Christian thought ought to be. Her Harriet is introduced as a woman doctor in her fifties who has been involved in Guides from

the beginning (presumably, given her age, as a Guider), served during the First War in Serbia, then ran a Guide company, but for the last ten years has been out of England doing medical work in unspecified parts of Asia. The first book's chapters follow her round the country as she catches up with what her former Guides are now doing (married, nursing, teaching, in advertising, in films) and what has happened to the movement in her absence; this gives a fascinating picture of what was going on in Guiding, and was of course written by someone who was now based at Guide Headquarters in London and who had her ear close to the ground. Christian makes it clear that Guiding was even then going through a crisis: some of her characters question what it is for, and ask whether girls still need it, should it change, and if so, how? Harriet is remorseless in her lack of toleration of the second-rate and the self-satisfied but given hope by the keen youngsters whom she does encounter, even if they are keen in unorthodox ways. At the end of the book Christian gives us a delightfully unexpected conclusion, when Harriet, instead of returning to her work out East, suddenly reveals that she is going to marry a doctor friend of long standing whom she has loved for twenty years but who had married a month before they met—his wife has now opportunely died. The sequel picks up her story as a married woman newly settled in a small cathedral town and recently appointed District Commissioner. Inevitably the book is dominated by preparations for, and then experience of, the Second World War, the last episode (and last chapter) ending in December 1940, possibly simply because that was the point at which *The Guider* folded because of wartime restrictions. Harriet is off East again but still full of hope for the future. Of course her story is as much propaganda as reportage, but it remains a valuable picture of what the Guides set out to do at a time of unparalleled national crisis.

Christian's last Guiding book was non-fiction: *The Big Test, The Story of the Girl Guides in the World War* (1947). It was presumably a work commissioned by the Girl Guides Association, by whom it was published. By then Christian appears to have distanced herself from the movement, possibly after some sort of row or at least shake-up at headquarters, perhaps because of disillusionment at the way things were now going. She had, after all, shared the common experience of six years of war, had lost her home if not family and friends, and had been writing fairly strenuously into the bargain, publishing ten books (all with Guiding themes) in the nine years from 1939 to 1947.

For whatever reason, there were no more Guiding books. She produced two adult historical novels, one story for girls, a children's book, and finally, as her last book, *The Sword and the Flame* (1978), an Arthurian romance which reminds us that the Arthurian legends run as an inspiration through all her books—the one book that Avril takes with her on running away, in *Greenie and the Pink 'Un*, is Tennyson's *Idylls of the King*, and the Wild Swans are particularly enthused by the Grail idea. There is a sense in which Christian's whole writing career pursues characters in search of a quest, always seeking for an ideal to live up to, and a definite feeling that, for her, Guiding came closest to providing it. Certainly her Guiding books are her best work, and the ones for which her name will deservedly be remembered.

PEG AND CHUMS: THE GUIDE BOOKS OF MRS A C OSBORN HANN

Tig Thomas

Mrs A C Osborn Hann's books have a realism about them which is matched by no other author, an almost documentary feel in their portrayal of ordinary Guides, which gives possibly the most accurate picture of what Guiding was actually like for many girls in the 1920s and 30s. Her uncondescending depiction of working-class girls has already been discussed and is a notable part of her books, but the authenticity of her world of Guiding is equally important. As her real-life District Commissioner says in the foreword to her first book, *Peg's Patrol* (1924), 'I have met the Guides in *Peg's Patrol*, met them in more than one company; heard them speak as they speak in this book, heard them laugh too, and laughed with them.'

The dialogue has the ring of truth to it, and clearly Mrs Hann's own East End girls have provided good copy: 'Life is full of surprises … I expect one day I'll wake up and find myself dead.' On a postcard home: 'Dear Mum, I've been to the sea, and I've seen the sea, and I've paddled in the sea, and I like the sea!' Malapropisms are affectionately recalled: a little recruit learning the Laws insists that a Guide is frisky (instead of thrifty) and *poor* in thought, word and deed. Letters, games, prayers and newspaper articles in the stories are often accompanied by a footnote explaining that these are real examples. The photos of real Guides—with beaming smiles and unflattering tunics—add a further layer of reality.

Hann's girls, unlike those of many other authors, are not converted into textbook Guides, although they may discover new strengths. On a trip into the country to Great Missenden, Hann's home in later years, the first thing the London Guides of *The Redheaded Patrol* (1936) want to do is find a shop and buy sweets. An enrolment is portrayed as a clumsy sequence of prompts and reminders, although no less significant for the young child involved. Neither does Hann write many Guiding set pieces: when some girls get cut off by the tide in *The Pluck of the Coward* (1926), they are not rescued by a line of gallant Guides hauling on a rope but instead have to sit in the rain ignominiously for five hours until the tide goes down again. However, their Guiding training enables them to bear this cheerfully, and their Captain sends encouraging messages to them via semaphore, to which they reply with a Guidey 'cheerio'.

Mrs Hann is also one of the few Guiding writers to show how captains can feel jaded and overburdened: 'She had not had much sleep the night before and was feeling rather tired. It is no light job getting a party of thirty girls down to camp, as many Captains know!' Nor is camp the idyll of wood fires and cliff top setting that so many story-books show. In *Peg's Patrol* the tin hut leaks, the girls get scared, they can't have a fire, and some patrol leaders neglect their patrols. Despite this, the story is full of good humour and gusto.

One of Hann's great strengths is her descriptions of Guide evenings, with their jokes, tests, practices and games: 'I'm glad you all know that Mary shouldn't have slept in her underclothing! The Forget-Me-Nots score that time.' Accounts of visits to disabled and bedridden Post Guides (which occur in several books) give fascinating details about how these girls are integrated into the community of Guiding:

'When the Captain says "Fall in" we in bed lie perfectly straight with our "eyes front". We form four and two deep by putting up four fingers or two; we do "eyes right" and "eyes left" and "numbering" just like the rest.'

Hann's predominant theme is the way Guiding can harness qualities that girls already possess and put them to good use. Many girls in her books, starting with Peg herself, begin as troublemakers filled with restless energy but transform into vigorous Guides. Sometimes, as in *The Redheaded Patrol* and *Rhoda the Rebel* (1925), the gradual assimilation of a girl into Guiding ways, through the patience of her Captain and fellow Guides, forms the whole plot of the book. In others the change happens within the first few chapters.

Her companies are always filled with a range of personalities. Unsatisfactory girls such as Polly the flirt remain within the movement, along with company clowns, exhibitionists and uneasy juniors. The difficulties of managing the lazy girl or the one who must dramatise herself are discussed in the tone of the captain who has seen them all: 'It's really an acute form of self-consciousness and the best treatment is to ignore her completely. I've known girls like that before.' The troubles of the girls are sympathetically described—in *Peg the Ranger* (1928), Peg has to endure Polly temporarily stealing her boyfriend. By the standards of ordinary Guiding fiction it is remarkable in itself that Hann's girls have boyfriends, let alone unfaithful ones—but then these are girls who have been working since they were fourteen, and Mrs Hann knows what their lives are like. Unusually for books of this period, they are not expected to assimilate middle-class standards: one Guide who is a shop assistant tells of playing a joke on an exasperating customer and reports that her manager 'spoke to me stern-like while she was there, but afterwards, my hat! He nearly killed himself with laughing!' With a more class-

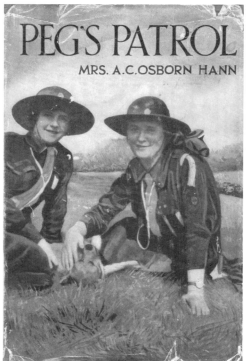

conscious writer, one feels, the girl's duty to show respect and deference to those of a higher class would have been firmly upheld. Health rules are matter-of-factly addressed to girls who live in houses without bathrooms and with poor heating: one Guide, Vesta, starts the racy-sounding Strip to the Waist Brigade whose girls must commit to having a proper wash all over every day (unsatisfactory Guide Hilda replies that she only washes the bits that show).

Most of Hann's stories have an urban setting, but one of her best books, *Captain* (1934), is the story of two middle-class girls who start a Guide Company in the small village to which they have moved. It opens with a gang of lawless girls coming up before the magistrate's court for criminal damage to their school, which they have incited their younger brothers to wreck. The two sisters spot the girls' potential and take them on as Guides and, ultimately, patrol leaders. The girls' transformation is perhaps wrought a little too easily, but the recognition that the same strong personalities that had led the girls into trouble could also make excellent Guides of them is a valuable one, and the description of the gradual building up of a village company and its everyday life is very readable.

Like many other authors, Hann took her most popular character into adulthood, with a series of books ending with *What Happened to Peg* (1932). *What Happened to Peg* is told in the first person— perhaps one of the few story-books for girls where the mother narrates the action (rather a clumsy device, giving rise to sentences like: 'The rest of this chapter was told to me by Peggy and Daphne but their accounts were so vivid I almost felt I had been to the party myself.') There is a sense of stress in these final books; Peg's dog Wag is lost, but there is no happy ending; his battered body is found in the fields, and who did it is never discovered. Peg's mother-in-law is found to have stolen a large sum of money from her employer and Peg assumes the debt of having to pay it back; an unsatisfactory Guide is dismissed from her job as a servant and disappears out of the story, saving Peg from the problem of whether or not to keep her in the Guides. 'That's just the worst of it! People always do expect a higher standard from Guides, and if one fails, it lets the whole Movement down so badly.'

Five jolly campers (*Captain Peg*)

Hann's books are not without their flaws. There is perhaps a weakness in the later character of Peg, who, once reformed, presents rather a Guide-perfect centre to the books. ('Peg, with her downright, honest nature was incapable of not "playing the game" as she understood it.') And at times Hann can't seem to resist idealising Guides: 'Thus Hope became a Guide, and then began for her what was really a new existence, where tears and troubles had no place, and where comradeship, fun and laughter reigned supreme.' (*The Pluck of the Coward*) Hann is also not skilled at building or sustaining a storyline—most of her books are episodic, dealing with various everyday aspects of Guide work. What is more, she occasionally seems to feel obliged to toss in dramatic Guiding rescues (possibly, I would guess, at the suggestion of an editor) which sit uneasily alongside the realistic tone of the books. In a beach rescue: 'Without an instant's hesitation she plunged in and with swift, strong strokes made her way to the lad … "It's all in a day's work," laughed Peg.' (*Peg the Ranger*) In *Peg's Patrol*, Guides on a train rescue a woman tied up in the next carriage who has tapped out SOS in Morse; the whole incident is over in one page.

Hann is indeed often far too brisk with material which would have been stronger and more plausible if developed more slowly. In *What Happened to Peg* the Guides enter a dramatic contest. They discover an unexpected talent in Hilda, the problem Guide in the Company, and spend a month rehearsing their parts and making their costumes. The day of the competition arrives and the Company travels to the contest and wins it by just a couple of points but then

realises that the adjudicator has added up her marks wrongly. There is a brief, agonised moment when one Guide urges that they shouldn't tell and another wonders if it is too late to do anything; then 'A Guide's honour is to be trusted' asserts itself, the girls rush after the adjudicator and explain what has happened, and the cup is re-awarded to the other company. It's a good storyline and in the hands of someone like Elsie J Oxenham it would have made half a book, but Mrs Osborn Hann takes just five pages to describe it all.

Mrs Osborn Hann's husband was an East End clergyman and she was clearly deeply devout (her second husband, whom she married after years of widowhood when she was seventy-seven, was also a clergyman). The connection of Guides to the established church is a strong part of her books (and we might guess that the recurring presence of the supportive, friendly vicar, who raises his hat even to the woman just out of prison, is based on her own first husband). Guides on a day out in *The Redheaded Patrol* visit a church, and their Captain reminds them: 'If you go into anybody's house, the first thing you do is speak to the person to whom it belongs. I want you to remember that when you go into this House.' The Guides kneel in prayer before exploring the building. In her last book, *Five in a Family* (1951), the text of all the company prayers is given in full, and the Guide camp erects a prayer tent which each patrol visits last thing at night for their own silent devotions. Yet her deep piety never causes her to lose her sense of humour, or her sympathy with the girls whose lives she shows. The previously mentioned foreword to *Peg's Patrol* commends Mrs Hann's book for being 'blissfully free of the rubbed-in moral lesson'.

Understanding, non-judgmental, lively and kind, Mrs Osborn Hann must have made a much-loved Guider. The same qualities inform her writing and make her still enjoyable to read.

ANNUAL GUIDING LIGHTS

Mary Cadogan

Girl Guide stories were to become bright and beautiful features of many annuals during the 1920s and 30s when authors and publishers realised the tremendous appeal for girls of camping and tracking, drilling, first-aiding and adventure-seeking. Most of these annuals were 'spin-offs' from weekly story-papers, in some of which Guide fiction had got off to an even earlier start.

Even before B-P was forced to recognise them, Girl Scouts had become suitable subjects for fictional treatment in some popular weekly papers. As a character in Catherine Christian's book *The Marigolds Make Good* was later to say, 'The first Guides … just jolly well started out with a copy of *Scouting for Boys* and their own common sense, and learned how to *do* things,' and magazine editors were not slow to see the potential for good story material in such actions. As early as 1909 the male editor of the *Girls' Reader* blazed the trail for a forthcoming serial which would 'treat of a wholly fresh phase of woman's activity,—viz. that of Scout life …' The story thus described was 'The Girl Scouts' by Evelyn Yates, which featured two sisters, Mollie and Virginia, who are vigorous young damsels of fourteen and sixteen 'clad in khaki skirts and soft felt "cowboy" hats', each carrying a sturdy pocket knife and a long pole.' (The uniforms and equipment of the early Girl Scouts were wonderfully improvised and varied.) Using Scouting know-how, the two heroines quickly restore order and happiness to a chaotic church-managed orphanage, and convert all and sundry to becoming followers of 'the hero of Mafeking'.

Another 1909 Girl Scout story came in the Amalgamated Press's boys' paper, the *Gem*. Here Charles Hamilton (best known as 'Frank Richards' and 'Martin Clifford') is writing about the reaction of 'Gussy', an upper-crust schoolboy, to the news that his cousin Ethel, hitherto an irreproachably subservient female, has now become a Girl Scout and, with others from her Curlew Patrol, is camping, unchaperoned and unassisted by adults, in some nearby woods. He is decidedly opposed to feminist ideals and equates the Girl Scouts with militant suffragettes. Convinced that the Boy Scouts from his school, St Jim's, can shame Ethel into ignominious defeat, he accepts her challenge to take part in a boy versus girl Scouting contest. However, Gussy's attempts to persuade Ethel of the error of her ways are somewhat undermined by the fact that he has to be rescued by her patrol from ragging by the boys of a rival school. And, in the contest, Boy and Girl Scouts share the final honours. Gussy is then persuaded that Scouting is—for girls as well as for boys—a positive influence. It is surprising that in a 1909 story the girls were allowed to do so well, as contemporary children's fiction, especially when addressed to boys, generally stressed masculine strength by exaggerating feminine weakness.

Girl Scouts, and later Guides, did not only feature in fiction in story-papers and their related annuals, however. The 1917 *Empire Annual for Girls* contains a long interview with Agnes Baden-Powell, the Girl Guides' first President, written by Norman R Vennew. This carries a photograph of her as a very dignified lady in majestic garb, with pearls and abundant lacy trimmings. She is certainly not wearing what she calls the 'distinctive uniform' by which 'our girls' are recognised. In contrast, when B-P's wife, Olave, later became Chief Guide, she was pictured in extremely smart uniform for a colour plate given away with *Collins' Girl Guides' Annual* 1929. (But Agnes too had her strapping side. In her 1912 preface to Dorothea Moore's *Terry, the Girl-Guide*, she comments that 'bright' and 'clever' girls were likely to find that 'prowess in the jungle, tracking Red Indians' had attractions which domestic routines or chats about 'hats or the new stitch in crochet' lacked.)

In the interview, Agnes talks of her work of 'travelling all over the country, making speeches' on behalf of the movement and generally 'stirring up enthusiasm'. She shows justifiable pride in the way in which the Guides have progressed: although the organisation is only a few years old, she reports that it is nearly 60,000 strong and growing rapidly not only in the UK but in Canada, Australia, New Zealand and elsewhere. Echoing her brother's concern about not encouraging hoydenism in girls, she stresses that the Guides' application of the famous 'Be Prepared' motto is often best demonstrated in working for 'the Home, Physical Development, Woodcraft and Discipline'. The interview is aspirational in tone, as its ending typifies: Agnes Baden-Powell reflects that '... it is delightful to know that our girls ... all over our great and noble Empire, are striving just as hard, just as splendidly, just as religiously as their fathers and brothers in the trenches to uphold the principals of God and Right, of Truth and Justice, of Freedom and Self-Sacrifice, for all that is highest, truest, and noblest in life.'

This lofty tone reflects the high-minded reputation that Guiding acquired fairly quickly. Although Guides were initially regarded as eccentric, goody-goodies and/or para-military, and early patrols had all kinds of filth thrown at them by suspicious onlookers, they nevertheless received support in high places, and the seal of respectability began to be stamped upon the movement when, in 1911, Her Royal Highness Princess Louisa 'graciously consented to become

Princess Mary

Agnes Baden-Powell

Patroness'. In 1920, King George V's daughter, Mary, became its President, and it is noteworthy that when the weekly paper *Schoolgirls' Own* began in 1921, its first issue contained a give-away photogravure picture of Princess Mary, in full Guide uniform.

This first *Schoolgirls' Own* also included a whole page of tips and chats under the heading 'The Girl Guide Corner' and the opening episode of a serial called 'The Girls of the Poppy Patrol'. This was by 'Mildred Gordon'. Many stories in the Amalgamated Press weeklies and annuals were published under this author's name: the flow of their Girl Guide fiction was attributed mainly to 'her' and to 'Muriel Holden'. In fact, Mildred Gordon was a male writer named J G Jones, and Muriel Holden was Ronald Jameson, who was also male! Whether or not they had much practical involvement with Guide groups is debatable, but they certainly wrote about them with untiring enthusiasm. They may well have had wives or sisters who ran Guide companies but it seems more likely that they gleaned their information less directly. The authentic pioneering atmosphere is often captured in their stories but technical detail is rather sparse. In contrast, the factual hints and tips about Guiding, published either anonymously or by 'Captain', which were features of both weeklies and annuals, often seem to have been written by Guides, or by someone with knowledge of their activities and aspirations.

Mildred Gordon's first serial starred Molly Marsh, the Leader of the Poppy Patrol, and her understanding Captain, Miss Robson. Molly's father is wrongly accused of embezzlement and sent to prison, but she manages to hold her head high and remain the Patrol Leader despite the nasty jibes of two snobbish girls who are against her because of her humble origins. Miss Robson supports her through thick and thin, and so do most of the Poppies and other Guides. Of course Molly, using skills and preparedness in true B-P style, eventually proves her father's innocence. She is complimented by the visiting Guide Commissioner:

> 'You, dear … have accomplished a great deal under difficult circumstances. The Girl Guides are proud to have such a patrol leader as you.'
> Molly's sweet face flushed with pleasure. 'Thank you,' she said simply. 'I shall always be proud of being a Girl Guide.'

Although a commendable character, Molly—unlike the usual Amalgamated Press heroines—was not exactly charismatic. Her exploits continued only until *Schoolgirls' Own* number ten, and then Mildred Gordon's second Guide serial started in the paper. This featured Stella Ray, who led the Robin Patrol in a town called Seaville, and was a much more dashing and colourful tale than the first story. Stella had the advantage of living by the sea—an adventure-ensuring device much used by future authors in the genre. She and her fellow Guides are called upon to respond to dramatic challenges such as steep cliff-side rescues, being trapped in caves with the tide rapidly rising around them, and the threat of capture by smugglers. Stella's patrol also copes with farming adventures (wild bulls!), camping vicissitudes and even rescues a baby from a burning building.

The first *Schoolgirls' Own Annual* was published two years after the weekly started, in 1923. It ran until 1943 and was a giant among the girls' annuals in size, style and influence. From 1923 until 1936 every *Schoolgirls' Own Annual* included at least one Girl Guide story and one article of practical advice for them. Strangely, after the 1936 issue, the Guides disappeared, no longer camping, rallying, practising first aid or demonstrating preparedness in the pages of the annual (except for a one-page article in 1941 on *Games for Girl Guides*).

HER FATHER'S HONOUR

A SPLENDID GIRL GUIDE STORY

By Mildred Gordon

It is mystifying that Guiding themes were suddenly dropped, particularly as the main creators of these, Mildred Gordon and Muriel Holden, continued to write regularly on other themes, both for the weeklies and the annuals. However, dipping into what we might call the *Schoolgirls' Own Annual*'s golden years of Girl Guide fiction we find many riches.

The first 1923 annual included five Guide features. There was a most attractive full-colour plate of the *Presentation of the Colours*; a whole page article, with pictures, about Babs Redfern (the ever-popular Cliff House junior captain) as a Girl Guide; a six page feature by 'Guide Captain' entitled 'How to Win Badges'; a play, *Proving Her Worth*, about a woodland Guiding adventure; and a Mildred Gordon story, 'The Guides of Peach Hollow'. As this is the first of the annual's Guide stories, it is worth looking at in some detail. Its heroine is fourteen-year-old Madge Burton who lives with, and looks after, her 'crippled' boot-repairing father (her mother died in a First World War German bomber raid). Madge, thanks to cookery skills and homecraft which she has learned from her Guiding activities, is a dab hand at domesticity. She is poor and hardworking, but never complains about her lot. (A curious thing about Madge and other leading Guide characters in the annuals' stories is that we never quite know whether they are still schoolgirls or are out at work. In those days, of course, most girls left school at fourteen, so these heroines could well have been working girls. Vagueness about their status might have been intentional as the readership of the annuals and weeklies was made up of both girls still at school and those who were working.)

Madge's acquaintance, Ann Duncan, scoffs when she sees her in Guide uniform: the story is here coloured by the early Guides' real-life experiences of hostility from some members of the public. Ann contemptuously calls the Guides 'Girl Guys'. When Madge pluckily saves rich Marian St Martyn from drowning, and then modestly fades from the scene, Ann claims credit for the rescue—hoping to obtain a reward from Marian's father. After several misunderstandings which result in Madge becoming unpopular with her troop, Ann's deception is discovered when Madge has to rescue *her* from drowning! Overwhelmed with penitence, Ann joins Madge's patrol and with her help becomes a reformed character and a true Guide.

The play *Proving Her Worth* in the same annual stars Barbara Redfern, Bessie Bunter and the girls of Cliff House who are in the woods to work on tracking and stalking for their Guide badges. The ever-ravenous Bessie has designs on the girls' picnic hamper, which gets mixed up with a hamper of similar appearance that contains a stolen baby! In the end Bessie proves herself a good Guide by rescuing the baby from a would-be kidnapper.

In the weekly papers and in the annuals Bessie typifies the inept Tenderfoot whom the other girls have to help and educate. The theme of the cack-handed Guide was, of course, to prove popular in hardback novels as well as in the more ephemeral publications, particularly in the hands of Ethel Talbot, whose stories we shall be looking at later.

The second *Schoolgirls' Own Annual* (1924) went to town over Guiding themes even more enthusiastically than the first. Its illustrated title page featured a much badge-adorned Girl Guide as well as schoolgirls and sports girls. Mildred Gordon contributed a story, 'Her Father's Honour', there was a two-page feature 'Out of Doors with the Guides', a three-page anonymous tale entitled 'The Lone Guide', and two pages of cycling hints in which every illustration was of a Girl Guide.

In the *Schoolgirls' Own Annual* the Guide input eventually settled down into one story and one factual article for each issue. The fiction *can* be seen as formulaic and repetitive, but to girl readers of the time the stories were without doubt appealing and inspiring.

Camping, of course, was an endlessly popular thread running through the Guiding stories in annuals, not just the *Schoolgirls' Own*. It provided so many excitements, including bogs, songs round the camp fire, pow-wows, the pitching of tents and field kitchens, and recurring crises which could be overcome only by Guide honour, grit and prayer! There were also opportunities to go tracking, to find specimens of unusual flowers and plants, and to do war service by picking sphagnum moss, a natural disinfectant to be found growing abundantly on British moorlands. In an early story, 'Luck', in the 1919 *British Girl's Annual*, Ethel Talbot's heroine comments: 'Picking sphagnum moss is ripping; quite apart from the jolly feeling that you're really doing something to help things along, there's always the chance of being bogged.' And in a 1940 *Girl's Own Paper* article, Princess Elizabeth says that she and her sister have been 'gathering sphagnum moss'. (Princess Elizabeth and her sister, Princess Margaret, were enthusiastic members of the Guide movement. The *Girl's Own Paper* feature mentioned above shows Elizabeth in Guide uniform with Brownie Margaret outside the Girl Guide Association's London headquarters. A letter from the elder Princess to her Captain is quoted: '… we have been knitting very hard for the Red Cross, the evacuees, and the soldiers … Please would you send me the details of the War Service Badge?')

Reading the *Schoolgirls' Own Annual*'s Girl Guide stories, it is sometimes a relief when these do not involve camping fulfilments and frustrations. In those which are domestically based, the leading characters often come from poor families. (It is surprising how many Girl Guides seem to have widowed and invalid mothers or fathers!) Family fortunes are restored by the enterprise of the Guides, through tracking, nursing, practising first aid, and other Girl Guide expertise. The heroines save their families from eviction from their humble cottage homes by finding lost deeds: other mechanisms for overcoming crises are to rescue the daughter—or the pet dog—of a rich landlord (there are iconic illustrations of a Guide climbing perilously down a rope over a cliff to retrieve a lost child or animal). Teenage villainesses seem surprisingly abundant in the towns and villages of 1920s and 30s England! They sneakily contrive to blacken the Guides' reputations, so that local farmers and landowners will withdraw previously granted permissions for the Guides to camp on their estates. Such deprivations, of course, would be a bitter blow to companies for whom the annual camp is the year's high-spot. Happily the *Schoolgirls' Own Annual*'s baddies almost always reform as a result of the heroines' selfless courage, and they then also become true Guides.

Girls Guides were also soon served by specialist Guide annuals, although none of these was as long running as the *Schoolgirls' Own* and other Amalgamated Press annuals. Some seem to have been simply one-offs. In 1923 C Arthur Pearson Ltd (the publisher of *Scouting for Boys* and *Girl Guiding*) introduced *The Girl Guide's Book*, edited by M C Carey, who was also Editor of the *Girl Guide Gazette*. Some of its fiction is by well-established girls' writers such as E L Haverfield, May Wynne and Dorothea Moore. Other stories and articles are by authors with military or other adventurous backgrounds like Vice-Admiral Mark Kerr, the husband of noted Guiding Commissioner Rose Kerr, and Sir Ernest Shackleton. There are Guide poems and articles about winning badges, life in camp and nature lore, but only one story is actually about Guiding. This, entitled 'Penelope the Practical', is by Dorothea Moore, herself, of course, a Guide commissioner. Penelope and her fellow Guides at the Manor School decide to 'go for the Child Nurse Badge, and attend to our Empire's future'. Suddenly the examination for this looms large and they are unprepared. Deciding that they must have a real baby to practise on, Penelope 'kidnaps' one, snatching it through the open window of a police station. She thinks—wrongly—that it has been abandoned. Fortunately, Penelope and Co, who seem particularly ignorant about very young children's needs, do not harm the baby in their efforts to practise child care, and—rather astoundingly—they do pass the examination and obtain the coveted badge.

There is a play for Girl Guides by K S Malden called *Midsummer Eve* which is about human and 'fairy' Guides. It stresses how a Guide has to be 'one on the inside' as well as the outside, and is a touch 'preachy'. For example, when Ida, who is a bit of a maverick, tries to impress her Captain by claiming to have the 'most badges', Captain replies rather dauntingly: 'Ah, badges ... They are of no importance ... if you don't make the knowledge useful to someone else.'

One of the most attractive features of this book is its full-colour frontispiece *Round the Camp Fire*, painted by A J Shackel, which suggests both the practical and the aspirational satisfactions of camp fire rituals.

Collins' Girl Guides' Annual for 1929 is a truly bumper book of 208 large pages. Its special feature is the colour give-away plate of Lady

Olave Baden-Powell, mentioned earlier. Authors include Katharine Tynan, Dorothea Moore, E M de Foubert, Jessie Leckie Herbertson and Marjorie Bevan, writing on school, adventure and historical themes. There are only two stories which specifically deal with Guide issues and these are both by Ethel Talbot. 'Gannets for the King' is a camping tale about two Guides collecting gannets' eggs for the king (and nearly having their eyes pecked out in the process!). However, all this fortunately turns out to be a post-prandial dream.

With 'A Test for Tenderfoots' Ethel Talbot, in serious mood—'Guides are friends of all the world'—sets the action in camp. Stella and the patrol which she leads explore a 'haunted' cave and eventually deal satisfactorily with smugglers. They recognise that 'there are two parts of you … one that's a Guide and fearfully scornful of spooks and silliness, but while you're a Tenderfoot there's quite a lot of the other part [fear] too'. Interestingly, throughout this story, the Guides refer to their (absent) brothers for standards of bravery.

Although the *Schoolgirls' Own* and the specialist Guiding annuals were particularly strong on Guiding themes, almost every annual had at least one Guide story in it in the 1920s and 30s, and authors like Violet M Methley and Ethel Talbot had to become increasingly ingenious at finding new themes for their stories. In *The Blue Book of Stories for Girls*, published by Thomas Nelson, Ethel Talbot contributes 'The Cross-Word Patrol' (which was also included in the 1925 *Bumper Book for Girls*). Phoebe is a Guide who wants her school, St Bride's, to start a company, but her school-mates are so obsessed with the current cross-word craze that they can't be bothered to get involved with Guiding. Needless to say, as a result of Phoebe's enthusiasm and deeds of self sacrifice, they eventually succumb to her persuasions.

Ethel Talbot was a sterling champion of the Girl Guide Movement, about which she wrote prolifically. She was perhaps at her best when tackling themes of 'hopeless duffers' who have to be helped, or 'outsiders' who have to be reformed by Guides and convinced to join the company. 'It's three cheers for the Guides. I've been thinking for some time that we ought to start a patrol at St Brides, and now I've made up my mind,' says a headmistress in Talbot's 'The Hallowe'en Ghost' (*Bumper Book for Girls*, undated). Ethel Talbot's Guides always operate to a quietly high standard in every way: in 'Guest of the School' (*Collins' Schoolgirls' Annual*, undated) a patrol help the police by their observational skills, and then: 'The Daffodils returned to school matters like everyone else—Guides never fuss.'

Talbot sums up her attitude to Guides in her book *Peggy's Last Term* (1920) when an experienced Guide says to the Tenderfoot who has let the side down: 'Don't you know when a thing is playing the game and when it isn't? Don't you know how to be sporting, and— clean, and—straight?'

Happily, most of the leading lights in the Guide stories of the annuals *do* live up to these high standards, and the stories featuring them provided inspiration, as well as entertainment, for many Guides, or would-be Guides, of the 1920s and 30s.

PATROLS

'We've no use for slackers in the Sunflowers.'
Jill of the Guides, Christine Chaundler, 1932

B-P chose six as the number for a patrol because 'this is the natural gang of the boy, whether for good, or for mischief', although Guiding allowed up to eight in a patrol. This certainly makes an ideal number of girls for a book, with the structure often being that there are two main characters, usually the Patrol Leader and the Second, and four less sharply delineated characters who need looking after and teaching. Many Guiding stories focus closely on one patrol. Christian and Talbot particularly tend to show patrols operating alone, while Hann and Chaundler prefer to show them within a company.

Many surprising flower patrol names appear in the pages of Guiding fiction, including Winter Roses, Goldenrod, Orchids, Bittersweet and Love-in-a-Mist. Later patrols also have bird, tree or occasionally animal names (one's mind slightly boggles at the thought of the patrol in Dorothea Moore's 1927 *Brenda of Beech House* who are called the Tits, and at Elinor Brent-Dyer's Cocks, but Margaret Middleton's Grasshoppers sound appealingly active). Some patrols pick their names for a reason: the Marigolds are red-headed, the Lychnis Patrol chose theirs because the name means a torch and they used to belong to the Guild of Torchbearers (*Cicely Bassett, Patrol Leader*, Winifred Darch, 1927). Scarlet Pimpernel is probably the most commonly recurring patrol name.

Patrols often choose mottoes suited to their flowers or birds: a Pimpernel patrol has 'Do Good by Stealth', the Swallows choose 'Swallows seek sunshine', while in J M Page's *The Three Elizabeths* (1950), a patrol leader announces: 'We're the Prickly Thistle Patrol, Scotland's Pride, you know. Wha daur meddle wi' me and all that.'

Patrol loyalty is intense—Patrol Leader Cherry, in Catherine Christian's *Cherries in Search of a Captain* (1931), turns down a chance to join a crack company of Guides because they will not also accept two younger members of her patrol who go to a council school. A common theme, often used by Mrs A C Osborn Hann, is that of a patrol taking on a 'difficult' member:

'Don't have "dirty Dolly," Peg,' begged Polly. 'She'll only be a disgrace to our Patrol. Why, I don't believe the kid ever washes!'
'Well, no one else wants her, that's the trouble, and I thought perhaps we might make something of her.'

(*Peg's Patrol*, 1924)

GUIDERS THREE: H B DAVIDSON, F O H NASH AND SIBYL B OWSLEY

Máiréad Campbell

Helen Beatrice Davidson, Frances Olivia Hartop Nash and Sibyl Bertha Owsley were all Guiders and all wrote Guiding fiction. Their extensive experience of the movement must have contributed to their affection for, and understanding of, girls—and their books give many insights into the world of Guiding, and present comfortable and cordial relationships between Guides and their Guiders. Above all, both the real writer Guiders and their fictional counterparts appear to understand the girls who are Guides; they appreciate they might trip up whilst marching, burn the potatoes at camp or make foolish decisions on occasion but believe that, fundamentally, they are good-hearted girls who value the personal development, the friendship and the fun of Guiding. Even troublesome girls, who are sullen or bad-tempered or selfish, are represented as having reasons for being so and are often redeemed through the influence of other Guides and Guiders.

Each of the three writers had her own particular interests and themes. H B Davidson's speciality is writing of girls who are 'at business', that is, who work for their living. In *Jane the Determined* (1929) our heroine, aged fourteen, arrives on the doorstep of her aunt's house following her widowed father's remarriage to a woman not much older than Jane. Jane acquires a job in a bookshop and goes to evening classes four times a week, as well as attending Guides. Eventually she goes to college to train as a teacher thanks to her own hard work, and encouragement (and a small legacy) from the owner of the bookshop. Geraldine, in *Geraldine, a Ranger* (1926), leaves her small country town for London and a job as a cashier in an Emporium and there are some interesting and lively descriptions of the 'behind scenes' of shop work. Geraldine also attends evening classes in shorthand, typing and advanced book-keeping as she wants to better herself, even when she and a boy from home come to an 'understanding'. She progresses to a cashier's job in a jeweller's and eventually becomes secretary to an MP, after being falsely accused of stealing from the jeweller's and ending up in danger of being homeless. Her cousin is also 'at business' and indeed her aunt tells Geraldine: 'We're all steady working people down this way.'

Quite striking in F O H Nash's books is the presence of unpleasant people, although they are usually redeemed or at least understood in some way. There is, for example, the young woman masquerading as a girl in *Audrey the Sea Ranger* (1931) who is involved in smuggling forged banknotes in the handle of a tennis-racket; although she is more sinned against than sinning, as her stepfather, the instigator of the smuggling, also wants to marry her off to his accomplice. Alix, in *Guides of the Glen School* (1948), mocks girls who join Guides, and her great chum Janet breaks a violin belonging to a musically talented girl and accuses another girl of committing the deed before leaving a fake suicide note and running home. She is described as 'poor, jealous Janet'. In *Second Class Judy* (1952), Val, a local Guide who meets Judy and her chums when they go camping, is boastful about her own patrol; 'We won't have a fat, slow Puma … Lumpy girls have to be Bears or Elephants and lanky ones Giraffes.' She goes on to be unkind about a Guide's fondness for romantic novelettes and to falsely accuse

scene from *Jane the Determined*

her grandmother's new handyman of being a villain. Judy herself lives with an aunt who makes her skivvy, forbids her any entertainment but Guides (and even that is begrudgingly allowed) and goes so far as to hide the letters from Judy's father telling her how well he is doing in Australia and how he hopes to send for her. At the end of the tale the aunt is represented as heading for a lonely old age. *Merrie Brandon* (1929) shows Merrie as mocking and teasing and, consequently, not very popular at school, but an older girl explains that she 'doesn't exactly mean to be unkind, but she's never had a proper home … and she went to a big school when she was quite small'. A girl who is lazy in *Audrey in Camp* (1923) is 'a very good sort in lots of ways—always good-tempered, and ready to give or lend anything she had—but if there was any work to be done Alice simply wasn't there'. Similarly, girls who aren't terribly good at Guiding can still produce odd bits of useful knowledge, as in *Second Class Judy* when a Guide gets a bat entangled in her hair and is rescued by another Guide who knows that the best way of getting rid of the bat is to duck the head of the bat-entangled Guide in a bucket of water.

Learning from working-class Guides is a particular theme in the books of Sibyl B Owsley. Guides in *The School that was Different* (1932) pay a visit to a 'slum' Company and find them to be capable and often outstandingly skilled Guides. *Dulcie Captains the School* (1928) has Dulcie visiting a fair at which a ride breaks and many people are hurt. A young working-class Guide applies first aid efficiently and calmly, despite her own injuries. 'To Dulcie was added the bitterness of knowing that, with all her breeding and education, her first impulse had been to turn her back on it without discovering first if her help were needed.' A maid in *The Guides of North Cliff* (1928) confides to one of the schoolgirls that she longs to become a Guide because the girls look 'smart and fine when you're in your uniforms—as if you couldn't do anything shoddy or underhand'. The schoolgirl, previously rather self-absorbed, offers to teach her Morse because she 'felt really sorry for Betsy, who wanted to do so much and who seemed to have so few opportunities'. Another maid appears in *An Absent-Minded Schoolgirl* (1928) and says to the schoolgirl, Rosemary, that leaving valuables lying about is unkind to servants as they will be blamed if they go missing; and furthermore, she wonders at the inefficiency of these older girls when she herself can produce a full Sunday dinner despite being only fourteen. Another pupil tells Rosemary that the Brownie Pack with which she helps out is, despite its own straitened circumstances, working to put together a selection of gifts for children in impoverished mining communities. Rosemary is very much impressed with these examples of capability and resolves to stop being absent minded.

I have outlined some of the particular interests of these three Guiding writers but it is the similarities that really make an impression, and I think they can be summed up as Understanding.

We have seen how Nash understands that people are not, generally, unpleasant for no reason or without consequence, and Davidson and Owsley are similarly understanding of human frailty. In *Geraldine, a Ranger* the girl who did steal from the jeweller's is persuaded to become a Ranger; and a rather lumpish and snobbish Old Girl in *The School that was Different* takes a shine to a hospitalised child and subsequently becomes a Tawny Owl so that she may continue her good works. The writers equally understand that not all Guides have the time or the money to participate in all the activities on offer. *The School that was Different* features new recruits on the very first page who are unable to afford uniform, and in Davidson's 1927 story *Bridget and the Dragon*, when someone proposes that the Guides stay at camp for a further few days, Bridget responds that 'some of the girls find it jolly difficult to get the money together for the week, even, and Captain doesn't like to

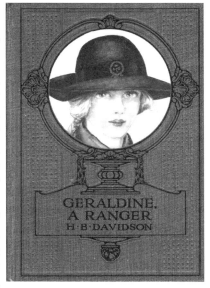

make any difference between us'. *Second Class Judy* sees our heroine having her camp fees paid, discreetly, from District funds whilst she earns her own spending money by clearing tables and washing up after school dinner. Even the simplest task can present difficulties for girls of modest means, as Judy's neighbour, also a Guide, explains to her in *How Judy passed her Tests* (1936).

> 'Lots of Guides haven't had the chances that you've had and some of them can't keep all these rules even if they want to. Maggie used to have to sleep with two elder sisters who wouldn't let her have the window open more than the tiniest crack even in summer-time, so Captain had to tell her that the next best thing is to open it as wide as it will go in the morning and do deep breathing exercises in front of it.'

In *Dulcie Captains the School*, Dulcie helps her mother run a boarding house for girls at the school. When the Company Leader complains that Dulcie hardly ever attends Guides she is rebuked by Dulcie's cousin.

> 'Goodness gracious, talk of Guides being unobservant! Why, you're blind as a bat. Don't you know that Aunt Sue can't afford to keep nearly enough servants? Don't you know that she and Dulcie are always tidying and washing up after all of you? … If you were real Guides you'd jolly well buckle to and help so that Dulcie would have time for all the nice Guidey things she'd like to do.'

All three writers, of course, also have a deep understanding of the minutiae of Guiding, and there are explanations and descriptions galore of Patrol Corners, the Court of Honour, the Second Class Guide tests, making camp gadgets, putting up tents, lighting fires, stalking, tracking, working for badges and a multitude of games and exercises. They also, though, understand that the movement must be examined and critiqued so that it does not become static, smug or hidebound. The Captain in *Guides of the Glen School* reminds her Guides of the serious nature of Guiding, but:

> 'I don't think that we've got to go about looking as if we'd got toothache …
> The Founder was the happiest and most amusing of men, and he always said that
> trying to "happify" other people was one of a Guide's first duties.'

Judy's Captain, in *How Judy passed her Tests*, is 'awfully keen on all the outdoor part and says that she can't stand "parlour" Guiding!' and later urges Judy to really think about the Laws and the Promise rather than just parrot them. *Merrie Brandon*'s Captain says, 'We may be selfish, or disobedient, or not quite straight in some way,' but that redemption is possible by 'some specially brave or unselfish act … some secret little struggle with yourself which will mean a real sacrifice'. Criticism from those hostile to Guiding is voiced in the books and Guiders themselves are not represented as faultless. The Captain in *Bridget and the Dragon* forgets to bring her Camper's Licence to camp; in *The School that was Different* the Guider 'was only too aware how her own quick temper and self-sufficiency were at variance with the ideals of the movement that she loved'. The most comprehensive discussion, though, takes place in *The Guides of North Cliff* when a girl becomes ill because of the thoughtlessness of a Patrol Leader. Matron, who has crossed swords with Captain before about Guiding, lets go and expounds her many thoughts on Guiding in the school.

> 'You know it's a tradition of the school that every decent girl at North Cliff is
> a Guide! A nice to-do there is if any girl refrains from becoming one! She's
> dubbed a slacker at once, both by you and the girls. It oughtn't to be so. It's an
> intolerant point of view, and it's not worthy of your movement!'

Captain takes Matron's views seriously and has a stern talk with the Patrol Leaders and Seconds. 'I'd rather see fewer badges and more of the real Guide spirit. You're lacking in humility, and I am too,' she says, and gives Matron full credit for her insight.

I invite you, then, to salute (or half-salute if you're not in uniform) these three understanding and entertaining women.

> Frances and Helen and Sibyl
> Enjoyable authors—no quibble!
> They wrote about lasses
> From all social classes
> Go on and give 'em a nibble!

THE STORY OF A COMPANY: THE 4TH EDINBURGH, ST SERF'S GUIDES

Alison McCallum

This is the real-life history of a hundred years of one Girl Guide Company, compiled from the Company log books, the Court of Honour minutes, and from the memories of some of the early Guides, as well as my personal memories of the later years.

1910s

My Guide Company was formed in Edinburgh in October 1910 and became known as the 4th Midlothian Guide Company when it was registered on 21 November 1911. It later changed to 4th Edinburgh and Leith and is now the 4th City of Edinburgh, St Serf's Guide Company.

One of the earliest minutes notes that some of the parents were worried that their daughters might become tomboys, as the first few Guides had asked if they might take their straight, tight skirts up an inch or so, for climbing fences.

The first Guide Captain, Miss Tait, wore a beautiful cockade of feathers in her hat, and always carried a walking stick as part of her uniform. In 1912 the Company had its first camp, sleeping in the village school at Romanno Bridge about twenty-five miles away. Early records report that the Guides set off to walk the distance with their equipment in a covered trek cart. The girls went camping again in 1913 and a photograph shows the Guides this time departing for camp on bicycles, with a little pony pulling a governess cart, loaded with all their equipment. The camps in those days had a military flavour as army bell tents were pitched in a semicircle with the colours in the centre. No camping was allowed during the Great War until 1917, when a large Area Guide Camp was held at Ninemileburn in the Pentland hills to pick sphagnum moss for war wounds.

The fields the Guides camped in were fenced with barbed wire, and Guides from one of our local companies were recognised for years by the neat 'L' shaped darns in the back of their tunics, acquired when misjudging the height of the wire while crawling under it. The girls slept on palliasses filled with straw from the farmer's barn and sewed together two blankets for a sleeping bag. To keep the damp off they put army ponchos on the ground under their bedding.

In 1918, Ann Redman (who joined the Company that year) reported that there were four Guide patrols: Thistle, Rose, Shamrock and Daffodil. The girls enjoyed signalling, first aid, emergencies, home nursing, nature, marching to music, country dancing and team games, which the patrols would

Alice Roberts, one of the early Guides

play with great gusto. They were slightly hindered in dancing and marching as the ramshackle hut in which they met would start to sway if they did it too vigorously, and they had to be careful on the platform in case they put a foot through the boards. Every year at the Church Sale the Guides acted as messengers, ran a parcel stall and also put on a Folk Dancing display. At Christmas they would invite around thirty very poor children to a party. They had games and a tea and the children were all given a present of sweets and a toy.

St Serf's Brownies were registered in 1918. They practised Morse, first aid, followed tracking signs, tied knots, tied up parcels, made handcrafts and learnt table laying.

1920s

It wasn't until around 1920 that our Company found a permanent home in our church halls at St Serf's Church in the Edinburgh district of Goldenacre. The Guides wore a uniform of long skirts, long blue tunics over the skirt, Guide belts, long black stockings and navy knickers. Petticoats were not allowed to show and Guide badges had to be well polished. The Patrol Leaders were very strict and inspected their patrols to make sure that the girls were smartly dressed.

On Saturday afternoons in the early 1920s the Guides had outings to the local woods. Carrying their poles and with their haversacks on their backs, they marched smartly for about a mile until they reached open country where they were able to do surveying and nature study. In 1920 our Guide Company set off for camp at Gorebridge in Midlothian. They loaded their entire luggage including a trek cart on to a lorry, and the Guides cycled the distance of about fifteen miles. Ann Redman represented our Company when she went to the First World Camp at Foxlease in Hampshire in 1924 with three other Guides from Edinburgh. She reported that in the evenings there were big camp fires with wonderful international displays, and the Scottish Guides sang Scottish songs and danced the Eightsome and Foursome Reels. Lady Baden-Powell and Miss Agnes Baden-Powell were at the camp and joined the Guides for tea.

In camp the girls wore camp tunics, ties and belts, with bare legs or black socks or stockings, to do their chores, but wore their normal uniform for the journey, parades and church. Shoes were brogues or gym shoes that could be black or white, and in wet weather they wore wellingtons and lightweight navy raincoats. As most of them had long hair, they wore tammies or bathing caps on wet days. Their Guide hats were very stiff and big, with three peaks that represented the threefold Promise. When the brims got limp the Guides would damp the rim and iron them, or in camp they would damp them and lay them on the tent wall overnight to stiffen.

1930s

By the time my mother was a Guide in the 4th Company in the 1930s, St Serf's had a very large company, so the older ones had to make a Senior Patrol to prevent the Company being divided, as it would otherwise have exceeded the regulation number. By this time the Guides travelled to camp by train. One of the joys of camp was cooking on a wood fire, which had to be replenished constantly by the Wood Patrol. The Water Patrol saw that there was always water in the wash tent and at the kitchen, and there would normally be a Cook Patrol, Health Patrol and Orderly Patrol. The Health Patrol would be responsible for taking care of the trench latrines and the Orderly Patrol would set tables and help the Cook Patrol to dish out the food at mealtimes.

St Serf's Guides enjoying outdoor activities in the 1920s

Camping in the 1930s

Patrols in 1938 included the Thistles, Shamrocks, Daffodils, Roses, White Heather and Harebells. Patrol cases were introduced for the Guides to keep their patrol possessions in, and we still have some of them in our Guide cupboard. Commissioners for the County Victory Shield inspected the Company in 1939, and the Patrol Leaders practised patrol drill. The Guides were instructed on the correct way to dress a burn and put on a sling in first aid. A lorry, some cars and trailers were offered for transport to camp, the last Company camp before the war.

1940s

Owing to the war the Guides met in patrols during the winter of 1939/1940; this was probably due to a combination of the blackout and lack of heating. Company meetings were resumed on 19 April 1940. There was a shortage of Guide badges, and flower badges were unobtainable so the patrols changed their names to trees: Silver Birch, Hawthorn and Larch. The Company was much smaller and it was decided to limit the number to twenty-four. Company camp was impossible, mainly because of the war. The Guide Captain was now in the WAAF, based in Gloucester, and in a letter to the Guides dated 8 August 1941 she said that when the Guides were cleaning their badges they should think of Captain cleaning eighteen buttons every morning.

Guide meetings were held on Saturdays during the winter of 1941/1942 and the Guides were encouraged to collect old keys and tinfoil for salvage. They decided to knit comforts for the forces if the wool was obtainable without coupons. The leaders learnt how to build emergency brick ovens to help provide hot food for people bombed out of their homes. In March 1942 there was a talk for Guides between the ages of sixteen and eighteen who were due to register (ready to be called up for service when they left school). The Patrol Leaders practised Blitz cooking (cooking on portable stoves or camp fires to assist bombed-out people) before demonstrating it to the Guides, and the Company had a day's hike in July in lieu of Guide camp. In November the Guides were asked for volunteers to be Invasion Messengers and in December their Christmas treat was again for poor children. Sick Nurse lectures were on the agenda in 1943 and camping was permitted again. It was decided that money received from the sale of second-hand tunics should be put into the Guide International Service. The minister attended an enrolment and gave the Guides a talk about Good Manners. At a November meeting there was pocket inspection, Morse practice with flags, and an international game finishing with Canadian Vespers.

The words to Canadian Vespers are:

As evening shadows gather,
Ere we close our eyes in sleep,
We would thank Thee Holy Father,
For Thy keep.
Keep our loved ones free from sorrow,
Be Thou ever close beside,
Help me play the game tomorrow,
As Thy Guide.

Morse message games seemed to be quite popular. An outdoor meeting was proposed for

Queen's Guide presentation, with Alison McCallum the Brownie at the left of the picture

early December to test stalking and tracking, and patrols were encouraged to start nature books.

In 1944 the patrols were the Red Rose, Harebell, White Heather and Thistle but due to the lack of available emblems it was again thought necessary to change the names. White Heather and Harebell remained and later records mention Lily of the Valley. Clothes rationing caused uniform problems when six Guides were due to be enrolled in November—the girls were dependent on borrowing old uniforms. It was agreed that there was too much Morse; the Guides wanted a new programme of games and some country dancing. There were many Second Class Guides in February 1946 and it was decided that each week a leader would teach them some part of their First Class.

In 1947 the Company enlarged still further and there were eight patrols. Captain, Lieutenant, the PLs and Seconds went to the Edinburgh Assembly Halls in March to be addressed by the Chief Guide, Lady Baden-Powell. There were no hat badges or other accessories in the Guide shop. There had been no Company camp for a few years and the good news in January 1948 was that Captain would try to find a camping site for summer camp.

1950s

The Company's first Queen's Guide badges were presented to twins, Margaret and Audrey Brown, in 1950. One of our Guides was invited as the Edinburgh representative to a Canadian camp. In 1957, to celebrate the centenary of the Founder's birth, Edinburgh county had a large Guide camp at Doune in Stirlingshire in the summer. The Patrol Leaders went ahead the day before to set up camp and the Guides travelled by train with all their kitbags which they then had to carry in the rain for what seemed like several miles. Each company had its own small campsite. Our Guides camped in ridge tents and it was fairly cramped. The four older Guides in my tent used my friend Kathleen and me as foot mats. The following year, in 1958, St Serf's Guides camped at Kingsbarns in Fife. We travelled in a furniture van which carried all the Guides and the camp gear to camp. Our old ridge tents had perished but new tents with the old tent poles were used for the first time and are still in use today. Water was collected from a trickle near the farm gate, although there may also have been a tap. One night the heavens opened and we were flooded out and had to sleep in the village hall. I remember the friendship, swimming in the sea, cows poking their noses in the tents and someone sitting on an unbreakable plate and destroying it. When we were at Church we learnt that nine-year-old Prince Charles had been created Prince of Wales. After the service the older Guides went to the newsagent to get a paper and bought the *News of the World*, which was immediately confiscated by our Guide Captain. The camp charge was £3, and it is minuted that a profit was made.

The Company numbers were now so large that we could only admit girls who had previously been Brownies. At this time we also enjoyed sausage sizzles, camp fires and Christmas parties, Hallowe'en parties and Burns' Suppers with the Scouts. Our Country Dance Team won the cup for the third time at the Edinburgh Music Festival in 1959. The Guide Company of around thirty-six members was presented with three All-Round Cords, five First Class badges and nearly seventy proficiency badges in 1958/1959. The 1959 Company camp was at St Mary's Glade at Duns Castle and cost £3 3/– (£3.15p). The report mentions that all the tradesmen were very satisfactory and that one Guide took dysentery and was sent home. The Guides shared a camp fire with a Boy Scout Troop camping nearby and unfortunately had slight trouble with local youths.

1960s

In 1960 the Company sent 1d (0.5 pence) per head for a Guide gift for Princess Margaret's wedding, to be spent on carpets. I attended several weekend camps at the Trefoil Site, our local training site, and one hot May weekend we camped with our new Captain who had succeeded in gaining her Camper's Licence. We made gadgets, including a bedding rack for airing our bedding. Long sticks outside the tent were useful to put our Wellingtons on when they got full of water as we splashed in the burn that flowed through the camp. After being up early doing chores in the fresh air we were ready for a breakfast of cornflakes, or porridge made the night before and kept cooking overnight in a hay box. French toast or eggy bread and a sausage or scrambled eggs and a half tomato might follow. The Cook Patrol had a problem of how to cope with food that was ready too early before we had had Colours, Prayers and the sung Grace.

Camper's badge was fun; the girls spent a weekend pitching ridge and bell tents and also screening toilets (these were canvas screens put up around chemical toilets, called Elsans). Around about this time a toilet block was built at our County campsite with Elsans in the compartments, and one girl came out having dropped her white Patrol Leader's lanyard into the chemical solution. (The same site has had flush toilets for many years now!) On one First Class hike a Guide had her lunch sausages eaten by the Tester's dog. Another Guide had the

Alison McCallum at the cook house, 1997

good idea of boiling her water before she left home and putting it in a thermos flask so that it wouldn't take too long to boil on her fire at the test. She later did her Patrol Leader's Permit and became a Queen's Guide. I was among a group of six Guides that she took camping in tents one Easter holiday—we woke up in the morning to find the water in the buckets was ice.

I was one of the six older Guides who attended Air Rangers for six months until we were fortunate enough to find a Ranger Captain to re-register our Ranger Company in 1962. We planned our own programme which included camping, ski-ing, canoeing, hiking, first-aid weekends and visits to places of interest including a local newspaper printing works, a potato crisp factory and a trip down a coal mine. I was very fortunate to be invited to represent Scotland at a mountain camp examining the flora and fauna in the Tofsingdalen National Park in the Dalarna region of Sweden near the Norwegian border.

1970s

Company camps were still popular and took place in various parts of Scotland including the Borders and Perthshire. In 1971 we had an extremely wet camp on a beautiful site above Blairgowrie that had superb woods, so at least our wooding parties had an easy time. The following year we camped near Peebles, and in 1973 my fifteen-month-old son accompanied us to camp near Ayton in Berwickshire, where a friendly farmer kept an eye on us.

1980s

By 1981 we were unable to travel to our Company camp near North Berwick in a furniture van as regulations had decreed this unsafe. The Guides and all luggage and equipment travelled by bus, but our flagpole was attached to the top of my husband's car for the journey. When the heavens opened on our return from the swimming baths in a local town, the Guides clambered back into their wet bathing suits and did a rain dance round the flagpole. Rubik's cubes were banned at mealtimes. Last thing at night, sometimes working in the dark with only the light of a small torch, we would serve out cocoa to warm the Guides before they departed to their tents, probably to wait for the leaders eventually to go to bed so that they could have a midnight feast.

1990s

Mapping, nature trails and compass work were popular events at weekly meetings in the 1990s. We also did origami and jewellery making and took the Guides to the Trefoil site for tree climbing and archery. Badge work was important and we practised our first aid. Swimming and skating evenings were always fun. We raised funds for charity at coffee mornings and also took part in the annual Christian Aid walks across the Forth Road Bridge. Camping was still extremely popular, and at one camp in 1997 we had to pick out the mouldy bread before making up cheese dreams for what seemed like an army. We have joined in international camps in Scotland, and in 1998 I was fortunate to be able to accompany seven St Serf's Guides when our Guide Division visited the lovely Lechtal valley in Austria. We walked, climbed mountains, dry tobogganed and swam in beautiful outdoor pools and also in Lake Haldensee. The highlight of our holiday was an overnight stay in a mountain hut when we climbed about twelve miles up a mountain near Bach and experienced an electrical storm during the night.

2000s

Guiding moves on and we had another big change in our Guide programme when group projects called Go For Its were introduced, the favourite being Chocolate. Other Go For Its include Fitness, Communication, Glamorama, Showtime, Team Work, Health and Beauty, and Lights, Camera, Action. The girls work at these in their patrols over a period of five to six weeks and give a presentation on the last evening. We still meet at St Serf's Church hall and have twenty-three Guides in our Company. Guides still enjoy camping and have been away camping twice this year. The girls enjoy sausage sizzles, rounders and water sports, as well as taking part in team games and working for Guide badges including the Baden-Powell Challenge, the highest award that a Guide can earn. This is divided into five zones: Healthy Lifestyles, Global Awareness, Discovery, Skills and Relationships, and Celebrating Diversity. Guides need to complete ten challenges, at least one from each zone.

Our patrol names often change each term as the girls become more inventive, but they are always themed; recently they have been A A Milne characters: Pooh (Bear), Tigger, Piglet and Eeyore. This term they are Ice Creams: Phish Food, Chunky Monkey, Jamaica Me Crazy and Cookie Dough. The Guides wear a Guide polo shirt or T-shirt with a gilet on top and some of them wear the Guide rugby shirt or sweatshirt with navy trousers or jeans. We do not have parties for poor children now, but have done lots of fundraising over the years and often take a table at our church's Table Sale.

TESTS

'I'd like to qualify for horse-woman and rifle-shot and pioneer, and pathfinder, and all the badges no-one ever thinks of getting, wouldn't you? I'm sick of doing things I know how to do—'
The Marigolds Make Good, Catherine Christian, 1937

Tests and badges feature very largely in Guiding histories—perhaps less so in Guiding fiction, where Guides are often too busy having adventures to attempt to pass anything, although both Elsie J Oxenham's and Elinor M Brent-Dyer's girls spend quite a bit of time discussing the various badges they hope to go in for. Tests can lead to adventure, however: many a tracking game in Guiding fiction includes the discovery of some suspicious strangers talking in lowered tones. The fire-lighting test is occasionally used as a plot device, as when poor Bunty of the Blackbirds, in Christine Chaundler's 1925 novel of the same name, is taken out on an illicit expedition by her patrol (very unGuidelike, this) to allow her to practise her fire lighting skills, and manages to set both herself and the common on fire. The Guide hike, a requirement for the First Class test, is used to notable effect in Forest's 1948 *Autumn Term*.

The biggest difficulty for most girls in passing the Second Class test was Morse, the bane of many a fictional Guide (and no doubt the real ones too). The Morse test was not abolished until 1957, and Guides are often shown struggling with it: 'You've been learning it by opposites,' Anne told her severely. 'I know some people believe in that method, but I should be muddled to the end of my life. I learnt by thinking of words with long and short syllables that fitted with the dots and dashes … B is BEAUtifully. C is CHARlie CHAPlin and so on.' (*How Judy passed her Tests*, H B Davidson, 1936) The girls in Nancy Breary's magnificently entertaining *It was Fun in the Fourth* (1953) have no time for Guide obedience, but display a nonchalant competence in Morse, expecting a schoolgirl to understand a message sent to her via tugs on a string tied to her leg while she is simultaneously carrying on a conversation with a teacher.

The image of patrols of First Class Guides, each with an armful of badges, with which early books often ended tends to be superseded in later books by the more realistic depictions of people's struggles to get through. 'Bother the thing … that's six matches already. I've failed my test.' (*The Rising of the Larks*, Cris Johnson, 1966)

'LEND A HAND AND PLAY THE GAME'
An Affectionate Look at Brownies

Claire Smerdon

I first encountered Brownies when I picked up Freda Collins' *Pow-Wow Stories* (1948), expecting North American Native legends. Instead I found a series of short stories detailing all a Brownie recruit would need to know. Enthralled, I coloured in the drawings of the 'Sixes' badges—the Elves, Pixies and Fairies, plus the mysterious Tylwyth Teg, and decided I did *not* want to join the broom-carrying Gnomes, 'Helping mother in our homes'. A jumble sale produced Sybil B Owsley's *A Madcap Brownie* (1929) and I was hooked—on Brownie stories, at least. By the time I persuaded a classmate to take me along to a Pack meeting, I could not only recite the Promise and the Law but also air my knowledge of the Union Jack. A pristine copy of *The Pack That Ran Itself* (Freda Collins, 1955) was my enrolment present.

My public library had no Brownie books, and I only realised more Brownie stories existed through those tempting advertisements in the end pages of my battered collection. Titles such as *Brownie Island* (Ethel Talbot, 1935) and *A Brownie from the Caravans* (Mrs A C Osborn Hann, 1933) were tantalising, but *How Audrey Became a Guide* (F O H Nash, 1923) did not appeal, despite the publisher's statement that it was 'just the book for the countless Brownies who are looking forward to being Guides before long'. At eight, I had no intention of becoming a Guide—the few Guide stories that came my way seemed to revolve around dramatic cliff rescues or unlikely Ruritanian adventures (or a combination of both) and certainly lacked the glorious domestic detail of my Brownie stories. Anyway, Guides were far too old for Brownie magic—and magic seems to define the gulf between Brownies and Guides. Skipping in a Fairy Ring does sound extremely childish, as Antonia Forest's twelve-year-old Marlow twins suddenly realise when Lawrie describes their Brownie days to a new friend, Tim:

'We were extremely good Brownies. Nicola was a Sixer.'

> '*Look out! We're the jolly Pixies*
> *Helping others when in fixes.*'

quoted Nicola dreamily …

> '*We're the fairies glad and gay*
> *Helping others every day.*'

countered Lawrie instantly.

Tim looked faintly sick.

'Did you really say things like that?'

'Yes,' said Lawrie, surprised. 'Those were our Sixes' calls. Why?'

'I suppose it does sound a bit mad at our age,' agreed Nicola, blushing, 'but that was years ago. When we were quite young.'

'H'm,' said Tim.

Autumn Term, Antonia Forest, 1948

Brownies began officially in 1914, to accommodate Guides' tag-along younger sisters. Initially called the 'Rosebuds', they were identified by pale blue hair ribbons, but the little girls rebelled against this cloying image and Baden-Powell came up with 'Brownies', inspired by Juliana Horatia Ewing's 1871 story *The Brownie and Other Tales*, based on traditional British folktales about little people who do good by stealth. Ewing tells the story of the impoverished Trout family, who lost their luck when the Brownie left their house. The Brownie 'came in before the family were up … and set out the breakfast, and tidied the room, and did all sorts of house-work. But he never would be seen, and was off before they could catch him.' Idle Tommy thinks that if the Brownie could be induced to return, the family's fortunes would improve, and asks the Old Owl where he can find the Brownie. The Owl tells him he must look in the pond and say the following rhyme: 'Twist me, and turn me, and show me the Elf— I looked in the water, and saw …' Tommy follows the Owl's instructions and sees nothing but himself; and learns that he must be the Brownie. The Owl then sends Tommy home, saying: 'And remember that the Brownies never are seen at their work … Perhaps because all good deeds are better done in secret.' Tommy and his younger brother take on the household tasks in secret, the Trout family's luck returns and they prosper. Baden-Powell adapted elements from the story to serve his newest organisation, thus creating a wealth of Brownie lore.

The traditional Brownie Pack consists of up to twenty-four girls, divided into Sixes named after the magical 'little people' of folktales. As the Marlow twins tell Tim, each Six has its own rhyme, sung to the same tune as the Brownie Song. An older (or more responsible) Brownie is appointed as Sixer. The adult in charge of the Pack is known as Brown Owl, assisted by Tawny Owl and by Guides known as Pack Leaders. Brownies dance in a Fairy Ring around the Totem (a Wise Owl perched upon a Magic Toadstool) and sit in the Pow-Wow circle to listen to stories. Like Guides, Brownies greet each other by shaking with their left hands; the Salute and the Sign (index and middle finger, as in the Salute, but with the hand held at shoulder height, also called the half salute) are made with the right hand. H B Davidson describes the early Brownie uniform in *Peggy Pendleton, Brownie* (1923): 'Peggy gave a gulp of excitement … here were a group of real Brownies … dressed in brown overalls, with brown shoes and stockings and mushroom-shaped hats.'

After a Brownie is enrolled, she works for her Second Class badge. I was mystified by references to First and Second Class Brownies. Wasn't the 'second class' at school more advanced that the 'first'? Sybil B Owsley avoids this confusion, by using the more magical names for these two badges and writing about the Golden Bar which must be earned before the Golden Hand. In *Pow-Wow Stories*, Freda Collins explains that the Golden Bar represents the Golden Ground a Brownie stands upon, having passed the prescribed tests, and the Golden Hand reflects the Brownie's ability to 'Lend a Hand'. A Brownie who attains the Golden Hand can 'fly up' to Guides following her eleventh birthday and receives a pair of Brownie Wings to sew on her Guide uniform.

With the modernising of Guides and Brownies in 1966, the uniform became less formal, and the Golden Bar and Golden Hand were replaced with more up-to-date activities. These changes led to a resurgence in the popularity of Brownies, reflected in the steady stream of Brownie stories published from the early 1960s through to the 1990s. The most prolific writers included Verily Anderson (1960s–70s), Pamela Sykes (early 1970s) and Dorothy Richardson (1980s), with Lynda Neilands continuing the tradition through the 1990s. Many of these books were published in popular and affordable paperback editions.

While the essential principles of friendship and helpfulness are reflected in today's Brownie lore, the specific rituals and badge requirements play a much more dominant role in the 'classic' pre-1960s stories. I have selected a few books published between 1923 and 1960 that illustrate the main themes found in Brownie stories and influenced my ideas— and probably those of many other children— about Brownies.

The typical 1920s–30s story-book Brownie frequently gets into 'scrapes' but is quickly forgiven because her intentions are good. She is small, freckled and athletic, popular in the Pack and loyal to her friends, and is known as

Ten Little Brownie Girls by Mrs A C Osborn Hann

'Georgie', 'Bunch', or 'Moppy', 'Peg' or 'Meg'—seldom by her Christian name. She lives in the English countryside, where her parents may farm, work on the Estate as a gardener or chauffeur, or run the village shop. Adults are generally sympathetic to our 'harum-scarum' Brownie, who sacrifices personal pleasure to do her duty and does not hesitate to put herself in danger to save others.

The earliest Brownie story-books I have read are *Peg Pemberton, Brownie*, by H B Davidson, and *Meg of the Brownies*, by Margaret Stuart Lane, both published in 1923. While Meg's story revolves around Brownies, her home on the Sussex Downs provides an essential background: 'There was something about Lindons Farm that always made people long to live there.' For her birthday treat, Meg hosts a picnic for her Brownie friends, and delights in introducing the town girls to the beauties of the countryside, the farm animals and pets. In addition to an appreciation of nature, the story emphasises kindness to animals, and both themes appear in virtually all Brownie stories hereafter, as does the befriending of a lonely child, here the neglected Ellen, whose father is 'against' Brownies. Meg solves the mystery of the disappearance of Ellen's father's fruit and 'lends a hand' by bringing Brownies and Guides to pick apples which will otherwise spoil. When Ellen's father is injured, Meg and her sister Lucy stop to help, although this means missing a Rally. The Commissioner praises their actions: 'I cannot tell you how pleased I am that these two girls should have sacrificed their pleasure in this way, in order to do their duty.'

In *Peggy Pemberton, Brownie*, Brownie friendship and Magic dominate; and again a lonely child is befriended by the Brownies, although this time the story is told from her perspective. Peggy's father departs for America, leaving his daughter at the Manor with relatives. On a solitary walk, Peggy encounters a Brownie who takes her to the Pack Meeting. Unfortunately, the cheerful Brownies are working class, as evidenced by their accents and clothing, far beneath the status of the young lady from the Manor. Her cousin berates her: 'What do you mean by talking to those village girls? You know that mother never lets us speak to strangers, and those are only village school children!' Peggy replies stoutly, 'But they're Brownies,' demonstrating the inclusive nature of Brownies.

Peggy's governess discovers her enjoying a lively Pack Meeting with her new friends. As a punishment, Peggy is forbidden to attend Brownies, but she continues to study her handbook in secret. Finally her uncle relents and Peggy is duly enrolled as a member of the Sprite Six in a ceremony held in a woodland glade on the Estate, followed by a magnificent treasure hunt. Later, on the train to London, Peggy demonstrates her ability to keep her head in an emergency, alerting the guard when an inebriated passenger accidentally sets his carriage on fire. When the conductor praises her 'very plucky action', her father, recently returned, replies proudly, 'Why, Peggy, that was being a real Brownie!'

The sequel, *Peggy's School Pack* (1925), begins well, with lashings of Brownie Magic:

> Never before had Brownies seemed so wonderful as when she hid for the first time in the 'Magic Forest' before rushing out with the rest of the Pack to join hands in the Fairy Ring round the Brown Owl, and to dance the Pack Dance, ending with the special Pack Howl.
>
> 'Who are you, little folk?' questioned Brown Owl, who had been wakened from her sleep in the middle of the Magic Forest.
>
> And the cry came from all round the circle:
>
> 'We are the Fairies who fly to greet you!'
>
> 'We are the Elves who come to help you!'
>
> 'We are the Gnomes who come to work for you!'
>
> Then altogether [*sic*]: 'Welcome to the Magic World of Brownies!'

The uniform immediately identifies kindred spirits.

Peggy becomes obsessed with attaining her First Class badge, primarily as a means of securing the Junior House Captainship, and, disappointingly, the story focuses on school activities and sports, before concluding with a heroic rescue. In later books we see less individuality (and less heroism) among Brownies; Freda Collins in particular places the Pack ahead of the individual. Both *The Pack That Ran Itself* (1955) and its sequel, *The Woodland Pack* (1957), focus on a small group of Brownies, whose personalities are summarised by their animal nicknames in a Blytonesque shorthand easily recognised by her young readers: 'Tortoise' is deliberate and thoughtful, 'Squirrel' is talkative and athletic, and so on. In *Amanda and the Brownies* (1960), Verily Anderson allows for greater individuality and even a smattering of realistic small-girl nastiness, caused because the Brownies care deeply about their Six and the new recruit evidently does not. Amanda could 'run faster than any of them and learnt new knots twice as quickly. Yet when it came to doing anything for the Six, she always seemed to do it the wrong way round, as if she was not trying.' It takes a serious accident for Amanda—and her Six—to realise the value of being a team player. While I found these short, plot-driven stories quite satisfactory, I greatly preferred the more complex characters and plot lines of my 1920s and 30s Brownie books.

My favourite Brownie book is Sybil Owsley's *A Madcap Brownie* (1929). While the story encapsulates most of the dominant themes in Brownie books, including the nurturing of a lonely child, I think its greatest strength lies in its characterisation. Unlike Peggy and other story-book Brownies, Moppy does not rescue babies from under the wheels of a runaway cart, extinguish fires, or pull children out of ponds, but frequently needs rescuing herself. Although she is always well intentioned, through her thoughtless ways she continually hurts those who care most about her. Moppy provides a realistic role model for little girls who struggle to keep their Brownie Promise. Brown Owl asks:

> 'You wouldn't wish to think of the Golden Hand except as something very fine, would you?'
> 'No!' faltered Moppy.
> 'Then do you honestly think you come up to the standard of a Golden Hand Brownie?'

Moppy befriends a lonely invalid, Betty, and introduces her to the Brownies. Brown Owl arranges for Betty to become a Post Brownie and Moppy helps with her badge work, thus illustrating the work required of a Brownie recruit and a Golden Bar candidate, as well as Moppy's own attempts to earn her Golden Hand. As a child, I savoured the detailed instructions that allowed me to recreate the same projects with a fair degree of success. Interestingly, over thirty years later Verily Anderson uses the same device of the Post Brownie (*Amanda and the Brownies*, 1960), not only to provide the Pack with opportunities to nurture and befriend, and show that physically challenged children can participate fully in Brownies, but also to incorporate illustrated instructions for badge work through the Post Brown Owl's letters. Here Anderson surpasses Owsley by including elaborate directions for setting up an aquarium and constructing a miniature dolls' Guide camp to entertain the invalid, easily outshining poor Betty's paper cut-outs!

While Amanda helps her Pack by training a new recruit, Betty's good turn means helping her mother with ironing. Domestic chores are key to the original Brownie story; Ewing's Old Owl compares helpful Brownies with idle Boggarts, 'who untidy instead of tidying, cause work instead of doing it', and upon enrolment, a Brownie promises to 'help other people every day, especially those at home'. In *A Madcap Brownie* and other stories of the era, 'helping' means ironing, darning, washing-up and cleaning, as required to earn the Golden Bar and Golden Hand. Before pitying the nine-year-olds burning their fingers with flat irons, we must remember that most of these story-book Brownies come from rural working-class families where such skills would be very useful, and while fussy Brown Owls obsessing over germs may seem quaint today, in the days before antibiotics a minor infection could have serious consequences.

While far from wealthy, country Brownies are portrayed as more fortunate than city children. In *Brownies All* (Sybil B Owsley, 1936), Brown Owl takes advantage of the District Commissioner's visit to direct her Pack's efforts to help less privileged children: 'We thought perhaps you'd tell us something about your London Packs … We're such lucky Brownies here in the country, with our flowers and trees and birds and ponds. We thought we'd like to do something to help London Brownies.' The Pack is less enthusiastic when Georgie befriends some London children and brings them to Brownies. Horrified by their unkempt appearance and 'wild' ways, one of the Sixers tells them they 'spoil the Pack'. Here Owsley not only illustrates the children's cruel snobbery, but also emphasises the responsibilities that come with the Golden Hand in living up to the Brownie Law and Promise. Georgie is astounded at the Sixer's behaviour: 'she couldn't feel friendly towards Mavis … and she stared at Mavis' Golden Hand. How could she? And a Golden Hand Brownie!'

Brownies were not allowed to camp, which leads to trouble in several instances when they attempt to emulate their Wolf Cub brothers and sister Guides. However, Brownie authors compensate by arranging numerous picnics, thus catering to children's fascination with food; most books contain at least one (if not several) descriptions of lavish feasts. Mrs Osborn Hann describes the Brownies 'admiring the cakes and the sandwiches, and revelling in the thought of the tea to come'. (*Peg, Junior*, 1931) When a country pack plays host to London Brownies, the town girls help gather wood, light the fire and boil a 'dixie', making tea to wash down numerous sticky buns. (*Bunch, a Brownie*, H B Davidson, 1927)

Rallies not only provide additional opportunities for feasting but also create awareness of the larger Guiding community, 'all members of one Great Company' as seen through the eyes of a Brownie: 'She would never, never be able to describe it—the strange feeling that grew in her as the March Past began, and all the world seemed to be full of long lines of girls, saluting the flag of the Empire.' (*Meg of the Brownies*)

Over the years, Brownie stories have provided entertaining and memorable illustrations of the key values of the organisation. It seems fitting to close with a description of the Flying Up ceremony, as one Brownie leaves the Magic Circle for the grown-up world of Guides:

> She stepped forward to face Brown Owl, who, standing by the Totem, addressed her in her usual clear voice.
>
> 'The time has come for you to take Wings and fly up to the Company. You have learnt many things in the Pack. Are you ready to learn more?'
>
> 'I am quite ready.' Peggy wondered why her knees felt so funny, but all the same she remembered to hold herself straight and upright, with her hands to her sides.
>
> Then the Pack burst into the Grand Howl, showing they could raise a considerable noise between them even if they had lost their biggest Brownies!
>
> 'I will never forget that I have been a Brownie.' Peggy's voice was quite clear and steady by now.
>
> Brown Owl bent forward and pinned on her Wings.
>
> 'Fly up and prosper.'
>
> She returned Peggy's salute, shook her hand, and then turned her to face her Six. Peggy shook hands with each Brownie in turn, and ran outside the Ring, pausing for a moment to return the farewell salute of the whole Pack.
>
> Then she ran lightly across the slippery floor of the big hall towards the horseshoe of the School House Company and the space that she was to fill in a few minutes by the leader of her new patrol.
>
> *Peggy's School Pack*, H B Davidson, 1925

'ROMPING IT GENERALLY'
Fiction in Guiding magazines

Máiréad Campbell

Do you know that there are more girls nowadays with hairy lips than formerly, and I believe it is due to the violent exercise they take, and romping it generally— it's no joke. No—if Scouting for girls is going to do good and produce lovable, splendid women, it must be on its own lines, and certain things must be given up and others cultivated.

'Girl Guides: A Suggestion for Character Training for Girls, Pamphlet B', 1909

Following the publication of *Scouting for Boys* in 1908, Scouts and Scoutmasters were rapidly provided with periodicals in the form of *The Scout*, first published in April 1908, and *Boy Scout Headquarters Gazette* from July 1909. Guides had to wait a little longer. In July 1910 C Arthur Pearson, who was already publishing Scouting papers, offered four guineas a week for the right to publish two pages of Guiding matters in the weekly *Home Notes*. This offer was accepted and the pages first appeared on 11 August 1910. '*Home Notes* was a funny little paper, and the two Guide pages were sandwiched in between comic pages for children … and fashion pictures of ladies sedately promenading in trailing skirts.' (Rose Kerr, *The Story of the Girl Guides*) Kerr further notes that 'the paper did not meet with universal approval as an official organ. Miss Lawrence, for instance, said it was not at all the sort of paper for the Roedean girls and their like.' Unsurprisingly, then, the arrangement with *Home Notes* was not renewed in 1911. A representative of Pearson offered to publish a Guiding monthly on his own account but the committee opted for the offer of two pages in the monthly *The Golden Rule* for two years.

It was not until January 1914 that Guides acquired their own periodical in the form of the *Girl Guides' Gazette*. From the outset, the *Gazette* reflected the real-life debate as to whether Guiding encouraged hoydenism and other non-ladylike traits in girls, particularly in its fiction. Countless fictional Guides had to win over antagonistic aunts and crusty colonels who believed Guides to be reckless tomboys, hell-bent on subverting widely held ideas of womanly behaviour.

In the very first story in the *Gazette* in April of 1914, 'Miss Priscilla's Conversion' (Alice & Claude Askew), for example, Miss Priscilla Verney refuses to let her orphaned niece, Lilian, become a Guide because she thinks that it will lead to unbecoming behaviour. 'I do not care for any of the modern movements,' she declares and goes on to opine that Lilian has no need to learn skills such as cookery as she will be a wealthy woman. The leader of the Guide Company is an utterly respectable woman, married to an officer serving in India, but she struggles to find new recruits because of the disapproval of Miss Verney, who exerts considerable influence in the neighbourhood. Lilian is robbed of valuable jewellery by those stereotyped villains, Gypsies, and is then tracked by the Guides to a chalk-pit where she has been left unconscious. The Guides apply first aid and restore Lilian to her aunt. Furthermore, the Guide leader's husband is to be awarded the VC. The respectability and usefulness of Guiding, Captains and Guides is established, there is a rush of new recruits and Miss Verney apologises handsomely

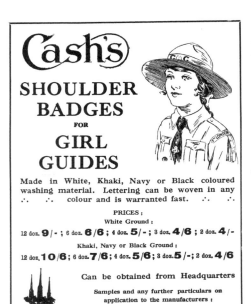

for her mistaken appraisal of Guiding. 'I understand now that the Girl Guides are not rough tomboys, but plucky, womanly girls, and that your organisation … helps girls to develop their character. It teaches them to be useful members of society. They learn what patriotism means—true bravery.' She goes on to offer her manor house as a venue for future Guide meetings and is happy for Lilian to join the organisation. It's clear, then, that from the earliest issues of the *Gazette* it was viewed as crucial to convince people of high social status of the value of Guiding, particularly as they were seen as 'natural' leaders of the movement.

This drive for 'respectability' coincides with the First World War and so it is not surprising that patriotism is, during this period, explicitly linked in some stories with the events of the war. 'The Sunflowers of Salixstone' (E Le Breton Martin), from October 1914 to March 1915, involves Guides capturing German spies, whilst the play *The Reformation of Bridget* (E J Powell), from December 1916 to February 1917, features an 'Oirish' housemaid who, as a keen but inept Guide, nevertheless manages to apprehend another German spy. 'I be loyal although I be Irish, so let's all sing "God Save the King" and confusion to Bill Kaiser!' she cries at the conclusion of the story. This was followed in June of 1917 by the short story 'A Good Turn' (Faith Mullett) in which yet another German spy is captured by Guides and tied up with girdles, as a result of which a local farmer realises that Guides, rather than being frivolous tomboys, are useful citizens who can take an active part in the war.

Spy mania reaches its height, perhaps, in the serial 'The Castlestone House Company, a School Story of Girl Guides' (Constance Gregory), which begins in January 1918. In the same issue there is an interesting announcement of a new rule: 'For the present, no Warrant to hold office in the Girl Guide Movement can be granted to anyone of Alien parentage whose parents are not properly naturalised British subjects.' Similarly, in the serial itself it is not only German spies against whom Guides have to contend but also, seemingly, foreigners in general. The girls at Castlestone House School form a Guide Company. Mademoiselle, who is disliked by some girls at the school, has been seen throwing mud at the Guides' Union Jack. Furthermore, when the girls discuss possible new recruits to the Company:

'Estelle does not strike me as being quite up to the mark. I shouldn't like her in my patrol, anyhow. She was in some fuss with Dot last term, and she didn't own up, but let Dot take all the punishment; that wasn't conduct "befitting an officer and a gentleman," was it?'

'Well, she happens to be neither—not even a Guide, yet, and, after all, what can you expect from a German? … One of her parents is German or Austrian, or something, her mother probably, and she has loads of relations fighting against us.'

Jingoism is, here, represented as both normal and logical as eventually Mademoiselle is unmasked as a member of a spy ring and Estelle is identified as the person who copied an examination paper.

The popularity of Guiding was such at this time that it was announced at the end of 1919 that during the year the circulation figures for the *Gazette* had risen from 5500 to between 7000 and 8000. In addition, in January of the following year Arthur Mee started publishing articles on Guiding in the *Children's Newspaper*, which had an estimated readership of one million per week.

In 1921 the *Gazette* became a publication for Guiders and Rangers and the first edition of *The Guide* was published in April, on St George's Day, at a price of 2d (1p) per week. 'What an opportune date for *The Guide* to make its bow!' the first page of the first edition exclaimed, perhaps to the irritation of Guides in places other

It slings on her belt—
it will help her
to win her
Photographer's
Badge!

Here's the camera that was made to help her to win her Photographer's Badge—the Girl Guide 'Kodak.' Portraits, landscapes and interiors are all hers for the taking with this camera. As conditions demand, she can use instantaneous or time exposures. Efficient —equipped with sliding lock, finger grips, focus catch and view-finder—the Girl Guide 'Kodak' is compact, handy and handsome. Dark blue, it has a case to match. A case that slings smartly on her belt—and both camera and case are stamped with the Girl Guide emblem. The Girl Guide 'Kodak' has the approval of the Girl Guides' Association!

★ *Remember that a good film will help you as much as a good camera. 'Verichrome' Film is the faster, master film. It gets clearer, richer pictures. It secures a wealth of detail in both highlights and shadows. It shows tone within tone, shade within shade. There never was a film like 'Verichrome' before!*

The **Girl Guide**
'KODAK'   *Complete with case* **27/6**

Please mention "The Guider" when replying to advertisements.

than England. *The Guide* aimed to promote 'character forming and developing good citizenship, which is more than ever demanded now that girls have the new power of the Parliamentary Vote'. Also promised were 'good serial stories by the best writers that we can get'.

To be frank, it took some time for the fictional aspect of *The Guide* to establish itself. Stories in the early editions are a mish-mash of, to modern eyes, shockingly racist tales of derring-do in outposts of Empire and short stories with no, or at most a tenuous, connection to Guiding. By the end of 1921, however, things had settled down and readers were treated to, for example, a two-part story from 20 to 27 August, 'Mollie Lone: A Story of Western Canada' (Winifred M New). Mollie, a thirteen year old who lives with her father in British Columbia, is bequeathed by a stranger a New Testament and a copy of *Girl Guiding*. Mollie is inspired by these and writes to London about becoming a Lone Guide and starts to learn the Laws and practise knots and so forth, before a Guide Company is eventually started in the town. In the last issue of 1921, there is an interesting summary of the status of Guiding:

> The Girl Guide Movement has grown immensely in popular estimation during the last few years, and shows indications of a far more widely extended sphere of usefulness as time passes. From the period when the Girl Guides were looked upon questioningly, if not with hostility and suspicion, to the present day, when they play so important a part in the girl-life of the nation, is indeed a far cry.

By the 1930s, whilst there are still traces of defensiveness about the purpose and usefulness of Guiding, such is the level of self-confidence within Guiding that fictional characters may challenge orthodox views of Guides as exemplars of honourable behaviour. Some of these challenges are relatively mild; in 'Thekla of St Osyth's' (Heather White, 1931), a school and Guiding story, Thekla is shocked at the dishonesty she sees in the other Guides such as dodging bus fares and cribbing in exams; whilst members of the Guide Company in 'Mirindy Comes to Town' (Jean Vaughan, 1931) gossip about a new girl's unbecoming hairstyle and spectacles. Both stories suggest that Guides are not always noble and kindly but that the Guiding movement can be a catalyst for change and an arena in which honesty, good manners and thoughtfulness are encouraged and will win out. In serial stories, such self-examination of the Guiding movement is more in depth and demonstrates the maturity of the organisation. 'The Cosmopolitan' (Heather White, 1931), for example, features Ouira and her family who are 'genteelly poor' and inherit a Swiss chalet in which they will (reluctantly) live for reasons of economy. Ouira becomes a Lone Guide and her cousin, Miramé, also a Lone Guide, lives with Ouira and her family. During their stay in Italy, Vesuvius erupts and earthquakes follow.

> The homeless and destitute of Italy … were pouring across the frontier in almost unbelievable numbers … The Swiss were being inundated by riff-raff with no visible means of subsistence … orders had been issued to all the frontier guards, to shoot on sight any persons crossing the frontier without proper credentials … it was suspected that some people were assisting these refugees and even taking money from them in order to let them escape from their own country.

Out hiking, Ouira and Miramé find a tunnel which refugees have been using to escape to Switzerland and they report it to the police. They later discuss it and Ouira says that they were right to inform the police.

> 'Fiddlesticks!' retorted Miramé. 'You're frightfully British, aren't you, Ouira? The British always look on themselves as the policemen of the world and generally think they ought to set a standard of morals. Why shouldn't the wretched refugees be allowed to escape as best they can? Their homes have been destroyed and thousands can't live upon charity all at once. If they can slip through into another country where the people are happy and prosperous I, for one, would aid and abet them all I could.'

Eventually, the two Guides co-operate in setting up an International HQ for Guides.

During the Second World War, many real-life Guides were involved in war work of various kinds, and this is reflected in their fictional counterparts in *The Guide*. Due to paper shortages, the number of pages in the magazine was halved shortly after the start of the war, but there were still plenty of stories to support the war effort. The war is given prominence, and it affects all aspects of life. Whilst the stories during the First World War were of fearless derring-do, the focus during the Second World War is on the realities of a war not confined to the battlefield. Rescuing some foolhardy Guides who are stranded overnight on an island, Marion is met by a Second with a torch. 'Be careful with that light!' Marion reminds her. 'There is a war on, you know!' ('The Camp of Adventure', Marjorie Norton, 1941) Planning a picnic, on an outing to repair a bridge rail which they have broken, a patrol ponders what to bring: 'What could we cook?' Sue asks. 'Can't get sausages; can't get bacon; can't get eggs.' ('Be Prepared 1st Brockenhurst!', 'Martin', 1941) The Kingfishers discuss doing good turns in disguise. 'I mean, suppose we ever got an invasion, and wanted to carry a message, or escape, or something, if we each had one or two disguises we had practised so that even the neighbours didn't know

To add interest to Summer Camps

GORRINGES

suggest a

Portable Gramophone

and a selection of Folk Dance Records

GORRINGES stock many other makes of Gramophone in addition to "H.M.V." and "Decca." We shall be pleased to send you current lists of Folk Dance Records and will register your name to ensure receipt of further lists as they are available.

Salon Decca No. 110, exponential tone production unit, strong single spring, British made, Salon motor, silent in action. 10-inch plush-covered turntable, playing up to 12-inch records. Fitted with automatic brake. The case is covered in durable black leather cloth, with copper-bronzed protectors. **£3 17 6**

New "Decca Rally" portable, with meta interior horn combined in one-piece British motor, both strong and silent. 8-inch nickel turntable, playing 12-inch records. Covered in lizard-grained leather cloth, in Brown, Blue, Red, Grey or Black, and fitted with nickel corners. **£2 7 6**

FOLK DANCE RECORDS

selected from specially compiled lists.

H.M.V.

B3674 Morris Dances. 3/-
Trunkles.
(a) Double Set Back.
   (b) Hunting the Squirrel.

B3675 Morris Dances. 3/-
(a) Rigs o' Marlow.
   (b) Rodney.
(a) Blue-eyed Stranger.
   (b) Country Gardens.

B3671 Morris Jigs. 3/-
(a) Ladies' Pleasure. (b) The Old Woman Tossed Up. I'll go and enlist for a Sailor.

B2954 Country Dances 3/-
Oaken Leaves.
(a) Mage on a Cree. (b) Hey, Boys, up go we.

B2959 Country Dances. 3/-
The Merry Milkmaids.
(a) If all the world were paper. (b) The Black Nag.

C1645 Country Dances. 4/6
Pop goes the Weasel.
Speed the Plough.

COLUMBIA

5503 Folk Dances. 2/6
Fourpen-halfpenny farthing.
Lilli Burlero.

5434 Folk Dances. 2/6
Haste to the Wedding.
Bonnets so Blue.

5733 Folk Dances. 2/6
(a) Hey Boys up go We.
   (b) Rufty Tufty.
(a) Mage on a Cree.
   (b) Parson's Farewell.

4615 Folk Dances. 2/6
Merry, Merry Milkmaids.
Old Mole.

DB82 Folk Dances. 2/6
Dick's Maggot.
Nonesuch.

Scottish Country
4055 Dances. 2/6
The Haymakers.
Cumberland Reel.

His Master's Voice, Model 102. The world's finest portable, rounded edges and corners, chromium plating. Universal automatic brake. Storage tray for 14 records. Astounding musical quality.
In Black **£5 12 6**
In Blue, Green, Red, Brown or Grey **£6 0 0**
In Red Leather **£8 8 0**

SMALL PRIZES
for Camp Games

In Gorringes famous Bazaar, the only one of its kind in London, you will find hundreds of ideas for competition prizes. Prices are as low as 6d. each for small games, toys and fancy goods.

His Master's Voice, Model 99. An amazing little portable, giving wonderful quality and volume at a low price.
In Black **£3 5 0**
In Red or Blue ... **£3 10 0**

FREDERICK GORRINGE LTD., BUCKINGHAM PALACE ROAD, S.W.1

One minute from Imperial Headquarters. 'Phone VICtoria 8600

Please mention "The Guider" when replying to advertisements.

us, we'd be able to feel much more sure of ourselves, wouldn't we?' (*The 'Kingfishers' See it Through*, Catherine Christian, 1941)

The impact of the war on the Guides, however, is represented as being more far-reaching than being careful with torches, cutting down on bacon sandwiches and fooling about with disguises. In 'Who Knows When?' (E M R Burgess, 1941) Dutch Guides, 'just two days before Germany brutally invaded the peace-loving and neutral land of Holland', foil spies and invading troops. They are evacuated to England where they join a company. The District Commissioner gives a speech: 'Who knows when our time of testing may come—swiftly, perhaps, and unexpectedly. Am I prepared? Are *you* prepared, each one of you, loyally to use your common sense, your powers of observation, the strength of your mind and body—unsparingly, in the service of God and your country?' This is not simply a 'play up and play the game' summons, though. The heroine of 'Jane Sees the Way Out' (M J Baker, 1941) is a Guide and is passionate about being unstinting in her war efforts. She 'knew quite clearly what the word "Nazi" meant and what the word "democracy" meant too'. She and her patrol have an allotment, she runs messages for the Home Guard, is a firewatcher and collects wastepaper as 'her way of insuring that she would never have to march around an arena on a hot summer afternoon with her arm raised in salute to a pale, stuffed figure standing behind a bullet-proof shield'. Such are her war work commitments, though, that her schoolwork suffers and she begins to look unkempt and exhausted. A teacher finds her crying and gives her a pep-talk about seeing the wider picture and making space for activities which are not, strictly speaking, war work but are just as important. Jane has 'starved that something inside you that wants beautiful things', and she realises that there is nothing wrong in giving over a little allotment space for attractive flowers or sparing a copper to purchase a postcard of a beautiful painting.

It is not just Jane who ponders the reasons for the war and its possible implications. In 'The House of Simon' (Carol Forrest 1941), a group of children is evacuated and meets Peter, a Rover Scout, who is likeable and has a range of practical skills, all learnt via Scouting. Katrina, twin sister to Matthew, 'took some things very seriously. One was Guiding or Scouting, another was the war. She was disturbed because Peter didn't seem to hold the strongly patriotic views she held herself … She thought of Matthew's solution, that there weren't any Scouts or Guides in Germany [and so the Fourth Law wasn't being broken by fighting against Germany], but, being more thorough than her twin, she turned it down as unsatisfactory. We might just as easily be fighting France, she thought.' She discusses her dilemma with Peter who says that 'Nazism is rotten at the core … Therefore we've got to get rid of it, or it's useless for us as Scouts and Guides to say we're going to make the world safe for the future. While it's there, there can't be any security. One day it'll smash the whole world.' In the same story, a Polish refugee gives his view to Tessa-Jane, Katrina's sister.

> "We will have no more of such wickedness!" we say—and we fight, in order that good may be restored. But while we fight we must not hate—or we shall have gone no further towards the final good.

Furthermore, it is recognised that the end of the war is not the end of the battle for the ideals held by the Guiding movement. 'Other Folk's Fortunes' (Catherine Christian writing as Patience Gilmour, 1941) features a number of young women who are Rangers, although not attached to a company, living in London. They discuss forming a sort of flying squad after the war, travelling to Europe to offer their help wherever it is needed. 'Out in Poland, and France, and Belgium, and the other countries there are so many Guides suffering, and lonely, and almost broken at this moment … I've seen films … that were never released to the general public at all, because they were so awful.' They are not, however, under any illusion that this will be a romantic escapade. 'Sleep anywhere, at any time. Eat anything—also at any time. Doctor yourselves when you feel ill with the simplest of remedies … Learn to mend your own shoes, make your own clothes, and do without everything you have ever taken for granted, like water out of a tap, and gas, and electricity—and even ordinary sanitary conditions.'

The reality of post-war life is, in the pages of *The Guide* at least, perhaps less dramatic. Whilst some real-life Guides were carrying out that post-war work described above (an article on the tenth anniversary of the Guide International Service describes Guides 'helping their friends and sister-Guides in countries devastated by war'), fictional Guides were represented in more pedestrian ways. A patrol use a dolls' house to practise domestic skills, a thief is uncovered, a Guide learns to swim and wins a race, a missing pony is retrieved. Suggestions that Guiding is not valued in wider society are resurrected too. The Robins in 'Anne of the Robins' (Brenda Morton, 1951) have lost their Captain and Lieutenant and are keen to acquire replacements, but the first woman they approach is dismissive: 'I have never approved of these youth organisations. All this play-acting of emergencies is no use. Life is real, life is earnest. Face up to real emergencies.' The same serial also shows class tensions when a new Guide, on being told that she has tied a knot incorrectly, snaps: 'Your father is only my father's ploughman.' There are also concerns about standards of public behaviour, seen in the same serial when one Guide and her cronies bring bags of chips to the meeting and refuse to leave them outside. The Second of the Wren Patrol in 'The Taming of Twig' (H M Crawford, 1951) sees Twig running off to explore on her own, rather than staying with her patrol, and says that she ought to be expelled. 'And let her go and fool about with those doubtful types from the new housing estate?' the Patrol Leader retorts. 'Not likely!'

By the 1960s it was not just 'doubtful types' from council estates and the eating of chips

causing anxiety. Just as in non-Guiding publications, the girls featured in stories in *The Guide* are represented as a bit hopeless, and even patrol leaders are not paragons of virtue. In 'A Badge for Belinda' (Marjorie Nisbett, 1961), for example, Belinda is something of a 'dud', and she is resentful of efforts to keep her in line. 'That was the trouble with Guides—they wanted you to keep so jolly tidy—and to work. If only Captain would stick to games and camp-fires, hiking and nature-rambles, it would be good fun. But having a PL like Hazel, always grumbling because you hadn't bothered to go in for a single proficiency badge, tweaking the buckle of your belt dead-centre before inspection, asking scornfully when you had last cleaned your nails and simply insisting that your Tenderfoot badge should really sparkle, well, it was enough, sometimes to make a girl give up the whole thing altogether!'

The sceptical older relative reappears in this period too. The Nightingale Patrol, in 'The Nightingale Room' (Moira Burgess, 1961), is a drama-oriented patrol, its last PL going to stage school; and its members disdain the collecting of badges in favour of getting up plays and other entertainments. The Nightingales' latest recruit is Sally who, bizarrely, turns up to her first meeting 'dressed like a 1910 Guide' because she has read *Scouting for Boys* and elderly Guiding stories from cover to cover whilst ill. She offers her grandmother's house and grounds as a meeting place and a venue for Wide Games but, it turns out, the grandmother has not given permission for these activities and, in fact, disapproves of Guiding; 'I have never thought Guides a suitable occupation for girls, and I never shall. A girl is better employed in learning the housewifely arts than in crawling about like a savage.' The Nightingales protest that they are proficient in both areas and the grandmother challenges them to turn a semi-derelict summerhouse into a home in a month. If they succeed in the challenge then she will allow Sally to join the Guides. Members of the patrol are in dispute, as some of them think that this challenge will take up time, funds and effort which could be expended on the patrol's well-established entertainments. Eventually all is resolved when the grandmother falls and injures herself in her bathroom and the patrol applies first aid and calls a doctor. Grandmother turns out to be witty and amusing and not only gives her blessing to Sally joining the Guides but also gives over the summerhouse as a patrol room. In addition, the competing interests of the Nightingales are brought together by their re-enactment of their efforts over the summerhouse as a slapstick comedy musical.

Another serial brings together the themes of recognising that Guides sometimes behave in an unGuidely manner, and concern at social changes in society in general. What is particularly interesting about this serial is that it represents working-class culture as both vibrant and viable. Kathleen, the central character in 'The Exile' (D H Ralphs, 1961), has moved with her family from the countryside to Helliford, a 'horrible northern town where everything was black with soot'. She meets another Guide, Spud, and is invited to a Guide meeting. Kathleen is unimpressed: 'Honestly, Mum, you should see that hall—it's just like a prison. Oh, but there was a horrible girl, just like a Teddy girl, with her uniform skirt so tight that I thought it would split every time she sat down ... And there were two others, just like puddings and they *never uttered* all evening—well, hardly ever—and when they *did* I could hardly make out what they said.' Her brother, John, calls her a snob and says that her attitude is incompatible with the ethos of Guiding. 'This is a lively, interesting town with a first class library, a Choral Society, Repertory Theatre, and lots of other things. Stop brooding about your precious state of mind and "look wide" as B-P said. The people here are friendly but they've got an idea that folk from the South are starchy and stuck-up ... and if they see many like *you*, it's not surprising!' Kathleen flees

to her bedroom in tears and is followed by her mother who tells her that 'there were ugly things in Wickham too—out of sight. Some of those pretty cottages were not so good inside. The people had faults, too, but we grew up with them, so we made allowances.' When Kathleen has to run an errand to the home of Marjorie, the Guide with the tight skirt, she meets Marjorie's parents, who are gregarious and generous, and her brother, who is a Teddy Boy. It is further revealed that Marjorie is unable to go on patrol hikes not because she is idle and wears unsuitable skirts but because she is committed to Choral Society rehearsals in her spare time. 'Look, Marjorie, I'm sorry if I've been maddening. Can't we start again? It seems silly to go on like this,' says Kathleen, and Marjorie agrees.

Some days later, when the patrol members meet for a hike, Jean, the Patrol Leader, muses about the bright red coat and unsuitable bag of two patrol members: 'I suppose *some* PLs somewhere can get their Patrols properly turned out for a hike,' she thinks ruefully, 'but I've never met them! Spud's shoes aren't very suitable either, but Mrs Tate has four other children and shoes are so expensive.' Coming back from the hike, Kathleen is taunted in the street by an older man, Thacker, who hangs around with the Teddy Boys, and when Kathleen's brother brings home Marjorie's brother the three of them discuss Thacker. 'The lads and me have never done anything wrong ... it's not illegal to talk on street corners and most of our homes are too crowded to ask a gang of fellows in,' says Marjorie's brother; but nevertheless he is suspicious of Thacker and thinks that he is plotting against the Choral Society. Kathleen and her family approach the choirmaster, Mr Pickering, to voice their suspicions in the light of an impending concert. Kathleen dismisses her mother's suggestion that the door stewards look out for Teddy Boys:

'That wouldn't work, Mum. A lot of boys wear these clothes—they *like* them, and most of them are quite ordinary, and well behaved.'
'That's true,' said Mr Pickering. 'They wear them for the choir practices.'

It transpires that there is indeed a plot against the Choral Society, instigated by a cousin of the choirmaster (jealous that the society might win a grant from the council) and foiled by Kathleen. '"Well, you're a real Hellifordian, now!" said Marjorie,' and Kathleen 'glanced at her mother and John, then at the circle of her new friends, and felt that this indeed was home'.

The Guide's last editions appeared in 1969, and their fiction is a rather odd mixture of non-Guiding serials and stories and some rather dull Guiding short stories. There is an interesting Guiding serial, however, called 'Libby for Leader' (Gwyn Sutton, 1969), in which Libby, a relatively recent wheelchair user, has been elected PL but feels ambivalent about it as she is not sure that she has been selected on merit:

> She longed to be the new Leader, but surely the Linnets had chosen her because they felt sorry for her? She was their Second. But then Valerie … had only made her Second because she had been longest in the Patrol. They were all sorry for her; they pitied her. And her handicap was still too new. She couldn't take pity. Then … she pushed her thoughts away and summoned a determined smile.

As in 'The Exile', there is a newcomer to the Company, Kay. When the patrol members discuss their good turn, gardening for Mr Briggs, Kay pipes up:

> 'Mr Briggs lives by the railway, doesn't he? The man with one leg?' There was an awkward silence. Everyone knew that Ben Briggs had lost his leg in a railway accident … And nobody talked about it; not straight out like that. But

Kay seemed to be different from everybody else in Castle Burry. She had even left Libby to struggle in her wheelchair, trying to get it up the ramp into the Guide hall herself.

At Mr Briggs' cottage, Kay overhears another member of the patrol talking about her ('She behaves as though there's nothing wrong with Libby—') and joins in the conversation:

> 'Quite right. And there isn't.'...
> 'But she can't walk.'
> 'So what—I can't sing. But nobody feels particularly sorry for me ... Lots of people can't spell or add up or swim or climb a rope, but nobody thinks they're odd. Stop trying to do everything for Libby, or she really will end up a useless piece of decoration for the Linnets.'

Libby ponders things and, after having a discussion with Kay, agrees to a trial run at being PL for three months. Later, the patrol considers working towards a patrol pennant and, in particular, the Explorer Pennant. '"Has it occurred to you there's just one snag?" Libby's voice cut across their happy comments, bitter and somehow defeated. "Whoever heard of an explorer in a wheelchair?"' Nevertheless, the patrol decides to go ahead with the pennant and selects a local set of earthworks to explore. On a trip to the Guildhall to research the earthworks, the patrol overhears a woman in a bus queue commenting about Libby:

> 'The poor thing!' she said, her voice oozing easy sympathy. 'Such a pretty girl, too. It's a shame.' Kay set her mouth grimly ... Why were people so thoughtless? And why did they always assume that the handicapped are deaf or mentally deficient? ...
> 'Beastly woman!' Mary muttered. 'I suppose if you were as ugly as sin, it would make everything all right!' ... Not so long ago, the Linnets would have been overcome with embarrassment at having attention drawn to Libby's handicap. Now they were indignant, ranged on her side.

Despite falling out of her wheelchair on the moors, Libby participates fully in the exploration and the patrol not only gains its pennant but also wins the Patrol Shield and is invited to present its findings to the local historical society. At the conclusion of the story they all, including Libby, look forward to going to camp, and Libby will remain as PL.

The last edition of *The Guide* was published on 26 December 1969 and was succeeded by *Today's Guide*. The fiction in *Today's Guide* seems rather half hearted; the 'serials' run for only a few weeks, rather than for months, and the contents of them and the short stories tend towards the mundane. Consider, for instance, 'No Apples for Mrs Salisbury' (Kenneth Moore, 1970), in which Mrs Salisbury's crab apple tree has failed so she is unable to make jelly for the fete until Guides collect bilberries for her instead; or 'Alice Saves the Day' (Joyce Chapman, 1970), which involves a woman accusing a Guide of stealing her purse, but it then being discovered that the purse has been left in a shop.

A switch to a monthly magazine format didn't really improve matters. In 'Ghostly, Spindly Legs' (Kenneth Moore, February 1980), for example, a 'ghost' turns out to be a young man

Tea ware for Guides

practising the trombone. Even camping, that stalwart of Guiding fiction, seems light on entertainment and excitement. In 'Come Sing and be Merry' (Rosemary Taylor, 1980), it rains, the Guides take a box of chocolates to the owner of the field, a lost pen-knife is found, someone's waterproof trousers turn out to be merely shower-proof and then they all go home. Similarly, 'Delights, Drawbacks and Disasters' (Lisa Morris, 1990) presents camping as a rather aimless activity; a small Guide weeps, another is sick through over-eating, two more sneak off to look for boys, none of them can cook and their sole activity is going on a ramble. Not even 'Galaxy Guides' (space Guides in the twenty-second century, a cartoon with no author credited) did much of interest. The non-fiction elements of *Today's Guide* were varied, interesting and progressive, including a problem page, features on Guiding around the world, and articles on sex, menstruation, the environment, the law and so forth; but, as in the world of non-Guiding magazines, demand for fiction seemed to be waning.

The last magazine aimed at Guides was *Guide Patrol*, a short-lived monthly which began in January 1992 and ceased publication in March 1994. From April 1992 it was announced that the magazine was to be published on a 'firm sale' basis, ie available only via a regular order from a newsagent or by subscription. There is one short story per issue and Guiding is frequently presented as a way of meeting boys. The 'being hopeless at camping' theme recrudesces in 'Under Difficult Circumstances' (Gillian Ellis, May 1993) in which most Guides have not brought suitable kit, it rains unceasingly, someone steps in a cowpat during a barefoot midnight visit to the latrines and someone else becomes hysterical when she is licked by a cow. The death knell was sounded in February 1994:

Sadly the March edition of *Guide Patrol* will be the last …

Tremendous effort has been put in by both volunteers and staff to continually improve the quality of the magazine but it has not appealed to the intended group: Guides.

A recent survey showed it was, in fact, being purchased and read by Commissioners, Guiders and Trainers, for whom the magazine *Guiding* is principally intended.

(February 1994)

I was both a Brownie and a Guide but I don't recall ever seeing these magazines as a child so, when I was given an excuse to wallow in Guiding periodicals, I jumped at the chance. If I'm honest I didn't know what to expect, although I suspected that the fiction would be rather pedestrian. I was pleasantly surprised to find a number of stories which are thoughtful and challenging and show an awareness of social changes. Some of the Second World War stories are outstanding in their understanding of a crisis, and in their representation of this crisis to girls as young as eleven or twelve. These stories read well today and give a good insight into the activities carried out by real Guides in a war that was all too real for so many Guides. I also enjoyed seeing the growing confidence of the Guiding movement, from its days as an organisation suspected of leading girls astray to one which felt able to speak for, and to, girls and young women with conviction that it would be heard. Many stories convey the fun and excitement that must have been felt by so many Guides as they strode out into the world in the company of like-minded girls and women. On the other hand, given that a number of stories explore social change, it was disappointing not to see girls of colour in Britain feature in fiction in Guiding magazines until quite a late date. The relatively poor quality of fiction in Guiding magazines in later years is reflected in non-Guiding magazines as story-papers died at a rate which would be alarming even in Midsomer or Brookside Close. Overall, reading the magazines gives an excellent insight into the significance of Guiding in the lives of girls and young women as the movement sought to establish itself as 'respectable', became bold enough to criticise itself, showcased Guides' contribution to the war effort between 1939 and 1945 and then addressed social change in the period after the Second World War.

Magazines are fascinating social documents, and those published by the Guiding movement are no exception; so if you have some lurking in a box in your loft, or you come across some in a charity shop, you could do worse than put aside an afternoon in your favourite chair and plunge into the world of Guiding.

Measure the tracks using whatever you have to hand

FIRST AID

'Mary registered a prayer of thankfulness that her Guide first aid outfit reposed in its usual pocket of her haversack.'
With the Speedwell Patrol, Marjorie Taylor, 1938

All Guides, of course, learn first aid. The Guiding handbooks from 1914 until at least 1938 were still telling how to splint a broken limb, although the new manual of 1946, *Be Prepared*, limits itself to slings and suggests all breakages be otherwise left untouched until a doctor arrives. Many fictional Guides, however, are almost frighteningly willing to spring into action. In Diana Pares' *Hawthorn Patrol* (1930), two Guides go to the help of an unconscious elderly lady with a broken leg. In a passage that is horrifying to a modern reader, they decide to splint the leg themselves, even though a doctor has been called.

> 'She'll be awfully cross when she gets better and finds that I've broken off one of the legs of her best bathroom chairs for a splint and tied it round with her nightdress …'
> There was a crack of tearing calico, as Jocelyn slit a petticoat into five long strips then handed them to her sister.
> Evelyn thought for a moment. 'Oh, I do hope I'm doing it right; it was all so easy when I was doing it for the test for my Ambulance badge, but now I simply mustn't make a mistake.' Aloud she said: 'You must put the bandages on, while I pull out her leg to the length of the other.'

One of the most famous cries in Guiding fiction occurs in Dorothea Moore's overblown *Judy, Patrol Leader* (1930), when Judy is rescued from a cottage in which she has been buried under a landslide with a sick baby: 'Please tell Billy's father that the baby came out of her fit. One up for the *Child Nurse Badge*!'
Christine Chaundler's Guides are less alarmingly competent: '"Oughtn't we to treat her for shock or something?" … said Theo, with vague recollections of some of the first-aid instruction the Guides had lately been having.' (*Bunty of the Blackbirds*, 1925) On the whole, however, Guides leap into action with disturbing alacrity: 'Please let sixpence drop in Uncle's cap,' chants Roy, recalling Ambulance badge mnemonics, after Catherine has fallen out of a tree in Joanna Lloyd's *Catherine Goes to School* (1945):

> '"P" for Pain, "L" for loss of power; well, I'm sure you lost that, if you ever had any; "S" for swelling, it doesn't look very swollen; "D" for deformity; yes, definitely; "I" for irregularity of the bone;

well it does look a rum shape; "U" for unnatural mobility; it doesn't look very natural, and "C" for crepitus. I can't remember what crepitus is, but I expect you've got it. Yes, I'm sure it's a fracture, Tiger. We must pad the splints first; we can use our jerseys for that. Find some wood for splints someone. Then bandages … Tiger's school scarf will do for one, but we want five. What about stockings?'

Catherine Christian acknowledges more realistic feelings when her Magpie Patrol go nervously to the assistance of injured passengers off a crashed train, and the Patrol Leader inarticulately states: 'We may be able to help. Just anchor your minds on that idea. It isn't going to be what we feel—it's going to be whether we can be of some use or not.' (*The Seventh Magpie*, 1946)

'IT BUCKS YOU UP AND MAKES YOU SMART!'

Guiding in the works of Elinor M Brent-Dyer

Ruth Jolly

Elinor M Brent-Dyer included Guiding as a major strand in her writing from the publication of *Jo of the Chalet School* in 1926 until the mid-1950s when she moved the Chalet School out to Switzerland and allowed its Guide Company to lapse. The Guide movement was only sixteen years old when she brought it into her fictional school, and it fitted seamlessly into her world: not surprisingly, since she wrote for girls, and Guiding could be said to have epitomised the attitudes, ambitions and aspirations of girls of that era.

By the time I became a Guide in the early 1960s, terms such as 'Guide's honour', while still entirely comprehensible, had a slightly quaint ring. In the 1920s, however, honour was a major preoccupation. Since schoolgirl literature of those days aimed to inspire as much as to entertain, the introduction of Guides into her main series gave a natural vehicle for such matters as honour, loyalty, bravery and clean living. 'It bucks you up and makes you smart!' says Grizel Cochrane in *Jo of the Chalet School*, hoping to persuade her new headmistress to start a school company—and as it turns out, 'Madame' is already thinking along just those lines.

While some companies may have allowed their Guides to roam the countryside unsupervised, building camp fires or bridges and seeking out opportunities to do good turns, such freedom would not have been appropriate at the Chalet School, where continental parents still expected their daughters to be carefully chaperoned. Add to this the tremendous emphasis on control which pervades the works of Elinor Brent-Dyer—one cannot help suspecting that she had discipline problems in her own teaching career, such draconian measures do her fictional schoolmistresses employ to remain in charge!—and it is not surprising that the 1st Tiernsee Company is shown mainly partaking of more orderly pursuits such as drill or ambulance work.

Guiding first appears in the series as a passing mention in *The School at the Chalet* (1925), where Wanda describes a book she has been given about a Girl Guide called Gilly, short for Gisela. This is surely *Guide Gilly, Adventurer* by Dorothea Moore (1922)—Elinor warmly commends this author in at least two of her books.

Then comes the decision in *Jo of the Chalet School* to start a company, and Madge Bettany's plans to acquire the necessary training. By *The Princess of the Chalet School* (1927), which begins one year after the end of *Jo of*, the Company is up and running, and the book contains detailed descriptions of Guide activities, especially badge work, and includes a moving description of the enrolment of Elisaveta, the eponymous princess.

> 'Elisaveta, are you ready?' Joey Bettany looked excited as she came to the Princess, who stood alone behind the horse-shoe formation in which most of the others were drawn up. The only exceptions to the rule were the colour parties, which had just taken their places in front of the other Guides, and now stood like images, holding the flags. In front of the Guides stood the Brownies, very thrilled

at this enrolment of a princess—the entire school knew who Elisaveta was by this time—and doing their best to look smart and workman-like.

Elisaveta, clad in blue jumper and skirt, with her yellow tie hanging loose— where the others had theirs pinned with the little metal badge that meant so much to them all—marched forward shyly at Joey's side.

Between the flags stood Miss Bettany in her captain's uniform, the other officer behind her, and, on one side, Crown Prince Carol of Belsornia, who had managed to snatch a week's holiday to come and see his little daughter enrolled. He wore his white and silver uniform as colonel of the Royal Guards, and his medals flashed in the sunlight, even though he stood, erect and still, eyes front, hand resting on his sword-hilt …

She came with Joey, very serious, and full of the promise she was about to make. They marched up to where Miss Bettany stood, and then Joey saluted smartly and took two steps back, standing at attention, while the captain asked the simple questions:

'Do you know what your honour is?'

'Yes.' Elisaveta's reply rang out, full of confidence.

'Can I trust you on your honour to be loyal to God and the King; to help other people at all times; and to obey the Guide Law?'

Up went Elisaveta's hand to the half-salute as she replied in clear tones, 'I promise on my honour to do my best to be loyal to God and the King; to help other people at all times; and to obey the Guide Law!'

'I trust you on your honour to keep this promise. You are now one of the great sisterhood of Guides.' The captain's tones were very comforting. There was a quiet strength in her voice which Elisaveta found restful.

The new Guide gave her left hand in the Guide grip, and then she half-turned on the word of command and saluted the colours. Finally she saluted the company, and then she marched back to her patrol with Joey, the badge in her tie, and a deep resolve in her heart to do her best to keep her promise and to do the Guides honour by her behaviour.

Then the command rang out, 'Company dismiss to patrol corners!' and it was all over.

One aspect of Elinor Brent-Dyer's view of Guides upon which people often comment is that she invariably has a mixture of bird and flower patrol names. In this same book we are told, 'After the company drill, the Cock and the Poppy patrols showed the work they had done in ambulance and stretcher drill, and the Cornflowers and the Swallows gave a good display of signalling, with the Morse code.' And in *Judy, the Guide* (Nelson, 1928) there are Daffodils, Wrens and Skylarks; while in *Carnation of the Upper Fourth* (*Girl's Own Paper* 1934) we encounter Swallows, Robins, Blackbirds, Daffodils, Daisies, Carnations and Pimpernels. Unusual though this may be in most people's experience, there was never a requirement that one or the other should be chosen. In the 1918 handbook *Girl Guiding*, Baden-Powell wrote, 'and so now a patrol can choose which it likes, a bird or a flower'—it was up to the founders of the patrol, not the whole company.

Princess of the Chalet School also makes constant reference to the behaviour of a good

Guide: Joey pledges her Guide honour to tell no one that Elisaveta is a princess; Joey and the Robin persevere with trying to help the hostile matron, because Joey is a Guide and the Robin a Brownie; Bianca is a Guide, so she cannot go down to breakfast leaving Jo's bed unmade.

More significantly still, Joey's Guidecraft is a major factor in her success in foiling the princess's kidnappers. Although Elinor (or EBD, as many of her fans affectionately call her) is careful to stigmatise the following of the abductors as a 'mad chase', for Joey herself, it is the skills learnt in Guides which lend her confidence in her ability to find her friend. 'She had always been good at tracking, and had learned to be very observant.'

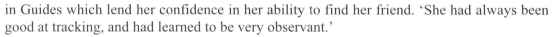

> When she had reached the bush she found that the ribbon had been tied so as to bend some of the smaller twigs together, and pointing up the mountain. The Guide sign for 'Road to be followed'! How thankful she felt that she had given up a whole Saturday afternoon once to teach the woodcraft signs to Elisaveta!

Princess is a school story, yet it could equally be considered a Guide story in its own right—since it contains every bit as much Guiding as, for example, *Guide Gilly*, a Ruritanian adventure story involving a Lone Guide at boarding school: more, if we are considering actual descriptions of Guide events, and not just opportunities to put Guide skills and attitudes into practice.

Guiding is now an established part of the Chalet School. In *The Head Girl of the Chalet School* (1928), however, it plays only a small part, although an interesting summary is given of the previous term's Guide activities; and the movement is seen as likely to benefit a dishonourable new girl—'After all … that's what Guides are for—to help people to play straight.' This theme is further elaborated in the fifth book, *The Rivals of the Chalet School* (1929), where we are treated to a cautionary tale of What Happens if Girls are Denied Guides— the headmistress of the rival school disapproves of them, and as a result her girls are dishonourable, snobbish and incapable of taking responsibility.

> 'But what more could we give them than they have had?' asked Miss Browne. 'They have a good library, games, a debating society. What more can they want? And what grieves me the most,' she went on, 'is the fact that foreign girls have shown them how to behave well. We haven't a girl in the school who isn't of British birth and training, and yet they have shown less sense of honour and responsibility than those Austrian and French and German girls in the Chalet School! *Why?*'
>
> 'I don't think it is altogether that,' said Miss Anderson. 'After all, we never

said anything about their not going out during their free time. But I do think they need something more than they have—the something more that Guides would give them. I am not a Guide myself, but I know what tremendous good they have done wherever they have been started. Miss Browne, won't you think about starting them here—in this school—once this dreadful time is over?'

'I may begin them,' said Miss Browne. 'But I am afraid it will be—too late.'

The Chalet Guides, incidentally, do not always show up well in this book. In Chapter IV we hear how they meet the girls of St Scholastika's on a narrow path, and, choosing to forget the school rule that they should fall into single file, force their antagonists off the path into long grass, condemning them to the terrible consequences of Getting their Stockings Wet. If the Chaletians had properly read their *Handbook for Girl Guides*, they would have recalled that 'when marching out, Guides are careful not to fill up the footpath, so march in single file if a large party—out of consideration for other people'.

The sixth book contains only a couple of passing references to the movement, but in the seventh, *The Chalet School and Jo* (1931), we are back to a long description of a Guide meeting:

> At half-past, came the Guide meeting … this was the first meeting of term, and they had to decide what badges they would take that term.
>
> 'Basket-worker for me,' proclaimed Joey that morning, as she was putting on her stockings. 'Also, I rather want a shot at Pioneer.'
>
> 'I will do Basket-worker too,' agreed Frieda. 'And I should like to take Boatswain, if I may. I have done the Turk's Head, and I know all the knots, and can swim.'
>
> 'Boatswain wouldn't be bad fun,' ruminated Jo. 'I think I'll have a shot at it myself. And don't some people intend to take Signaller?'

The rival school has by now set up its own company, and the Chalet girls are told:

> 'You all know that St Scholastika's has started Guides this term, girls? … I want you to extend a helping hand to them. We are an old company in comparison with them; we have several Guides with the all-round cord, and several who hold the first-class badge. They are all novices in the movement, and I want you to help them—tactfully, of course—as much as ever you can. To that end, Miss Browne and Mademoiselle have arranged that this term you shall go camping together at the week-ends, as soon as the weather permits. Two patrols from each company will go every week-end, with the exception of the Oberammergau week. You will go in strict rotation, and while in camp you will be expected to give a helping hand to the new Guides, so that they may be able to catch up with us as far as possible.'

In fact these weekend camps are never described, and it may be no coincidence that the next book is entirely about a Guide camp—perhaps Elinor realised that this plot line had too much potential to be covered in a single chapter. All we hear at this point is a throwaway comment from Joey: 'In some ways, I suppose it has been a jolly good term … The week-end camps were topping, and the Saints have made a jolly good beginning as Guides.'

And it is in this book that the girls assume the charge of the young orphan Biddy O'Ryan, only possible because they do so as Guides, giving them access to Guide funds (presumably in a boarding school there was little other use for their weekly subs!), potential support from the Guide Company at the other school, and the Guide Captain as a responsible adult.

In book number eight, *The Chalet Girls in Camp* (1932), we have a Guide story per se, though Guides and Guiders are already known to us as pupils and mistresses, so it becomes a fascinating synthesis of the two genres. Here at last, in this safe, remote Austrian valley, the girls can go off by themselves and act autonomously. And they do. They go to the farm to fetch milk; they go wooding; the older girls go fishing on the lake at daybreak; and all this without a Guider in sight, though the grown-ups are of course near at hand to get them out of the resulting scrapes, even to the convenient arrival of Drs Jem and Jack just when some wilder spirits have stirred up a hornets' nest!

Interestingly, in this book the Guides perform no heroics. The adventures of the Guide camp are all well within the bounds of probability, and the camp could be pretty much any Guide camp at any era—though in my day we no longer had the comfort of palliasses to sleep on! The disastrous attempt to help by doing the laundry particularly resonates with me: in my experience, attempted good turns were seldom understood or appreciated by the grown-ups they were intended to assist.

Certainly EBD must have camped herself, to have the atmosphere so perfectly; and how well she integrated it into her beloved Tyrolean setting! Who could forget those evening sing-songs, and the 'unbidden audience' of locals who 'stole away' after what they came to expect as a nightly event? How true to life is the reaction of the 'voluble farmer's wife':

> … who exclaimed at their dress, at the size of Rufus [the dog], and at their daring in camping out thus. She took them into the kitchen, and made them sit down and drink big mugs of sweet rich milk, warm from the cow. Even Rufus was given a bowlful, much to his joy.
>
> 'For well-wishing and good luck,' she remarked, as he lapped it up. 'But, *mein Fräulein*, what if the rain comes?'
>
> 'Sit in our tents,' said Joey, finishing the last of her milk with an effort, for the mugs were generous ones, and had been brimful. 'We shall be quite safe and dry there, *meine Frau*.'
>
> The good woman shook her head. It was more than she could understand. However, these were undoubtedly foreigners, and one had heard of the mad ways of foreigners before this. Of her own accord, she offered to send over six dozen eggs the next morning, when her man would be going that way on an errand.

In the next book, *The Exploits of the Chalet Girls* (1933), EBD reverts to keeping Guides as an important background theme: the girls remain keen, Joey Bettany complaining bitterly that she is allowed to work for only three Guide badges at a time! And the Guiders prove very efficient when one of the girls (not a Guide, of course) accidentally sets herself on fire. However, in *The Chalet School and the Lintons* (1934), it is perhaps surprising that she fails to contrast Guide honour with the extremely dishonourable behaviour of Joyce and Thekla. This is the

Disaster in camp (*The Chalet Girls in Camp*)

more remarkable since the book contains frequent minor references to the movement, including a significant mention in the Head's beginning of term speech:

> '… Miss Wilson tells me that she expects as many of you as possible to qualify for Cook's and Laundress' badges this term.' Here she cast a laughing glance across at the tall, pleasant-faced mistress who sat at one end of the little dais.
>
> Miss Wilson rose to the occasion. 'It's high time you all had those badges, girls,' she said. 'I know we have a few; but I want to see every Guide with them.'

And it is specifically stated that Joyce was already a Guide before joining the school, and that her membership was transferred, which makes it the more strange that EBD fails to point the moral. But her remit was to write *school* stories, so she may have been wise not to overuse the Guiding theme.

In *The New House at the Chalet School* (1935) we find minor mentions once more, though Guiding is significant in the important episode where young Daisy Venables asks for help: 'The small, wistful face at her elbow brightened. "I *thought* you'd help. Besides, you're both wearing the Guide Badge. Guides always help, don't they?"' And number twelve in the series, *Jo Returns to the Chalet School* (1936), has only a single, passing mention—the lowest profile yet.

However, book number thirteen, *The New Chalet School* (1938), in which the School joins up with its erstwhile rival, St Scholastika's, makes up for this. Just as EBD had used Guides— or the lack thereof—to symbolise, and in part explain, the initial contrast between the rival schools, so now she uses a Guide event to exemplify their eventual oneness—although this time it is left to the reader to draw the inference. The final chapter, 'One at Last', shows 'Saints' and 'Chaletians' no longer distinct, united in the sisterhood of Guides.

> It was the last day but one of term, and the annual garden-party with which the summer term always closed was in preparation. They generally entertained their guests with some performance, and this year it had been decided to make a Guide affair of it. The Rangers would see to Kaffee und Kuchen, and the Cadets were to have a couple of stalls in aid of the free beds at the Sonnalpe which the school had maintained ever since the opening of the Sanatorium. The Brownies were to give a display, and it had been decided that they should present the story of Grace Darling, which would bring in a good deal of their Brownie work such as semaphore signalling, knot-tying, simple bandaging, laying tables, and making beds, while little Marie Varick, whose ambition it was to be an elocutionist some day, would tell the story first so that Continentals should know what it was all about.
>
> The Guides were more ambitious. They were to represent hospital work in wartime, and would show stretcher and first-aid drill; sick-nursing—including making of beds with patients in them; invalid cookery; tying of knots for nooses and lowering work; interpreting; short-hand and typewriting and book-keeping, since, as 'Bill' had pointed out, to run a hospital you must understand the financial side as well as others; and, finally, tent-pitching …
>
> As for the few unfortunates who, for one reason or another, were not members of the movements, they would act as hostesses. There *were* only a few of them,

for the School ran three large Guide Companies, as well as the Ranger and Cadet Companies, and all the Juniors were Brownies.

In the next book, *The Chalet School in Exile* (1940), the school becomes caught up in the prelude to World War II, and leaves its beautiful Tyrolean location for good. But before we move on to examine the importance of Guiding in the 'English' part of the series, some mention should be made of the depiction of the movement in EBD's other pre-war works.

EBD produced only one Guide book as such, and *Judy, the Guide* (1928), though sufficiently well received to run to a second edition, has not proved one of her most enduring works; the fact that it was not part of any series was doubtless against it. In fact it rather falls between two stools, since for some reason she chose to import her heroine from a Canadian Outback origin, and the story is at least as much about how Judy becomes integrated into the quite alien boarding school community as it is about Guides. However, Judy's origins have one great strength, and that is that she has fairly plausibly never heard of the Guides, which gives an opportunity for detailed explanations of the Law and Promise; there is another comprehensive description of an enrolment, and of course numerous references to badge work, and to that universal bugbear of pre-war Guiding, the Morse Code.

The main plot centres round the persecution of Judy, on somewhat flimsy circumstantial evidence, by Muriel, Patrol Second of the Wrens, and her following. This feud gives ample opportunity for the stigmatising of various behaviours as 'unGuidelike'—a worse condemnation than 'unsporting'; and the keeping of the Guide Law is seen as more important than the law of the land—'[Talking libellously] is a criminal offence, Muriel. Also, it is most unGuidelike.'

Guiding and school life are completely integrated: before an enrolment special hymns are sung in school assembly, and the Guide Captain joins the girls in their Common Room for a talk, which on the occasion described takes the form of a patriotic story, with the moral: 'Now, Guides, those men have a message for us. It is this: "Hold on in difficulties, and don't whine." *They* didn't!' The story she tells is drawn from the early days of the British Empire, and the value of Guides in helping the girls to 'think imperially' is reiterated later in the book.

In the end, the dispute between Muriel and Judy is taken to a Court of Honour, since the mistress who is also the Guide Captain 'felt that she could deal better with it as Guider than mistress'.

Miss Carthew waited till the last Guide had vanished; then she took her seat in the centre of the circle. Standing with hands at the salute, they all solemnly repeated the pledge.

'I promise on my honour that nothing which is reported here shall be repeated by me outside this Court of Honour.'

The captain gravely spoke her reply. 'I trust you on your honour to keep this promise.'

Then they sat down, and Thekla, the secretary, read aloud the minutes from the last court. They were approved and signed, and one or two notices were then given out. Tests were discussed, and the Saturday fortnight hence was decided on for the examinations. When this was over, there was a momentary silence. Every one knew that now the real business of the meeting was at hand, and every one mentally braced herself to meet it.

Then Miss Carthew spoke. 'I want to talk about the lack of the true Guide spirit that I have noticed this term in our company,' she said slowly. 'I am sorry to have to say it, but it seems to me that every day it gets worse. There is no feeling of being "a sister to every other Guide." It seems to me that many of us are in danger of completely forgetting the fourth law. We talk of "the great sisterhood of Guides." I can't think that our company has been anything of a sisterhood this term. What makes it worse is that some of the people who are showing this lack of the Guide spirit are Guides who, in the normal course of events, will become cadets next term.'

The portrayal of the Court of Honour is accurate and detailed, but the outcome is inconclusive: the aggrieved Patrol Second refuses to accept Guide Judy Carey's word of honour, on the grounds that she is not English! The matter is not resolved until the real—and quite unforeseen—culprit is revealed at the end of the book.

While it might have been expected that the Court of Honour would have provided the resolution of the impasse, its failure to do so is true to the characters as they have been portrayed, and perhaps to real life. It also gives an excellent opportunity to contrast the practical and spiritual aspects of the movement.

> 'The badge work has been very good this term,' [the captain] announced, 'but I am afraid our company spirit has been poor. Remember, Guides, that it is better to have few badges and the real Guide feeling than many badges and no Guide feeling at all.'

Guiding is also a sub-plot in *Heather Leaves School* (1929), part of the rather loosely connected La Rochelle series which shares some characters with the Chalet School. Heather, a slangy and rebellious schoolgirl, is removed from her boarding school by her father and provided with a governess. We are told that:

> If she stayed at Ripley she could be a Guide, and she had always longed to be one, ever since she had read Miss Dorothea Moore's delightful stories of Guides. Of the fact that, as she was, she was scarcely fit to be one, she made nothing. She

knew the Guide Law, of course; but the clause that dealt with courtesy meant nothing to her. Neither did the one about 'A Guide obeys orders.' It wasn't the Law she had been thinking of, but the fun to be got out of Guides.

In fact the new governess turns out to be a Guide, and makes short work of the suggestion by the Rector's priggish eldest daughter Cressie that Guides are 'an excuse for unladylike behaviour'.

> 'That's nonsense!' said Miss Christopher crisply. 'The Guides are just the reverse. They insist on courtesy for one thing—it's a part of the Guide Law.'

A company is formed, but we hear little more of it, apart from the occasional hope that it will help cure Cressie's character defects.

Refuting the common criticisms levelled at Guiding seems to have been important to Elinor Brent-Dyer at this era. As well as Cressie's strictures quoted above, we have the example in *Judy, the Guide* of a girl who is not permitted to join the Company because her 'uncle-guardian was old-fashioned, and declared that Guides were just an excuse for hoydenish behaviour in girls'. A similar point of view is held by the unpleasant vicar's wife in *Jean of Storms*, EBD's one adult romance (serialised in the *Shields Daily Gazette* in 1930, and published in book form by Bettany Press in 1996). In her view, 'the children learn all kinds of military ideas from the Company', and the movement is 'apt to make the girls discontented'. This belief is strongly refuted by the heroine, Jean, who declares: '"It teaches the girls loyalty, honour, oneness, and self-reliancy. As soon as Allison is old enough, she shall be enrolled as a Brownie, and I only wish every girl I know belonged to us." … "Also," she added mischievously, "both Princess Mary and the Duchess of York are Guides, and surely, what is good enough for them is good enough for us!"'

Carnation of the Upper Fourth might have been another contender for 'Guide book per se', had the author not been already established as a school story writer. Like *Judy, the Guide* it is about a school in which the Guide Company is very important; and once more a major theme is the persecution of a new pupil by one of the Guides. One unusual feature is that in this book, we actually see the girls taking part in a tracking exercise. The Chalet girls do track, but only ever off-stage:

> 'What about tracking games?' suggested Gertrud.
> 'All right if the thaw is quick. If it isn't, well, it's all wrong,' replied Grizel. 'You know what it's like then—knee-deep in mud! Matey would have a fit if we brought the babes into anything of the kind. As far as that goes, she'd have a fit over any of us. The cleanest person can't help looking like a tramp after tracking through mud and puddles.'
>
> *The Head Girl of the Chalet School*

How thankful they were that, as Guides, they had all had plenty of tracking practice! Joey and one or two of the elder girls could move as noiselessly as poachers when necessary …

> *The Chalet School in Exile*

Perhaps it was hard for EBD to invent circumstances in which they could have done so, given the restrictions of their boarding-school setting and especially of the protective continental culture; badge requirements, however, made it necessary that they should have acquired these skills. The Guides could not even pass their Second Class test without knowing how to stalk and track, and the elaboration of this in *Girl Guide Badges and How to Win Them* (8th edition, 1925) instructs the patrol to 'let its members scatter and bring back their solitary observations after a given time'—not easy to reconcile with strict chaperonage.

Probably the fact that Carnation attends a day-school, and in the freer atmosphere of England, makes it easier to include this essential ingredient of Guiding: and the activity provides the scenario for two important episodes—Guide rescues fellow-Guide from drowning, with the bonus of some effective resuscitation procedures (was Holger Nielsen *really* performed at that era by two people in combination?), and the next step along the long slippery slope of dishonourable behaviour for the anti-heroine Birdie, who not only plans a shocking breach of trustworthiness for a Guide outing, but actually fails to turn up to carry it out, having received a better offer elsewhere!

Guiding is in fact crucial to the 'Birdie' plot strand: sentence is finally passed on her at a Court of Honour, and her expulsion from Guides and from the school are simultaneous. Once again EBD is portraying a world—or a life, perhaps—in which Guiding is a big part, but not quite at the centre.

Caught on the rocks
('The Robins Make Good')

For a Guide story with no element of school, we must look to 'The Robins Make Good' (*Girl's Own Paper*, 1936, republished in *Elinor M Brent-Dyer's Short Stories*, GGBP, 2004), the only short story about Guides EBD seems to have written. It is a standard 'Passing Patrol Rescues Small Boy from Deadly Peril' situation, saved from banality by the author's talent for painting a dramatic word picture. The Guides, of course, manage to reach the child by forming a human chain, with a rope of Guides scarves ('mercifully Guide scarves are made of stout material'), knotted together with reef knots, for added security.

A tall pinnacle of rock stood here at the foot of the steps, and clinging to it was a little boy. Every now and then he vanished from sight as the foam of the raging sea dashed over him, and it was plain that he could not hold on much longer … The rock was a good three feet away from the steps, and the sea was tossing madly over the strip of sand that on fine days lay between it and the sea-wall; even Rosalie and Ursula, who were tall and strong for their fifteen years, could never have kept their feet.

It was Lois who was inspired.

'Barbara, run for help!' she shouted.

Barbara, the fleetest member of the company, turned and fled down the promenade towards the coastguard station which, mercifully, was not far away. Then Lois turned to the others.

'Scarves—quick!' she said.

It seemed impossible that the girls could have pulled off their scarves so quickly, but they had them free and were busy knotting them with reef-knots into a rope almost before she finished speaking. Lois tied this rope firmly to her belt.

'Rosalie next,' she said, as she took a step down. 'Then Ursula; then the rest, and Sybil last.'

They did not require to be told what to do. Rosalie gripped Lois's hand 'sailor's grip.' Ursula took hers; then Janet hers; and so, till they had a living rope of the six of them. The last one, Sybil, tied the other end of the scarf-rope to her belt and slung her arm round the nearest railing, determined to hold fast at all costs.

At this point, EBD's sense of realism and the fitness of things seems to have taken over. The Guides are hanging on like grim death, unable to pull the boy to land, when a gigantic fisherman looms up and takes the shivering victim off their hands. But Lois the sea-captain's daughter is soaking wet and exhausted—so who should appear but the District Commissioner with her car, smiling and ready to take the girls home and speak a few well-deserved words of commendation: 'You are worthy of our Sisterhood, every one of you!'

To the rescue
('The Robins Make Good')

For Elinor Brent-Dyer, it is indeed hard to keep the grown-ups out of the picture. But her Guides are nonetheless plucky, resourceful and committed, and quick to apply the skills they have learned to the emergencies which inevitably confront them in the world of fiction.

Returning to the Chalet series, we come now to the wartime books, in which EBD continues her very idealistic portrayal of Guiding; and this comes as no surprise, since it reflects exactly the role and attitude of real-life Guides during the Second World War. What could seem more relevant during the blitz than the first-aid skills they had all so carefully mastered, and what more useful in that era of make-do-and-mend than the virtues of thrift and perseverance? And in the fight against Nazism, the carefully inculcated values of truth and honour were again a perfect match. In a highly symbolic moment, the refugee pupil Emmie Linders, fresh from her and her sister Joanna's flight from Nazi Germany, is provided with a Guide uniform before she tells their story to their enthralled schoolfellows. (*The Highland Twins at the Chalet School*, 1942)

The wartime books also contain many references to the application of Guide skills, from the ability to make clove-hitches in the dark when on the run from the Nazis in *Exile*, through the use of a Guide knife to force a way through a hedge in pursuit of putative spies in *The Chalet School Goes to It* (1941), to the vital recognition that a suspicious character is using Morse Code—'Crumpet' had learned this from the Guide handbook—in *Chudleigh Hold* (1954), a spy story which, though published much later, is referenced in one of the wartime Chalet School books.

In the weekend camp in *The Wrong Chalet School* (1952), the main Guide episode of the post-war English books, a change of emphasis may be discerned. After the emotional intensity of wartime, a more pragmatic spirit pervaded the fifties. 'Make-do-and-mend' was still a necessity, but 'pick up the pieces and move on' had become an aspiration. Moreover, it was not an era when concepts of honour or duty to God—or, indeed, the Queen—were often discussed; and this shift is reflected in Elinor Brent-Dyer's portrayal of the movement. The chapter gives a vigorous and attractive account of the pitching of camp, collecting of driftwood, preparation and serving of a meal, and rest afterwards—and then veers off into an afternoon's swimming, where one of the Lieutenants rescues a Guide from a group of jellyfish—an episode which need not have been in any way Guide related.

Why did Guiding fade so suddenly from the Chalet School world over the transition from England to Switzerland? For it is a sudden disappearance in effect, even though the fading is actually gradual. From *The Wrong Chalet School* where the camp has a whole chapter to itself, via *Shocks for the Chalet School* (also 1952) where Guiding is briefly affirmed as demonstrating leadership and teaching qualities, and *Bride Leads the Chalet School* and *Changes for the Chalet School* (both 1953) where there are only passing mentions, we arrive at the first two Swiss books, *The Chalet School and Barbara* (1954) and *The Chalet School Does it Again* (1955), both of which mention the girls' keenness to restart Guides in their new location—and indeed in *Barbara*, the eponymous heroine expresses a longstanding and wistful ambition to join. But no Guide company is ever formed in the Chalet School in Switzerland, and all we have by way of explanation is a rather lame comment in Chalet Club News Letter 15: 'The Chalet School Guide Company has not carried on in Switzerland because there is little or no time for it. The English branch has, however, a flourishing Company.'

A clue may perhaps be found in Elinor M Brent-Dyer's own Guiding record. Research at Guide Headquarters shows that she held two official appointments: she was Captain of the 3rd South Shields Rangers from 15 October 1926–11 November 1929, and Captain of the 6th Hereford Rangers from October 1936–11 May 1939 (not a Lone Ranger Unit as is erroneously stated in her biography, *Behind the Chalet School*). Her warrant record also states that she signed forms for the 22nd Hereford Guide Company around 1942–1945, as the acting Captain had no authority to sign official paperwork. EBD's active involvement in the movement did not therefore continue beyond the end of the Second World War.

Furthermore, considerable changes took place shortly after she ceased to play an active role. The uniform changed: the cotton overall was replaced in 1947 by the bright blue cotton shirt and navy blue skirt, and the navy blue soft felt hat was replaced by the beret. More significantly, in 1957—just two years after the publication of *Does it Again*—there were considerable changes to the Second Class test, including the removal of the clauses requiring semaphore and Morse Code. It may well have seemed to EBD that it was safer to cease describing the organisation, once she could no longer be confident of the details. Or perhaps she had simply lost enthusiasm.

It would not, however, be true to suggest that the *influence* of Guiding is entirely lost. Once a Guide, always a Guide—and Mary-Lou is still carrying her Guide cord with her everywhere in *A Chalet Girl from Kenya* (1955), although it must be at least a year since she attended a meeting. The consequent saving of Emerence's life is well within the traditions of Guide story-books. And strangely enough, in *Excitements at the Chalet School* (1957) it appears that the school still possesses its Guide tents, and has brought them out to Switzerland but presumably never used them! So clearly EBD also remained a Guide in her thoughts, even after she had ceased to be one actively.

One final mention comes in *The Chalet School Wins the Trick* (1961). This centres on a group of (as it turns out) future pupils, whose relationship with the school gets off to a disastrous start when they try to light a fire on the cricket pitch in emulation of the Camp Fire movement. The chief protagonist, Audrey, explains to her companions her enthusiasm for Camp Fire (as described to her former school by an American mistress on an exchange visit) and where it differs from Guides, which she had originally longed to join. The whole episode seems rather contrived, and whereas in an earlier book the girls might have been redeemed by the power of Guides, at this late stage it is the School's influence that 'wins the trick'.

Perhaps more than any other comparable author, Elinor M Brent-Dyer created a whole world into which we are transported as we read her books. Because it is a complete world, Guides cannot be more than a strand within it. But where Guiding is a significant part of that world, the strand is well interwoven and its influence pervades the whole.

CAMP

'It smelled like camp too—that delightful aroma of hot canvas
and bruised grass … [and] the subtle tang of wood smoke.'
The Swallows See it Through, C R Mansell, 1955

In the early days Guides simply went off to camp with no fuss, but very quickly
the approach becomes regularised. Kit-lists, camp rules, consent forms, health
certificates, approved camp sites and inspections by the Camp Adviser are all
part of camp preparation. Every detail is covered:

'It's quite a safe bathing place where we're going, isn't it, Grace?'
'Grade B according to the local C A,' Grace remarked obscurely.
The Makeshift Patrol, H B Davidson, 1932

Camps contain hospital and mess tents, washing shelters and latrines. Patrols
are appointed to various jobs, and the Captain and Lieutenant given orderlies. In
some stories, a Guide stands on guard outside the Captain's tent all day, ready to
carry a message. In others, they even post night sentries.

Certain foods dominate camping stories in both fact and fiction: eggs cooked
in orange skins are a common motif, but the two particular favourites are dampers
and cheese dreams.

'What fun!' exclaimed the girls. 'And what do we do with the
cheese?'
'Make cheese dreams.'
'What?'
'I'll show you!'
An exciting hour followed during which the girls of Low
Meadows cooked and ate the tastiest things they had ever known …
the glorious savoury that a fried sandwich of bread and butter and
cheese could produce was a revelation.
'Won't Mum just love this!' mumbled Puss, too entranced to wait
until her mouth was empty. 'I'll turn cook and show her when I get
home!'
The School that was Different, Sybil B Owsley, 1932

The same book tells how to make dampers from a simple flour and water
dough: 'You'll peel that green stick quite clean and you'll roll the dough round it
in spirals and bake it over hot embers. If it's properly cooked the bread should
slip quite easily off the stick.'

Camp cookery can be remarkably competent, or an opportunity for mishap.
In Elisabeth Mumford's *Judy Joins the Jasmines* (1934), the scrambled eggs are

seasoned with bicarbonate of soda instead of salt. In contrast, the admirable Guides in Margaret Middleton's *The Guide Camp at Herons Bay* (1927) produce an impromptu meal for forty visitors as well as the Company, including 'one sizzling panful after another of crisp brown chips'. In Ethel Talbot's *Peggy's Last Term* (1920), an enterprising patrol serves the rest of the Guides hedgehog baked in clay, only detected when someone finds a spine in her portion.

The pits, of course, are a feature of every camp. Near the camp kitchen would be an incinerator, the grease (or wet) pit, the refuse (or dry) pit and, somewhere else entirely, the latrine pit, screened by poles and canvas. The latrines are rarely mentioned in fiction, although Baden-Powell, who was much concerned with good hygiene and regular bowel movements (for which he uses the unique term of 'rearing'), goes into frank detail when discussing sanitation and urges Scouts and Guides 'when rearing away from camp' to take a spade with them. Other Scouters had similar preoccupations. Philip Carrington, who wrote *The Boy Scouts' Camp Book* in 1918 (and was my great-uncle), peppers his book with the initials KYBO to remind boys to 'keep your bowels open' and suggests that a Scoutmaster would do well to administer a mild laxative to every boy in camp on the first day as 'this will … cut off altogether the plague of headaches, boils, pains and debility that may otherwise crop up on the third day'.

Regular camp features include a rest hour and making camp gadgets, usually of an impressive standard: 'The Commissioner stood dumbfounded at the palatial racks for cups and plates and cutlery that had suddenly shot up. Miss Stephens inspected the lashing and found it almost perfect.' (*Cecile at St Clare's*, Margaret C Field, 1929) Washing can be river based, or in a camp washstand. 'A sponge and a brook are jolly fine in the morning,' says a Guide in *The Caravan Patrol* (Nancy M Hayes, 1926), and most camp sites seem to feature a place to swim. Tracking games may follow, frequently offering Guides the opportunity to have an adventure. In the evening comes the singing: 'In their wildest dreams they had never imagined anything nearer paradise than their first camp sing-song.' (*The Quest of the Sleuth Patrol*, Vera Marshall, 1931)

Most Guides sleep on palliasses, narrow sacks filled with crackling straw or hay. No one seems to attempt to weave a mattress on a camp loom, as shown in *Scouting for Boys*, or to follow B-P's description of how to make a framed camp bed lined with evergreen branches, for which the first instruction is 'cut down a fir tree' (visions of denuded plantations if a whole company attempted this). If a toothbrush has been forgotten, they will of course make one out of a frayed twig, although this doesn't occur to poor Bunty in Christine Chaundler's *Bunty of the Blackbirds* (1925), who gets herself into trouble (and an adventure) when she attempts to slip off to buy one. Unless it is raining heavily, Guides will sleep with their flaps open—no one wants to be a fuggy beast.

The final act of the camping day often involves a Guide slipping out in the rain to slacken the guy ropes that will otherwise snap or pull their pegs out of the ground as they contract in the wet (not a problem these days when guy ropes are made of nylon). Margaret Middleton even wrote a short story ('Herne the Hunter') about a camp ghost who slackens Guides' ropes for them!

'KICKED OUT'
Guiding in Antonia Forest's Marlow novels

Antonia Syson

'Do you think they'll put us in the Log-book?'
'Probably. On the second page. "L. and N. Marlow. Kicked out, Monday 27 October."'
'It sounds like an epitaph,' said Lawrie sadly. (*Autumn Term*, 1948)

Kicked out' may sound like an epitaph, but it is not an ending. Nicola and Lawrie Marlow's Guiding career lasts a mere three chapters in the first of ten Marlow novels, yet it reverberates in the plots and themes presented by the whole series. Antonia Forest's sequence of novels resembles traditional Guiding stories in that the books are preoccupied with moral excellence achieved through self-discipline. But where earlier Guide-centred stories present Guiding as a solution to the difficulties of adolescent self-discipline and self-knowledge, Forest uses her Guide plot to unfold these problems without providing any clear resolution. Forest's entire Marlow series provides remarkable insights into the practice and theory of Guiding, and shows how Guiding raises problems of make-believe and discipline which are central to a wide range of literature written for both children and adults.

The need to 'Be Prepared' is famously pivotal to Scouting and Guiding. Baden-Powell saw imagination as the key to helping boys and girls prepare themselves for whatever might arise. He believed that envisaging a wide range of eventualities could give people a kind of prior experience that would make them readier to meet an emergency in the service of their country and the Empire. He also realised that imagination is central to childhood play and saw that both moral and practical training would be made fun by entwining disciplined work with games and stories which could exploit the pleasures of fantasy. 'Being prepared' involves knowledge as well as fantasy, though, because moral integrity is essential for true readiness to serve. Unless a Guide knows what it means to act rightly, she isn't prepared. Knowing how to light a camp fire with only two matches is the least of it.

Autumn Term structurally balances the formalities of a Guide Court of Honour with the formalities of Mark Twain's *The Prince and the Pauper* (1881). Pauper and prince are acted by Lawrie and Nicola at the end of their first autumn term at boarding school; they have been suspended from Guides at the end of their first half term. On one level the successful staging of Twain's novel offers redemption after a series of failures that culminate in the Court of Honour. But the *Prince and the Pauper* also gives the novel a second chance to address the questions raised during Nicola and Lawrie's brief spell in Kingscote's Guide Company. In this chapter, we'll look first at that sojourn with the Guides; then we'll see briefly how the Twain adaptation handles similar problems of discipline, knowledge, and imagination. Finally I sketch (and sketch is the word) some broader implications of *Autumn Term*'s Guiding plot, including parallels between Forest's treatment of the naval Marlow family and Joseph Conrad's story of a disgraced young merchant navy officer, *Lord Jim* (1900).

Part 1: 'There's really nothing else we *can* do'

Autumn Term belongs in a category of Guiding stories which carefully avoid any assumption that girls will *necessarily* join Guides or will carry out their Guiding duties with the required quota of enthusiasm. According to this kind of narrative, Girl Guides are made, not born, whether it's an inner-city church group which needs to be won over into forming a company (Hann's *Peg's Patrol*, 1924), a school company gone rotten through slackness (Christian's *The Marigolds Make Good*, 1937) or a squire's daughter who changes from camp-saboteur to courageous guide (Hayes' *The Plucky Patrol*, 1924).

If this were a more typical Guiding story, Lawrie and Nicola would eventually see the error of their ways in treating Guides as a poor second best to netball, and would find in their new patrol the means to self-discipline and productive, courageous endeavours which would enhance their school and family life. They would discard the too-pragmatic mentality with which they join ('We thought as there wasn't anything else we could be good at this term, we'd better have a shot at Guides') and they'd learn, as their sister Ann puts it, not to 'worry so about being good at things'. Instead things go horribly wrong and they are ignominiously 'kicked out' (as they see it) or (in the Guide Captain's terms) suspended, with the promise of a way back in if they 'have really thought about what Guiding means' in a year's time. When that time comes, the twins are horrified by an invitation to rejoin ('scalded with embarrassment', *End of Term*, 1959).

Guiding is evidently not the answer for Lawrie and Nicola, but the novels take the principles of Guiding very seriously indeed. In giving the twins a hasty exit from the Kingscote School Guide Company, the novels do not reject the Guiding ethos or spirit. We are shown, rather, how difficult it is to maintain that spirit given the inevitably imperfect personalities involved. Unlike the groups seen in some more optimistic Guiding stories, the Kingscote Company fails to get its young members really to think (as the Guide Captain, Miss Redmond, puts it) 'about what Guiding means—not merely winning badges and scoring points against other Patrols'. As we learn in *The Cricket Term* (1974), their sister Ann has long taught Lawrie and Nicola that honour, symbolised in the Guide trefoil, must be kept bright at the back as well as the front. *Autumn Term* shows how Guiding activities may actually distract children from understanding what this deep sense of honour means, even while the ethos of Guiding conceives of this fundamental personal integrity as a central goal in the endeavour. We see some of the difficulties inherent in the underlying principles which sustain the Guide and Scout movements. Self-discipline, loyalty, and competence (that is, 'Being Prepared' to act bravely and *obediently* under pressure) are to be achieved through consistent practice and training, and Baden-Powell saw how to make repetitive work appealing to adolescent imaginations by telling stories of heroism under fire and devising games that teach practical skills: 'The Guides' Law binds you to be LOYAL, KIND, OBEDIENT, AND CHEERFUL … Most of your time will then be spent preparing yourself to carry out these things under difficulties, and in playing Scouting games and practices by which you gain experience.' (*The Handbook for Girl Guides*, 1912) But the pleasures of the imagination, which illuminate the ideals of Guiding and allow children to practise disciplined behaviour in the form of play, are unruly: imagination and discipline don't always blend as seamlessly as Baden-Powell hopes they will.

When Nicola and Lawrie rush hotfoot into the activities needed to attain Second Class, their cynical friend Tim hits the problem on the head. 'All for the honour and glory of the Patrol,' says Lawrie of their fire-lighting, bed-making, Morse Code-tapping work. Tim thinks she knows better: 'Honour and glory of the Marlows more like.' The twins' demise as Guides is caused partly by Lawrie's eagerness to bring these aims together. Lawrie wants to help make the Marlows glorious by making the patrol glorious. Tim's acerbic comment reminds us of how tempting it is to pair 'honour' with 'glory', as if the terms are interchangeable—as if honour lies in external recognition rather than inward integrity. As Joseph Conrad's Captain Marlow asks in *Lord Jim*, isn't there a risk that the task of maintaining one's honour might 'reduce itself to not being found out'? *Autumn Term* explores the danger that adolescents will blur the lines between the 'glory' of badge winning, designed to appeal to their flowering imaginations, and a deeper sense of honour, which depends on integrity and obedience as well as courage. None of *Autumn Term*'s central characters entirely lacks this more fundamental sense of honour (unless one counts poor Marie Dobson as a central character), but all except Ann Marlow are distracted from it by a more superficial concern for appearances.

Lois Sanger, who ranks among the most subtly drawn villains in English children's literature, is the character whose conscious moral choices—or rather whose moral errors—determine not only the Guiding story in *Autumn Term*, but also (to a great extent) the main plots of two other Marlow novels, *End of Term* and *The Cricket Term*. In her quest for public honour, Lois dreads being overshadowed by the Marlow family. Lawrie gradually comes to half-understand Lois's sensitivity, and in her passionate enthusiasm both for Guiding and for Lois personally, she tries to make up for any harm done Lois by her sisters (Lois has recently been evicted from the netball first eleven after her dubious sense of integrity is shown up through a quarrel with Rowan Marlow). Drawing on parallels from fiction (*The Flight of the Heron*, 1925), Lawrie sympathetically sees Lois as 'disgraced and disinherited' in being dispossessed of a rightful place in the hockey team (Lawrie at this point is aware only of a gossip-circulated account, not of Lois's actual dishonesty). So, when Lois has a First Class test hike turned into a patrol outing, Lawrie decides that it's up to the twins to 'be a credit to the Pimpernels and make them top Patrol'.

What the twins don't understand is that being 'a credit to the Pimpernels' involves following the Guide Law of obedience. 'In order to learn their duties thoroughly and smartly, companies must work together many a day, till it requires no effort or thought to be able to carry out their officers' orders to perfection.' (*The Handbook for Girl Guides*) Neither their time as Brownies and Guides, nor the training in naval ways that they have received from their father, has solidified the idea that acting honourably means that they should not pick and choose which orders to obey and which rules to follow. The twins first disobey Lois by bringing all sorts of superfluous things for the hike, including the matches which will later appear as evidence implying they have set light to a local farmer's rick-yard. It's apparent that Lawrie sees being prepared as making sure that the patrol has

A GUIDE OBEYS ORDERS OF HER PARENTS,

PATROL LEADER, OR CAPTAIN, WITHOUT QUESTION

matches and other equipment; she hasn't understood the more fundamental idea of 'preparedness' in the sense of self-discipline and integrity. The twins then disobey Lois again at a pivotal moment during the hike. At the Court of Honour afterwards, Nicola admits to having heard the order in question, but explains, 'I didn't think she meant it.' The Guide Captain, Miss Redmond, rebukes her for using this as an excuse: 'No one gives an order unless they mean it.' This silences Nicola as it occurs to her that 'her father was apt to say the same thing'.

Part 2: 'Does *she* think she's a heel too?' (*End of Term*)
Much of the drama in this whole episode derives from the problem of knowledge—both self-knowledge and general moral awareness. The *logic* of Guiding aims to bring together the external and interior aspects of honour—to unify honour in the sense of 'moral integrity' with honour in the sense of 'glory'. But in Forest's Kingscote world the *practice* of Guiding focuses on external glory, so that individuals risk losing sight of an honour that goes beyond 'not being found out' (to return to Conrad's Marlow's phrase in *Lord Jim*). Nicola admires Lawrie's enrolment ceremony: 'Her small, distinct voice saying the Promise made it sound like something real, not just a mumble of words to be hurried through because it was a formula which had to be said.' Lawrie makes a successful start as a Guide because she is a talented actress. But in an organisation that prizes the visible perfection of ritual display (in patrol inspections and so on), this special talent can be misleading, as it may be confused with a deeper understanding of the morality which underpins Guiding.

Lawrie takes to an exaggerated point the motivation exploited by Baden-Powell in the Scout and Guide handbooks, where girls are invited to imagine acting courageously under siege as nurses in the Boer war (or in other extreme situations), and are spurred to develop their characters so as to be ready to live up to their own imagined expectations of themselves: 'Just imagine what your line of action would be in a far-off colony—what you would do—if you were just finishing your supper and you suddenly heard that the enemy had shot down a lot of our men.' (*The Handbook for Girl Guides*) The ease with which Lawrie moves from reality to the world of her imagination will prove both help and hindrance later in Forest's series. In *The Marlows and the Traitor* (1953) she is ready to escape when sudden danger erupts, because her world already has room for high adventure. But because she is not 'prepared' in the fuller sense, she panics when a more mundane emergency faces her—losing her bus fare—and runs out in front of a car.

After Lois's betrayal, Lawrie indulges in a playful fantasy which inverts her earlier dream, romancing 'gently and pleasantly about the possibilities of pulling Lois Sanger out of the river just as she was being whirled towards the weir … and afterwards, in the San, a feverish and conscience-stricken Lois would … confess everything … and then they would be reinstated, and Lawrie would be decorated with the Bronze Cross'. She rounds things off with a more extreme, vindictive vision that rejects Guide honour altogether, paving the way for the moment in *End of Term* when the twins rebut Miss Redmond's offer of a return to the Guiding fold: 'Only I wouldn't save her. I'd jolly well let her drown. And I'd let her see I was letting her drown, what's more.'

Things start to go wrong on the patrol hike when Lois fails a simple test of competence—asked to examine a map, she doesn't spot the missing compass directions; Nicola can't help showing that she has noticed the intentional omission from the map, and Lois, humiliated by

this, decides that the test 'was a bit unfair'. The novel is much more interested in the way Lois denies responsibility than in her practical mistake. Still, it's worth noticing that Nicola explains her success in spotting the problem by describing precisely the kind of repetitive habituation aimed at in the way Guiding develops practical skills. Nicola's training has come not in the Guides or Brownies, but from the naval discipline of her father, Commander Marlow, who 'often shows us maps. He says compass directions are the first things to look for.'

Lois soon makes a second practical error of judgment in map reading, and again denies responsibility, passing the mistake on to her Patrol Second: 'What a pest! The map takes us all the way round by the cliff and we lost a lot of time that time you would turn right, Jill. They can't help knowing we didn't read the map properly.' Lawrie picks up on Lois's worry about what the Guiders will or won't know: Lois is concerned with success at the test rather than excellence for its own sake, and Lawrie enters into the spirit of Lois's aim by suggesting a way that she and Nicola could help conceal Lois's errors. The narrative subtly indicates Lois's double failure as a leader here—she takes the younger girls astray morally as much as she does cartographically. Influenced by Lois's preoccupation with what the Guiders will notice, and by Lois's own indifference to truth, Lawrie doesn't realise that she is suggesting a way to cheat at the test.

Lois's reaction shows that she *is* fully aware of what Lawrie's suggestion means. Her immediate response is to see whether she would get caught cheating: 'There were no Guiders' hats in sight.' She hesitates, but she doesn't openly acknowledge the dishonesty, and her words give Lawrie and Nicola the impression that she is needlessly worried about their safety: 'I don't expect you ought to go wandering off alone.' While she wavers, the twins charge off to go ahead and light the camp fire on the beach. It never occurs to them that they are acting dishonourably—trying to steal honour for Lois, in a sense (in fact Nicola later hotly denies stealing when she half-thinks Peter is accusing them of this). Lois realises her mistake in letting them go, but chooses to send the least competent patrol member after them, Marie Dobson.

Marie provides readers with a glimpse of what it might feel like to have no individual integrity at all. Either following or refusing Lois's order would require Marie to overcome certain private terrors, so she instead puts her energy into avoiding the task set her and into concealing that avoidance. Forest's narratorial voice intervenes to make a rare explicit moral judgment in describing Marie's response to fear: 'It had never occurred to Marie that for the sake of her own self-respect she should confront her personal hobgoblin, however much her teeth chattered and her knees shook.' Marie is the anti-Guide.

Marie's attitude to physical dread neatly inverts—or rather perverts—the Guide logic of using imaginative play as a means to build reliable courage. Her habitual avoidance tactics are intensified versions of the techniques that we later learn are familiar to Lois, though where Lois uses deceit to maintain her reputation for bravery and talent, Marie lies in order to avoid testing her skill or developing any ability in physical activities that frighten her: 'When illness could not serve, she was swift to invent a plausible story.' Her own personal self-discipline has been developed not in the kind of practical competence and courage valued by the Guides, but in using her imagination to hide behind. 'Now, crouching in the straw, counting a hundred slowly … the necessary story took shape easily enough.' It is no coincidence that Forest uses the word 'story' twice in this section, not 'lie'. The word reflects the ties between lying and more respectable imaginative invention, and it reminds readers how common it is for people to avert their eyes from sordid behaviour by using euphemisms (think of W S Gilbert's Major-General singing 'I'm telling a terrible story, but it doesn't diminish my glory'). Marie's seasoned deceptiveness and Lois's manipulations of the truth allow them to maintain a semblance of public honour (the 'not being found out' kind of honour), while they make Nicola and Lawrie appear wilfully or thoughtlessly disobedient, impervious to the kind of discipline that is essential to Guiding.

Lois tells an elaborate almost-true lie when it comes to the Guide Court of Honour two days after the hike, blurring the lines for Nicola between moral ambiguity and factual ambiguity. Nicola becomes confused, wondering whether Lois is describing a genuinely different perception of what happened, rather than deliberately lying. 'It was so nearly what had happened that her own vision of what had taken place was blurred. Perhaps Lois was right.' A little later in the chapter readers are given direct access to Lois's thoughts, and glimpse the complexity of her self-knowledge and moral perceptions. We hear her rehearsing in her mind a far more honest and accurate version of the hike, seriously tempted to admit to Miss Redmond 'what really happened', once she sees that the Guide Captain already has a none too high opinion of her: 'It might be easier, almost, to say: Look, they didn't exactly run away. They wanted to get the fire lit and I didn't stop them in time. I did almost say they could go.' When Lois visualises herself being honest, two things stand out: first, she comes close to admitting things because 'it might be easier' for her to do so. Second, even when she imagines admitting 'what really happened' she leaves out a crucial bit of the story; she glosses over the fact that (as Ann later describes it) 'it never came out at all about Nick and Lawrie going through the farm so that Miss Leslie shouldn't know that Lois had muddled the map'. Lois still doesn't fully acknowledge that she allowed the twins to help her cheat on a test.

Lois's degree of self-awareness clearly fascinates Forest. She attributes the same fascination to Patrick Merrick when he hears the story and its sequel in *End of Term*, where his interest is connected with his thoughtful Catholicism—he imagines how it would feel to confess Lois's actions; later in the series Forest draws attention to his sensitivity to 'full knowledge, full consent' as the definition of mortal sin (*Cricket Term*). Patrick wonders aloud, 'How does she make it all right for herself? Or doesn't she? Does *she* think she's a heel too?'

Autumn Term suggests that some of the time, at least, Lois does indeed think she's a heel. We hear Lois's thoughts and find that her imaginative processes are not unlike Lawrie's, but that she has intervals of clarity and full self-knowledge. After failing to grab the moment when she might admit what happened, she briefly imagines obliterating the memory of the hike through her hard work with the Pimpernels. 'Captain would probably say something like: you've done very well since that unfortunate hike, Lois; we're all very proud of you. ... Perhaps she'd say that; perhaps not.' Lois's fantasy shows that the way back into her own self-esteem is through praise from those in authority. But her mind never travels far from reality. She knows that it's

from *Autumn Term*

perfectly possible that this fantasy won't come true. A similar double vision of make-believe and reality belongs to her appraisal of what Miss Redmond has in fact said: 'Captain had been pretty venomous—rather unfair in some ways—' At this point the paragraph breaks off to provide a memorable one-line chapter ending:

'*Unfair*,' thought Lois derisively. 'Don't be such a clod.'

Part 3: 'Tom has always pretended to be a prince and so he gradually gets into the way of it' (*Autumn Term*)

Once the Marlows have gone home and hashed out the hike events with the rest of the family, the Guiding story appears to be over. Nicola and Lawrie give up their preference 'to be cleared in a blaze of glory and have their badges handed back and Lois Sanger's nose rubbed in the dust', since 'Father obviously thought it wasn't worth making a fuss about'. Their brother Peter parodies popular children's fiction to mock Ann's horror at the thought that Lois will continue as Patrol Leader after revealing her unworthiness: '"Honour of the school at stake, what?" said Peter with a grin.' The narrative hints that Commander Marlow looks at the female sphere of Guides as merely trivial make-believe, compared with the real masculine work of the Navy; this contrast is highlighted by Nicola's realisation that her eldest brother won't enjoy going to see a war movie about a sinking ship when he has recently come close to actually being tipped into the English channel: '… one couldn't expect Giles really to enjoy seeing people hanging on to a raft.'

The sequel to the hike in *Autumn Term* comes not in another explicitly Guide-focused episode, but in the Third Remove's end of term production, devised by Tim to maintain the form's prestige after they are sidelined from the Third form's fundraising bazaar. Forest uses the form play as an opportunity to continue exploring the themes of make-believe, honour and discipline raised by the Pimpernel Patrol hike. *The Prince and the Pauper* turns out to be an ideal choice of text, and not only because it makes the most of Nicola and Lawrie's appearance as identical twins.

A key theme in Twain's novel (and Forest's) emerges early in the casting decisions in *Autumn Term*, when Lawrie opts to play Tom Canty, the beggar boy who finds himself masquerading first as prince, then as King Edward VI. 'She could not find words to express her instinct that Edward's part was too straightforward to be interesting, whereas with Tom you must make the audience see that he was pretending all the time and at the last coming almost to believe his own pretence.' Twain is interested in the way that this blurring of lines between imagination and reality can be a positive force, providing a kind of make-believe experience that motivates and prepares for real crises—but he also shows how this can also lead to a loss of identity that may result in amorality or even immorality.

Tom Canty shows most confusion about his real identity at the moment before he denies knowledge of his mother (*The Prince and the Pauper* chapter XXXI); displayed to the public before the coronation in a 'recognition procession', Tom exults in the thought that 'all these wonders and these marvels are to welcome me—me!' He has lost track of what 'me' means. When his mother spots him and correctly identifies him, she's thrust aside by members of the retinue just as 'the words "I do not know you, woman!" were falling from Tom Canty's lips'. Yet his near-betrayal of his mother recalls him to reality, and prepares him to welcome the real Edward's appearance gladly. Both his earlier imaginings and his recent compulsory pretence of royalty help Tom rise to that occasion. When Edward comes forward as the true king in Westminster Abbey, Tom manages to prevent Edward's immediate arrest because of the regal authority with which he forbids it (*The Prince and the Pauper* chapter XXXII)—he has learned to wield real power through all his make-believe practice.

Conclusion: '… if you were in the Service you *had* to be sort of person who coped' (*The Marlows and the Traitor*)

Baden-Powell's hope of using imaginative stimulation to form character—the kind of character, moreover, that would be disciplined enough to rule Britain's Empire—raises a set of concerns which are pivotal to a broad strand of English literature, and which are especially resonant for children's fiction. Children's literature has a strong tradition of didacticism. Writers such as Forest evidently do not aim to provide simplistic moral guidance for their young readers. But Forest, like many twentieth-century children's authors, probes the effects that storytelling may have on children and adolescents who are gradually developing a complex moral awareness of the world around them. When we set Baden-Powell's project alongside broader debates about how imagination affects behaviour, Guiding is revealed as less marginal than it may at times appear.

Commander Marlow dismisses Guiding as an unnecessary 'extra', but during the remainder of Forest's novel-sequence it is the family's naval background that helps keep readers focused on the problems raised during Nicola and Lawrie's short spell as Guides. The twins' brother Peter, a Dartmouth cadet, suffers a recurrent inner struggle which has a lot in common with the sufferings of the proto-Scout Jim in *Lord Jim*. Forest never explicitly refers to Conrad as she does to many other writers; she would surely have read *Lord Jim*, given her love of sea-tales, but it's hard to know what to make of her use of the Marlow name, also that of a major Conrad character—coincidence or subtle allusion? Conrad's novel was published in 1900, just a few years before Baden-Powell established the Boy Scouts, and its themes are markedly relevant to Baden-Powell's theory of Scouting and Guiding as laid out in the handbooks; Jim even uses catch phrases that later became firmly associated with Boy Scouts and Girl Guides in the popular consciousness, such as 'Honour Bright'.

Conrad's Jim helps us see clearly how the problems of make-believe, courage and discipline explored in *Autumn Term*'s Guiding narrative are closely bound up with Peter's repeated need to confront his 'personal hobgoblin'. While training as an officer for the merchant navy, Jim 'would forget himself, and beforehand live in his mind the sea-life of light literature'—his personality becomes a vacuum, filled by make-believe. He later tells Conrad's Captain Marlow that ever since he had been 'so high'—'quite a little chap', he had been preparing himself for '… all the difficulties that can beset one on land and water … He had been elaborating dangers and defences, expecting the worst, rehearsing his best.' But when he finally finds himself in a real emergency, Jim discovers that he is unprepared: 'I was so lost, you know. It was the sort of thing one does not expect to happen to one.' This crisis exiles Jim from the sea, as he is judged to have joined his fellow-officers in disregarding their 'plain duty' by 'abandoning in the moment of danger the lives and property confided to their charge'. At the start of *The Marlows and the Traitor*, the novel that follows *Autumn Term*, we learn that Peter Marlow has recently suffered a similar moment of paralysis (though on a far smaller scale) during a sailing accident at Dartmouth. This incident makes Peter dread something like Jim's exile from the sea, that he will be 'kicked out' of Dartmouth for being a 'useless worm'. 'Because it wasn't the sort of thing you could guard against; a crisis blew up, and either you coped or you didn't; and if you were in the Service you *had* to be the sort of person who coped.'

Peter accordingly tries to remake his character, constantly challenging himself in the hope that by ignoring his fears he will eventually banish them. His identity is fundamentally at odds with itself. Peter's reaction to a strong dislike of the sea (surprising in a would-be naval officer) nearly gets Nicola drowned when he decides not to mention to her that the path they're about to take is impassable in a storm: 'He didn't want to sound as if he were afraid of getting his feet wet.' (*Marlows and the Traitor*) A similar, more extreme crisis occurs when he refuses to acknowledge his terror of heights in *Falconer's Lure* (1957), which results in his being frozen with fear on a cliff face with Nicola and with Patrick Merrick. But the novels suggest that it is not just a kind of cowardice that keeps Peter quiet on these occasions. He *is* afraid of admitting his fears (or even a perfectly reasonable sense of caution), but more importantly, he hopes by confronting his terror to refashion his personality and make himself into 'the sort of person who coped'.

Forest's novels remain ambivalent when it comes to judging Peter's attempt at disciplining himself in this way—in this instance as so often, the novels are more inclined to invite questions than to lay down the law. They reveal clearly the dangers of Peter's strategy by showing how he takes this self-discipline to excess. Yet Forest's novels do not dismiss the worth of self-discipline, training one's behaviour or character partly by remaking one's perceptions, in accordance with the logic of Guiding. The value set on self-discipline emerges frequently in the novel sequence: we see it in Nicola's successful work with her Lower Fourth cricket team, in which she steadily builds on their real strengths, rather than being led astray by fantasies of hitting 'double centuries in forty-five minutes, mostly in sixes'. (*The Cricket Term*) The same non-judgmental approach stamps Forest's approach to the force of imagination. Flights of fantasy can increase someone's self-knowledge and perhaps their courage, or they can allow a person to avoid the self-awareness necessary for discipline or integrity. *Peter's Room* (1961) takes this dual function of fantasy the furthest, showing the younger Marlows and Patrick immersed in Brontë-style Gondalling. Patrick Merrick uses his imagined *alter ego* to confront tough possibilities about himself, but also to avoid direct communication as he discards one close friend and builds a new romantic friendship. Nicola firmly asserts the limits of imaginary role playing, pointing out, for instance, that one thing the Marlows and Patrick are *not* going to discover is what it was like to be Emily and Anne Brontë playing Gondals—'You're you, not them.' Yet when her beloved merlin, Sprog, dies suddenly, Nicola is comforted by the memory of Emily Brontë's 'long-ago sorrow' for her little cat.

Ann Marlow, whose imaginative response to the Brontë stories dwells on the family responsibilities foisted on Charlotte, is portrayed as very nearly an ideal Guide. In this way, Forest is able to maintain her non-judgmental picture of Guiding and allow its ideas to generate a set of themes for prolonged exploration, without either dismissing Guiding principles or making Guide activities overtly central to the whole Marlow series. The final glimpse we have of this ideal Guide, *as* a Guide, casts a benevolent light on the organisation; I'll give Forest's own narrative the last word in this chapter. When required by new school rules to give up Guiding, Ann is perfectly ready to move on, and shocks her younger sisters by her indifference to the many badges she has won. The playful aspect of Guiding—the showier side of attaining 'honour and glory' in the form of badges won through tests—has served its purpose. What remains to Ann as she approaches adulthood is the trefoil badge, which symbolises the 'back and front' unobserved excellence that she prizes so highly. Nicola surprises Ann with her friendly, suspenseful concern as she waits to hear whether Ann will give up the Guide badge along with the others; she's eager to see if her elder sister will remain fundamentally the same person, or if her outgrowing of Guides is the sign of some prodigious change—nothing less than a collapse of integrity.

> They had heard so much over the years about the symbolic importance of the trefoil, and the necessity to clean back as well as front in order to keep your honour bright, that they awaited Ann's answer almost with anxiety. 'Oh no, I couldn't possibly give that back. That's quite different.'
> So the heavens had not completely fallen.
>
> *The Cricket Term*

ENVOI: 'THE FUNNIEST BEGGAR ON EARTH'

Tig Thomas

Robert Stephenson Smyth Powell (B-P) was born in Paddington on 22 February 1857. His father, whose first name was Baden, was a professor of geology and a clergyman. Professor Powell died when Robert was three, leaving his formidable widow, Henrietta Grace, to the business of raising her eight surviving children.

Henrietta's best assets, as she coolly recognised, were her social connections, and she focused all her energies on being accepted by the highest society possible. She added her husband's fashionably German Christian name to their own surname of Powell, an inspired move which gave her sixth son an instantly recognisable set of initials when he became famous, even if it did leave her eighth with the unfortunate name of Baden Baden-Powell. She held important dinner parties at which the interests of her children were ruthlessly advanced. Clothes were of the finest quality, accoutrements gold, a first class piano hired for the season. This awareness of the importance of the look of things was later to be used to brilliantly positive effect by B-P in his formation of the Scouts and Guides.

Robert went to Charterhouse, where he developed his first bushcraft skills scouting in the woods that surrounded the college. His mother intended him to go on to Oxford, but he failed the exams, a fact he tended to gloss over, and instead took up a military career. He joined a crack regiment, the 13th Hussars, and sailed for India as a sub-lieutenant in 1876 aged nineteen. He threw himself into doing well at his job and getting noticed, shrewdly realising that amateur theatricals offered a way to stand out from the crowd, and ended by acting before the Viceroy.

For the next few years he moved around points of the empire—Afghanistan, India, South Africa, always looking for the 'small war' in which he could prove himself as an officer. On his first trip to South Africa he was sent out scouting in preparation for action against the Boers and spent a glorious month living rough. He rode for 600 miles, checking army maps, sleeping under the stars and noting the lie of the land. There was something in the life of an army scout that drew on all his strengths; he loved living life on the edge of his nerves; he relished unconventionality, and often referred to his pleasure in the 'flannel shirt life' in contrast to the stuffiness of formal dinners in starched white shirts; he was an inveterate practical joker and must have enjoyed turning his talents for deception and trickery to serious use. In the meantime he was supplementing his army pay with his writing and sketches. He was a fanatically hard worker all his life, who claimed he got thirteen months out of a year because he rose at five to do three hours' work before breakfast. He boasted of receiving a commission for

Centenary statue of Lord Baden-Powell, Poole Quay

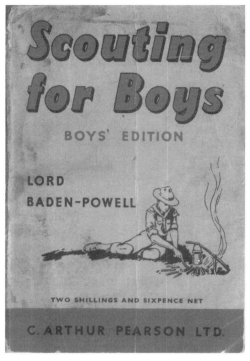

a book on Thursday, and sending off the completed manuscript on the Sunday.

In 1896 he returned to South Africa, where the tensions and factions that fomented the Boer War were coming to the boil. B-P was given the job of reconnoitring the Matapos area, with an outstanding native scout Jan Grootboom, and it is from this time that many of the scouting stories that appear in *Scouting for Boys* came. Posted back to India in 1897, he started training his men in reconnaissance and scouting, and appointed scouts within his own regiment, giving them as a badge the fleur de lys that is used on a map to indicate north. He also found himself with a lot of spare time, so he started on a second book about scouting. He was still working on it when he was posted to South Africa in 1899, aged forty-two.

He was immediately caught up in the Second Boer War, sent to a small town called Mafeking, which he found himself having to defend from besiegement by a superior force of Boers. It was the chance of his life. All B-P's skills of showmanship came to a head in the Mafeking campaign. He had the knack, not a noted one in the army of the time, of taking a situation seriously, but treating it with a certain nonchalant humour. Sir Arthur Conan Doyle in his history of the Boer war quotes a typical exchange:

> The Boer general, at the beginning of the siege sent out a message. 'Surrender to avoid bloodshed' was his message. 'When is the bloodshed going to begin?' asked Powell. When the Boers had been shelling the town for some weeks the light-hearted Colonel sent out to say that if they went on any longer he should be compelled to regard it as equivalent to a declaration of war.

B-P's tactics for holding the Boers off from making any direct assault were unorthodox, almost playful, and effective. He had no mines, but ostentatiously laid down minefields using over 300 dummy boxes filled with sand, then set off pre-laid charges, leaving the Boers convinced the areas were dangerous. Soldiers in the outer defensive trenches were told never to leave or enter the trenches without easing their way awkwardly around non-existent barbed wire. Dummies were placed around the town's defensive walls to draw fire and suggest larger numbers.

He also had to govern the town. The Boers did not fight on Sundays so B-P organised a series of amusements to keep up morale, often with himself as ringmaster, showman or leading (usually female) actor. He also acted as chief medical officer and quartermaster. Rations were dealt out, including soup made from half a horse. Violet face powder from the stores was used to eke out the oatmeal porridge, and ordinary flour was bulked out with ground-up horse-hooves.

The British public lapped up stories of B-P's insouciance and resourcefulness, loving the account of his famous laconic message: 'All well. Four hours' bombardment. One dog killed.' (In fact the message, smuggled out by natives, started life in longer form and was abbreviated by the agent in the telegraph office.) His initials were equated with British Pluck. When Mafeking was finally relieved after 217 days (in typical Boy's Own narrative style his brother Baden was among the relieving force), he found himself a hero. He was promoted to become the youngest major-general in the British Army.

The first biography of him appeared while the siege was still in progress:

> He is a hero in the best sense of the word, living cleanly, despising viciousness equally with effeminacy, and striving after the development of his talents, just as a wise painter labours at the perfecting of his picture …
>
> Ask those who know him best what manner of man he is, and the immediate answer, made with merry eyes and a deep chuckle, is this: 'He's the funniest beggar on earth.' And then when you have listened to many stories of B-P's pranks, your informant will grow suddenly serious and tell you what a 'straight' fellow he is, what a loyal friend, what an enthusiastic soldier.
>
> Harold Begbie, *The Story of Baden-Powell*

Practically the last thing B-P had done before the town was sealed off was send off the proofs of his book on reconnaissance, *Aids to Scouting for N.C.O.s and Men*. Within a few months it had sold 100,000 copies. It had a breezy, anecdotal style, far removed from the usual self-conscious seriousness of the army writer. Boy readers must have been thrilled to be taught that when sleeping it is better to keep one's gun tucked behind one's knees rather than under one's pillow where a thief will expect to find it. To learn that it is wise never to choose the *best* hiding place as an observation post, because that is also the place the enemy will look first, had as much appeal to the boy playing cowboys and Indians in Surrey woods as to the army scout on the north-west frontier. In typically boyish style B-P even included some games at the end to help train the scout. The book urged preparedness, and recommended learning signalling and playing observation and tracking games. Some of the games even suggest breaking up into patrols of six men.

From 1900 to 1903, B-P was sent to set up the newly formed South African Constabulary, himself designing their dramatic uniform of broad-brimmed hat, short sleeved shirt and khaki shorts, and probably personally picking its motto of 'Be Prepared', although he insisted the men had chosen it themselves.

Then in March 1903 he was posted back to England to take up the prestigious but deskbound position of Inspector-General of Cavalry. Soon afterwards he was invited, as a national hero, to inspect the Boys' Brigade, by its founder, William Smith. The two men got on, and talked for hours about what could be done for the British boy. William Smith knew *Aids to Scouting* and suggested B-P might write something similar for boys. B-P, ever alert to new projects and enjoying the company of boys, started to think about the problem. In 1900 a true-blue boys' magazine, *Boys of the Empire*, serialised *Aids to Scouting* under the title of 'The Boy Scout'. The proprietor offered prizes for scouting competitions designed to improve observation skills, but, with a shameful self-promotion, these consisted of tracking down newsagents who did not stock the *Boys of the Empire*!

Baden-Powell next met with the American Ernest Thompson Seton, who was trying to promote his own organisation, the Woodcraft Indians. Many of Seton's ideas, including individual patrols with totemic names and working for non-competitive badges, were used by B-P in Scouting, a fact which later caused Seton some bitterness. B-P was also influenced by an incident which happened to his friend Brigadier-General Allenby. The Brigadier-General was riding home one day when, from the branches of a tree overhead, his son called out to tell him he had been ambushed and was shot because he hadn't been observing closely enough. The general looked up to see not only his son, but also his son's governess in the tree. The governess, Katherine Loveday, explained that she had been using *Aids to Scouting* to teach the boy observation and deductive skills.

By 1907 Baden-Powell had formulated most of his ideas, and tested them out at the famous camp on Brownsea Island with thirteen boys from the public schools, and nine working-class boys from local Boys' Brigades. He never intended, at this stage, to start his own organisation. He was simply responding to the many existing organisations that had asked him for some ideas (one of his earliest suggestions was helping old ladies across roads). He published *Scouting for Boys* first as a series of pamphlets. Backed by his image as a hero, the idea spread like wildfire. The nation that had bought *Aids to Scouting* was ready for more. Moreover, Baden-Powell had a unique combination of skills that ensured his success. He was a dedicated hard worker and imaginative thinker who put everything he had into solving the issue of keeping boys properly engaged, but, crucially, also enjoying themselves. He had a genuine, unaffected belief in the code of honour, but he also had in abundance an unquenchable appetite for fun and adventure of a daring and outdoorsy kind. Tim Jeal, in his biography of Baden-Powell, pinpoints how B-P brilliantly 'drew in material from every conceivable sphere that could interest a boy, from knights in armour to espionage'.

If the games were fun, the demands were serious: the eight—later expanded to ten—Laws were carefully framed not to be prohibitions but definitions. The first one, for example, states that a Scout's honour is to be trusted, and therefore, as B-P said, if a boy did not act honourably, he ceased to be a Scout. But if the expectations were high, the individual touches were inspired. Who could resist joining an organisation where the punishment for swearing was to have a mug of cold water poured down the offender's sleeve? The earnestness of church organisations had no chance against a movement packed with amusing names, games that involved getting dirty, code words, tracking signs, secret languages and elaborate ritual. In May 1908 *Scouting for Boys* became available in book form. It was an immediate and huge success. In the book B-P suggests boys form themselves into Scout patrols and appoint their own leader and then, when several patrols have joined together, see if they can find a Scoutmaster to lead them. This bottom up approach illustrates how he still saw Scouting as something which might shape boys' characters in everything they did, rather than a specific organisation.

By October 1909 B-P was being knighted for services to his country, with particular reference to his role in setting up the Boy Scout movement. The investiture was followed by a rally at Windsor Castle for 33,000 Scouts, for which B-P—ever good at the inspired gesture—devised the grand rush, when thousands of boys charged the royal party, stopping dead a few yards from them. By 1910 he had resigned from the army and gathered a handful of men around him to run the Scouts. Gradually, a structure of councils and committees was created, and systems for appointing Scoutmasters, accrediting camps and setting up troops were devised. In this same year he formulated his plans for the Girl Guides and the two movements grew side by side.

In 1910, aged fifty-five and having had at least one proposal rejected, B-P finally found his boyish girl who could join him in rigorous outdoor life. Olave Soames was born in 1889, and was given her unusual name because her father had planned for a boy, to be called Olaf. Dances and flirtations bored her, and she swam, boated, shot, ratted, bicycled, played squash, billiards, football, and hockey and rode to hounds with unending vigour. She was just twenty-three when on trip to the West Indies she encountered 'the only interesting person on board, the Boy Scout man'.

The story is often told of how Baden-Powell had caught a glimpse of her two years before they boarded the ship, and thought her the perfect specimen of vigorous English girlhood with her straight back and swinging pace. When they first met on board the HMS *Arcadia*, she was astonished to be asked if she had ever walked near Knightsbridge barracks. They had secret assignations and wrote each other many love letters, hers noticeably more passionate than his. Several of his biographers have speculated that B-P was not heterosexual or homosexual but asexual—certainly he seemed to view sex as something only necessary for the procreation of children. Olave had a habit of getting engaged, then breaking it off a few days later. Perhaps the young girl and the older man found in each other not only a helpmeet but also a partner who was not very interested in the physical side of things.

Their wedding was restrained and private. Of his family, only his sister Agnes attended. For a later public reception, 100,000 Scouts contributed a penny each to buy them a car.

Olave was the ideal companion for B-P. She could keep pace with him mile for mile and be the comradely and frank, not over-feminised, companion that he sought. Their son, Arthur Robert Peter, always called Peter, was born in 1913, followed by Heather in 1915 and Betty in 1917. Olave does not appear to have been very maternal, but she idolised her husband: 'My darling husband was the person who mattered most in my life,' she wrote, adding rather chillingly: 'I always put him first, and the children came a long way second in my affection.'

A few months after the birth of their third child, B-P moved out of the marriage bed to sleep on a balcony, in an attempt to break a pattern of having bad dreams. He never returned. Before he went to bed, he and Olave would lie in each other's arms, talking over the day, a habit they called 'armchairs'. Olave seldom bought new clothes and loved wearing uniform. Visitors to their house, Pax Hill, were expected to wear no makeup or nail varnish, and Heather and Betty found life difficult at boarding school when they arrived with piles of old-fashioned vests and combinations instead of more modern underwear.

Olave had hoped to be involved with the Boy Scouts, but that didn't work out; and in 1915 she threw herself into organising Guiding, despite initial rebuffs by the well-established committees. She was given the job of recruiting county commissioners and bent all her forceful and charming personality to the task.

The First World War could have proved a disaster for the Scouting movement. A huge proportion of Scoutmasters went away to the front and never returned. But somehow the movement had such a grip on the public by this time that it survived. Over 60,000 war work badges were awarded to Scouts, and eleven older members of the movement won VCs. B-P tried to rejoin the army but was advised he was doing his most valuable work where he was. In 1920, he held the first Scout International Jamboree at Olympia which 8,000 Scouts from thirty-four countries attended. In a typically B-P imaginative touch, the floor of Olympia was covered in a foot of earth so that tents could be pitched. At the jamboree B-P was named Chief Scout of the World, a title only ever held by him.

Philip Carrington, early Scoutmaster and author of *The Boy Scouts' Camp Book*

In 1922 B-P wrote *Rovering to Success*, his books for older Scouts. B-P described the book, in a moving note to his eight-year-old son, as a very long letter written to him, the son, because he feared Peter (who had been born when B-P was fifty-six) might not still have a father when he was sixteen.

Sadly, B-P didn't seem able fully to love his own boy. His thrill at having a son was modified by the fact that Peter grew up sickly, bored by games, and—shocking for B-P and Olave—interested in girls. The relationship with his father foundered further when he subsequently failed to make the grade at Sandhurst, and instead he joined, or was organised into, the British South African Police. B-P had to give up his old dream of seeing his son succeed in his own regiment; and his close friend Colonel Spilling who had proposed making the three B-P children his heirs was so shocked that he cut Peter out of his will, leaving a fortune of £20,000 only to the two girls. The girls seem to have survived better—they set up a rival society called the BYT, or Bright Young Things, for people who had nothing to do with Scouting. Both daughters were, however, deeply involved in Guiding in later years, and Betty was awarded a Silver Fish, like her mother, in recognition of her extensive services to Guiding.

For the rest of his life, B-P devoted himself tirelessly to the movements he had created, as Scouting and Guiding grew beyond anybody's possible predictions. As World Chief Scout he travelled constantly, usually accompanied by Olave, while their three children were left at home under the care of Scouting servants, and later at school. Endless committees had to be set up and run, policy decided, infighting contained, strategy approved. When it wasn't a matter of settling national policy, he travelled simply to meet his Scouts and Guides the world over, to whom he was a hero figure and the epitome of good Scouting. Betty, their daughter, said, later in life: 'It can be given to very few families to be loved by millions of people of many nations.'

Wherever they went they were met by cheering crowds. Both Olave and B-P were unaffectedly charming, had a great ability to take endless pains and to remember people, and cared wholeheartedly for the movement. B-P also had remarkably inclusive attitudes for his time: to a complainant who objected to prayers from the Koran being read at a World Camp in the 1920s, he replied, 'They were broad minded enough to listen to our Scriptures; it was not so very much for us in return to listen to a chapter from the Koran. You probably know the Koran yourself and will agree that it contains very fine ideas and inspiring words …'

Honours were piled upon them: B-P was awarded a peerage in 1929 and took the title Lord

Baden-Powell of Gilwell (Gilwell was the Boy Scouts' camping and training centre). In 1932 Olave was made a Dame, attending the investiture in her uniform. In 1933 B-P went to Italy to try and persuade Mussolini to allow the Boy Scouts to continue, and shortly afterwards he did the same in Germany, where Scouting had been abolished in favour of the Hitler Youth. He had an audience with the Pope and secured his endorsement of the movement, in the hope that he might prevent the breakaway Roman Catholic organisations starting up in Canada—one country, one movement was always B-P's cry. His health was failing but he still accompanied his wife on her journeys around the world, even when convalescing after a prostate operation. In 1935 they went to Kenya, fell in love with the place and decided to retire there. At the Fifth World Jamboree in Holland in 1937, B-P, then aged seventy-nine, said goodbye to his beloved Scouts, acknowledging that he would not attend another.

B-P and Olave returned to England for that summer and wound up their affairs, then sailed for Africa just at the outbreak of war. B-P painted, read and wrote. Olave joined Swahili classes, and when war broke out took over the work of Colony Commissioner of Guides, where she was proud to see mixed-colour camps taking place.

B-P was becoming increasingly frail, and he died on 8 January 1941, aged eighty-three, having made his peace with Peter a few months earlier. Olave was heartbroken, but devoted the rest of her life to Guiding (she died in 1977 aged eighty-eight). Baden-Powell was buried in Kenya, having refused a burial in Westminster Abbey.

His grave bears an image of a stone in a circle, the Scout tracking symbol for 'I have gone home'.

GLOSSARY OF GUIDING TERMS

Note: Guiding was and is a constantly evolving movement. The conditions for qualifying for badges have changed over the years, and terms have altered their meaning. It would take up far too much space to document every modification. Where a word has changed its definition over time, we have tried to choose the one that applies to the period 1920–1935, which might be said to represent the Golden Age of Guiding fiction. This cannot be a complete glossary but we hope to have included most of the terms that might appear in Guiding fiction.

All-Round Cord This was awarded to a First Class Guide who had also passed seven proficiency badges. The Cord was blue and white for a Guide, blue and red for a Ranger.

Badge of Merit A gilt wreath with a white ribbon, this was given to a Guide who had done her duty exceptionally well, although not with grave risk to herself. It was renamed the Medal of Merit in 1925 and the design changed to a green enamel laurel wreath.

Bartimaeus Company A company for Blind Guides, named after a blind man in the Bible

Billy A lightweight can, with a handle like a bucket, which could be slung over a camp fire. Also known as a dixie.

Blue Cord The equivalent of the All-Round Cord for a Guide or Ranger in an Extension company

Blue dip A Guider holding the blue teaching diploma, which enabled her to train other Guiders

Bronze Cross The highest Guide award for gallantry, first awarded in 1912 and last in 1989

Brown Owl The leader of a Brownie Pack

Cadets Guides over sixteen who plan to become Guiding officers

Camp Adviser A Guider who could issue camp licences to Guiders, held a list of recommended and approved camp sites and often visited and inspected camps. They were introduced in 1923.

Captain The head of a Guide company. The term was changed in 1917 to Guider although this was not enforced until 1943 and the old usage persisted even after that. She had to be at least twenty-one, have passed her Second Class test and have three proficiency badges. She would then receive a warrant from Headquarters which gave her power to enrol her own Guides and see them through tests. She wore a navy blue cockade in her hat and was entitled to wear the First Class badge without having actually fulfilled all its conditions, although many conscientious captains did take all the tests.

Chief Guide The head of the Guiding Association, a post created in 1918 and held by Olave Baden-Powell until her death in 1977

Colours The national flag (in the UK the Union Jack) or the company flag. From 1910 to

1930, this was a dark blue flag with the First Class badge in the centre and the company name written in white above. After 1930 this was replaced by the World flag, which had a blue background with a gold trefoil on it.

Colour party A party of Guides appointed to hoist or lower the flag, or to carry it ceremonially, eg to church. The colour party consisted of three Guides, one to hold the flag and one either side.

Commissioner Executive officer of the movement at a senior level. At the top of the organisation there were commissioners for each branch of the movement, for overseas and for the four countries of the UK. Below them, in descending order, were commissioners at county, division and district level. The District Commissioner is the one most frequently met with in fiction, and was the head of the organising committee of any district, in charge of registering captains, companies and patrols, and generally supervising the movement. She also often performed enrolments. She wore a silver cord on the left shoulder and a silver cockade on the side of the hat.

Commandant A Guider in charge of a camp

Company The name in the UK for a group of Girl Guide patrols under a captain/Guider. In the US the same group of Girl Scouts is called a troop, and in Australia a unit.

Company flag *see* Colours

Company Leader An occasional appointment, the Company Leader was senior to the Patrol Leaders and wore an additional third stripe on her pocket.

Corporal Early term for the second-in-command of a patrol; the name was changed to second in 1917.

Court of Honour This acted as the committee or council for a Guide company. It was usually held before or after each Guide meeting and its proceedings were confidential. It made any important decisions affecting the company as a whole, including deciding on the future events, planning enrolments, the awarding of badges and classes, and of course any disciplinary proceedings. It was attended by Guiding officers, patrol leaders and seconds.

Enrolment The ceremony by which a girl is invested as a Brownie, Guide or Ranger and given her badge. Before enrolment a would-be Guide is known as a recruit. A Guide had to have attended at least four meetings and passed her Tenderfoot test before she could be enrolled.

Extension Company or Extension Lone Originally all companies for those with special needs or some form of disadvantage, including companies in poor schools and orphanages, but after 1926 companies for Guides who had some form of mental or physical disability. The name was later changed to Post Guides.

First Class Guide The First Class Guide test had fourteen steps including camping, swimming, passing tests relating to cooking, child nursing, and needlework, training a Tenderfoot, using a compass, taking other Guides on a half-day's hike, knowing how to read a map, perform first aid on drowned and burnt people and change the sheets of a bed with a patient in it.

Flying up A Brownie was said to fly up to the Guide company if she was a First Class (also called Golden Hand) Brownie who had passed her test before she was eleven years of age.

Founder Baden-Powell is often referred to as the Founder.

Foxlease The first training centre for Guiders, in the New Forest in Hampshire. Foxlease was presented to the movement by an American, Mrs Archbold, and financed by a gift of money from Princess Mary, the movement's President. Foxlease stands in sixty-five acres and is also a major activity centre and camp site. The First World Camp was held there in 1924.

Full salute The Guide salute when raised to the forehead. The full salute was used when greeting a Guide senior to oneself, or when saluting the colours or at the playing of the National Anthem.

GIS The Guide International Service, formed in the aftermath of the Second World War to offer service overseas in countries ravaged by the war. It consisted of adult Guides, specially trained for the job. The GIS ran from 1942–1952. See the excellent book *All Things Uncertain* by Phyllis Stewart Brown which details the work of the GIS.

Gold Cord An award for an exceptionally high-achieving Guide, above the All-Round Cord in difficulty

Golden Bar Brownie One who had passed her Second Class test. Among other things, the test involved knowing the composition of the Union Jack, and passing tests in health rules, handicrafts, observation, knots and road safety.

Golden Hand Brownie One who had passed her First Class test. This involved, among other things, knowing semaphore, the points of the compass, how to do up a parcel and deliver a message, and what to do if clothing catches fire.

Good turn Guides were expected to do a good turn every day, in secret and for no reward. B-P suggested Guides knotted the ends of their scarves until the good turn had been done, to remind them to do it.

Guide handshake Guides and Scouts use the left hand to shake hands with other members of the movement. B-P said the idea came from an African tribe where only the bravest warriors used the left hand to greet with. It is also said to be the hand nearest the heart and so stands for friendship.

Guide's Own A church service held in camp, conducted by the Guides and Captain/Guiders themselves

Grand Howl A Brownie salute for very important occasions, consisting of the Brownies saying tu-whit, tu-whit, tu-whoo three times, each time a little louder, while rising up from a crouch to a leap, before finishing at full salute.

Grease pit Part of the rubbish disposal system, this was a small pit dug to contain wet waste, especially the greasy residue in water or pans after cooking. It might have a light frame of leaves laid over it to act as a trap to separate the grease from the water. This frame would then be burnt daily.

Green cord This showed the wearer had qualified as a Camp Trainer.

Guide Cord A length of cord, traditionally three feet long, carried in preparation for any emergencies. It was usually worn hanging in a coil from the belt, although some early Guides wore their cord wound around their waist.

Guider The adult in charge of a company, a term used after 1917: *see* Captain.

Half salute The Guide salute made at shoulder height, the normal one in use for a greeting

Investment Rangers were invested, rather than being enrolled

Jamboree A term adapted by B-P to mean a gigantic Scout gathering. The first Scout Jamboree was held at Olympia in 1920, where Guides ran the first-aid tent. Nowadays both Guides and Scouts have Jamborees.

Kim's Game A popular game to train observation skills where a Guide must memorise the objects on a tray and then recall them once it is removed. It was invented by Rudyard Kipling in *Kim*.

Lah Lah Lah The Brownies' chant, referring to the initial letters of the Brownie motto Lend a Hand

Lanyard A white cord from which a whistle or knife could be hung, worn slung round the neck of the Guide or Guider's uniform and looped to the belt at one side

Laws B-P formulated the ten Guide Laws, keeping them more or less exactly the same as the Scout Laws. At the first camp in 1924 he suggested an eleventh Law: a Guide is not a fool.

Lieutenant A girl of at least eighteen who acted as the second-in-command to the Captain/ Guider. In fiction she is sometimes nicknamed Leff or Lefty and sometimes Loot, suggesting both the British and American pronunciations of the name were in use.

LINK An organisation for Guides between eighteen and thirty unable at that point to continue active Guiding but wishing to remain part of the movement

Lone Guide A Guide unable to join a company in person. A Lone Guider sends her regular letters.

Middies Loose white blouses, usually with a sailor collar, worn over a skirt as uniform by the early US Girl Scouts

Motto The motto of the Guides is the same as that of the Scouts: Be Prepared.

Olave House *see* World Centres

Our Ark *see* World Centres

Our Cabaña *see* World Centres

Our Chalet *see* World Centres

Pack Leader A Guide who assists the Brown Owl with a Brownie pack

Parade A formal parade, where the Guides drill, carry the colours and march in formation. A Church Parade involved the Guides marching as a company to church with their colours.

Patrol Badge If a proficiency badge had been won by all members of a patrol, they were entitled to sew the badge on to their patrol flag. This can also mean a badge that had to be taken by the patrol as a unit and could not be won individually. In 1925, there were two such: Folk Song and Dance badge and Hostess.

Patrol A group of Guides, usually six or eight, under a patrol leader and a second

Patrol Corner The place in the company meeting hut which belongs to one patrol, decorated by them and containing their patrol equipment and displays

Patrol Leader The leader of the patrol, appointed by the Court of Honour

Patrol pennant A small white flag, with the emblem of the patrol appliquéd on to it on both sides, which was attached to the staff of the Patrol Leader. Later, in the 1970s, it was a blue pennant-shaped badge which might be gained for a number of skills and which was worked for by the whole patrol.

Patrol home A place outside the company meeting place where a patrol can get together. Suggestions in *Be Prepared* (1946 edition) include a barn, empty house or even a bit of a public park.

Pax Lodge *see* World Centres

Post Guide A Guide who, through some form of disability, cannot join in the normal life of Guiding. *See also* Extension Company.

Proficiency badges Badges for which a Guide might work on her own to develop and test her proficiency in specific skills, such as various forms of handcrafts, many physical subjects such as rowing, riding or hiking and many practical skills such as map-reading, nursing and cooking. Certain proficiency badges had to be passed before the Guide could be a First Class Guide.

Promise The Guide Promise has three parts which detail a Guide's commitment to do her best to serve her God and her country and to keep the Guide Law. The Promise may vary in different countries, but generally contains these three parts, although many countries now accept a substitute for 'God'.

Punk Light, highly flammable stuff, such as dried gorse and birch bark, that was used as the first item when laying a fire

QM Quartermaster, the Guide or Guider in charge of stores for camp

Queen's Guide Award introduced in 1946. To become a Queen's Guide, the Guide had to be under sixteen, be a First Class Guide, have a series of good reports from her captain and have carried out a series of further tests demonstrating service to overseas and home. The test was completed by carrying out an unspecified 'Be Prepared' test to be set by the District Commissioner.

Rally Usually a gathering of companies of Guides where displays and demonstrations are put on

Rangers The senior level of Guiding for Guides over sixteen, in the 1920s divided into Land and Sea Rangers, joined by Air Rangers in 1945; later all combined into one movement

Recruit A girl wanting to join the Brownies or Guides who has not yet been enrolled

Red Dip A Guider holding the red teaching diploma, the higher level, who was qualified to teach other Guiders and could wear a red cord

Revels Brownie celebrations which might include games and competitions

Salute Now called the Guide sign, the holding up of the three centre fingers to symbolise the three parts of the Promise. Before 1967 the Brownies only held up two fingers as they had a different two-part Promise.

Sangam *see* World Centres

Scarf The Guide scarf (officially always called a tie) was triangular and forty inches long (big enough to become a sling or bandage). In the early days of Guiding the tie was worn with a point of the triangle at the back and two loose ends at the front, with the ends knotted if the Good Turn for the day had not yet been done. From about the 1930s the triangular tie was folded into a strip two-and-a-half inches wide, then doubled over so that a normal tie knot could be replicated, with the loose ends tied in a reef knot under the back of the collar. Later the triangular bandage was abandoned in favour of a simpler style.

Scout's pace Twenty paces running and twenty paces walking; B-P said this was the fastest way to keep up a steady pace over a long distance.

Second The second-in-command of a patrol, whose job was to support the Patrol Leader and take over from her in her absence. Seconds were called Corporals until 1917.

Second Class badge The stage a Guide reached after completing the Tenderfoot badge. The test had twelve steps, including understanding Morse or semaphore, lighting a fire with only two matches, following a trail, making a bed, knowing six knots and understanding simple first aid.

Senior Patrol Before the creation of Rangers, and occasionally after, where no Rangers were available, some companies formed senior patrols consisting of Guides over sixteen.

Shoulder knot Ribbons or tapes of patrol colours which were worn on the left shoulder

Sign The clues one reads in tracking to detect the path someone has taken; either those deliberately left by Scouts or Guides who have gone ahead in tracking games, or those inadvertently left by someone's passage, for example broken twigs and footprints

Sign Another name, especially used in Brownies, for the half salute

Silver Cross The second highest award for bravery, given to a Guide for gallantry with considerable risk to herself

Silver Fish In 1911 an award given to any Guide who had passed her First Class and achieved a number of proficiency badges, at first twenty, later reduced to fifteen. In 1917 the award was changed to one given for outstanding service to the movement.

Taps The song traditionally sung at the end of a meeting or camp day, which was introduced to the UK by the American Girl Scouts at the First International Conference in 1920. Its words go:

> Day is done
> Gone the sun
> From the sea, from the hills, from the sky
> All is well,
> Safely rest,
> God is nigh

Some versions have 'from the earth' as the beginning of the third line.

Tawny Owl The second-in-command to the leader (Brown Owl) running a Brownie Pack

Tenderfoot The rank a Guide takes when first enrolled (from the name given to an inexperienced pioneer or backwoodsman, whose feet have not yet been hardened by many days' walking). The Tenderfoot test included understanding the Laws, Promise, motto and meaning of the good turn; the composition of the Union Jack; being able to whip the end of a rope and tie three knots.

Thanks Badge Instituted in 1911, this was a trefoil with three white enamel moons, and was given by a Guide or company to anyone, usually not themselves a Guide, who had done them a service.

Thinking Day 22 February, Olave and B-P's shared birthday, a day set aside by the Girl Guides and Girl Scouts for thinking of the worldwide community of Girl Guides, Girl Scouts and Boy Scouts

Tie *see* Scarf

Trefoil The Guiding badge, a representation of a clover leaf, symbolising the three sections of the Promise. Different variations of the badge exist for the different branches of the movement.

Trefoil Guild An organisation for people over the age of eighteen who have been involved in Guiding or Scouting but are not, at the time they join the Trefoil Guild, taking an active role

Tweenie A Brownie recruit

Waddow Hall A training camp site in the north of England at Clitheroe, similar to Foxlease, which was acquired in 1927

WAGGGS The World Association of Girls Guides and Girl Scouts

Warrant The qualification obtained by a captain or lieutenant to run a company. A captain had to have trained her company for at least three months before a warrant could be issued to her.

Whistle signals Captains, lieutenants and patrol leaders all carried whistles to send messages to other Guides. Two of the most commonly used were the message to call patrol leaders to the captain, which was three short blasts and one long, said to represent 'Leaders come HERE'; and the signal to call all Guides, a succession of short sharp bursts, standing for 'run, run, run!', or 'Guides, Guides, Guides!'

Wide Games Tracking and scouting games played outside

The World Centres International Guide homes in different parts of the world: Our Chalet in Switzerland; Pax Lodge in London; Our Cabaña in Mexico; and Sangam in India. The London one was originally Our Ark, then Olave House.

World flag *see* Colours

BIBLIOGRAPHY OF GUIDING FICTION

Note: We have done our best to make this Bibliography comprehensive (it has been compiled with the help of Hilary Clare; Tig Thomas; Karen Stapley, the Girlguiding UK Archivist; and twelve collectors of Guiding fiction, two of whom are also Guiding Commissioners). However, we recognise we may well have missed out some titles, and if anyone identifies any gaps we would be grateful if they would write to, or email, the publishers. Our criterion for selection has been to include all girls' fiction that is principally about Guiding. In addition we have endeavoured to list books which contain a significant Guiding content (at least a chapter), or that add to our understanding of how Guiding was portrayed in fiction. We have not included every book in which an author mentions Guides briefly, nor have we attempted to list the many annuals and collections of short stories which feature Guiding. Unfortunately, constraints of space mean we are unable to include Brownie stories in the list.

AUTHOR	TITLE	DATE	PUBLISHER
ABBOTT, K Nelson	*The Camp at Sea View Meadow, a Girl Guide Story*	1929	Blackie
ALDIS, Janet	*A Girl Guide Captain in India*	1924	GOP
ALLINGHAM, Emmie	*Joyce the Second*	1929	Pilgrim Press
ARMSTRONG, M Vera	*Tracks to Adventure, a Series of Tracking Adventures*	1947	Brown, Son & Ferguson (new edition)
	Twenty Tales	1949	Girl Guides Association
	Rival Camps	1950	Warne
	Maris of Glenside	1953	Warne
	Trefoil Tales	1956	Pearson
BARCLAY, Vera C	*Campfire Yarns and Stunts*	1932	Brown, Son & Ferguson
BATTY, J A Staunton	*The Honour of the Company*	1922	Wells Gardner Darton
BERRY, Jane	*The Guides of the Chalet School*	2009	Girls Gone By Publishers
BOURCET, Marguerite	*Be Prepared* (translated by Mrs Mark Kerr)	1932	C A Pearson
BRADLEY, Anne	*The Widening Path*	1952	Girl Guides Association
	The Problem Patrol	1957	Lutterworth
	The Guides in Hanover Lane	1958	Lutterworth
BRADLEY, A W	*Won by Pluck*	1925	Pilgrim Press
BREARY, Nancy	*It was Fun in the Fourth*	1948	Nelson

BRENT-DYER, Elinor M	*The Princess of the Chalet School*	1927	Chambers
	Judy, the Guide	1928	Nelson
	The Rivals of the Chalet School	1929	Chambers
	The Chalet School and Jo	1931	Chambers
	The Chalet Girls in Camp	1932	Chambers
	Carnation of the Upper Fourth	1934	RTS
	The New Chalet School	1938	Chambers
	The Wrong Chalet School	1952	Chambers
BRUCE, Joyce	*The Twins to the Rescue*	1923	Pearson
BRUCE, Katherine	*Peace Comes to the Chalet School*	2005	Girls Gone By Publishers
BURGESS, E M R	*Hilary Follows Up*	1939	Blackie
	Cherry Becomes International	1946	Stockwell
	Ready for Anything	1948	Stockwell
CALDWELL, Patricia K	*Prefects at Vivians*	1956	Chambers
CALLENDAR, Reginald	*Pamela, Guide and Captain, a Story for Guides*	1932	A & C Black
CHANNON, E M	*The Honour of a Guide*	1926	Nisbet
	Her Second Chance	1930	Nisbet
CHATWYN, Alys (Ernest Protheroe)	*Two Schoolgirl Guides*	1924	Epworth
CHAUNDLER, Christine	*Bunty of the Blackbirds*	1925	Nisbet
	Greenie and the Pink 'Un	1928	Every Girl's Paper
	The Luck of the Scallop Shell	1929	Brown, Son & Ferguson
	Jill of the Guides	1932	Nisbet
	The Amateur Patrol	1933	Nisbet
CHRISTIAN, Catherine	*Cherries in Search of a Captain*	1931	Blackie
	The Marigolds Make Good	1937	Blackie
	Baker's Dozen (Thirteen Stories for Girls)	1937	GOP
	Bringing up Nancy Nasturtium	1938	GOP
	A Schoolgirl from Hollywood	1939	Blackie
	Diana Takes a Chance	1940	Blackie
	The Pharaoh's Secret	1940	Lutterworth
	Harriet, the Return of Rip van Winkle	1941	Pearson
	Harriet Takes the Field	1942	Pearson
	The 'Kingfishers' See it Through	1942	Blackie
	The School at Emery's End	1944	Pearson
	The Seventh Magpie	1946	Blackie
	(reprinted as *Sally Joins the Patrol*, 1948)		
	Phyllida's Fortune	1947	Newnes

HANGING
LARDER

CLARKE, Linda M	*The Guider's Book of Potted Stories*	1932	Brown, Son & Ferguson
COGGIN, Joan (Joanna Lloyd)	*"And 'why' not Knowing"*	1929	Methuen
COWPER, E E	*Corporal Ida's Floating Camp*	1920	SPCK
	Celia Wins	1921	Collins
	The Mystery of Saffron Manor	1921	Blackie
	Wild Rose to the Rescue	1922	SPCK
	Cross Winds Farm	1927	Chambers
	Camilla's Castle, a Story for Rangers	1928	Blackie
DARCH, Winifred	*Poppies and Prefects*	1923	OUP
	Cecil of the Carnations	1924	OUP
	Gillian of the Guides	1925	OUP
	Cicely Bassett, Patrol Leader	1927	OUP
	The Lower Fourth and Joan	1930	OUP
DAVIDSON, H B	*Pat of Whitehouse*	1924	Sheldon Press
	The Guides Make Good	1925	Sheldon Press
	The Ardice Fortune	1926	Sheldon Press
	Geraldine, a Ranger	1926	Nelson
	The Camp Across the Road	1927	Sheldon Press
	Bridget and the Dragon, the Story of a Girl Guide Camp	1927	Nelson
	Meg and the Guides, a Country Story	1928	Sheldon Press
	Jane the Determined	1929	Nelson
	The Castle Tea-Garden, a Story of Girl Guides	1930	Sheldon Press
	The Makeshift Patrol	1932	Sheldon Press
	Sea Rangers of the 'Rodney'	1933	Sheldon Press
	Brenda in Belgium	1934	Sheldon Press
	Adventurers in Camp, a Sea Ranger Story	1935	Sheldon Press
	How Judy passed her Tests	1936	Sheldon Press
	Billy Goes to Camp	1937	Sheldon Press
FIELD, Margaret C	*Cecile at St Clare's*	1929	Warne
FOREST, Antonia	*Autumn Term*	1948	Faber
FORREST, Carol	*The House of Simon*	1942	Pearson
	Patteran Patrol	1944	Pearson
	Two Rebels and a Pilgrim	1945	Pearson
	The Quest of the Curlews	1947	Newnes
GAUNT, Penelope	*Kitty Goes to Camp*	1932	Sheldon Press
GILLIONS, Ethel	*The Double Fours*	1936	RTS

DRIP SAFE

Can of water

Tiny hole

Towel →

Flower Pot

Tray of water

GILMOUR, Patience (Catherine Christian)	*Three's a Company, a Story for Lone Guides*	1935	GOP
	Seven Wild Swans, a Story for Rangers	1936	GOP
	The Quest of the Wild Swans	1941	Lutterworth
	The Cygnets Sail Out	1943	Lutterworth
GIRVIN, Brenda	*The Girl Scout, being the Adventures of Aggie Phillips and her Amateur Patrol*	1913	Frowde/Hodder
	Betty the Girl Guide	1921	OUP
	June the Girl Guide	1926	OUP
	Schooldays (one story only)	1930	J F Shaw
GLOIN, Anne	*Like Measles—It's Catching!*	1974	Girl Guides of Canada
	(Collection of diary entries from a range of Brownies, Guides, Rangers and Cadets)		
GLYN, Caroline	*The Unicorn Girl*	1966	Gollancz
GORDON, Pat	*Madcap Petrina*	1934	Hutchinson
GREEN, Mollie M	*Schoolgirl Janet*	1947	Blackie
GREEN, Vera M	*Joan to the Rescue*	1928	Brown, Son & Ferguson
	(First Aid stories, not specifically Guide)		
GREGORY, Constance	*The Castlestone House Company, a School Story of Girl Guides*	1918	C Arthur Pearson
HANLEY, Phyllis	*Winning Her Way*	1924	Epworth Press
	Girls' Grit	1926	Epworth Press
	Bridget of the Guides	1927	Epworth Press
HANN, Mrs A C Osborn	*Peg's Patrol*	1924	RTS
	(republished as *Pam's Patrol*, 1950, Partridge)		
	Rhoda the Rebel	1925	RTS
	(republished as *Rosemary the Rebel*, 1955, Partridge)		
	Smiler, a Girl Guide	1925	Black's Girls' Library
	The Pluck of the Coward	1926	Black's Boys' and Girls' Library
	The Sunshine Shop	1927	Partridge
	Peg—Lieutenant	1927	RTS
	Peg the Ranger	1928	Whitefriars Press
	Captain Peg	1928	RTS
	Peg and her Company	1929	GOP
	Peg Junior (Brownies)	1929	Every Girl's Paper
	Peg's Babies	1931	RTS
	June Runs the Company	1932	J F Shaw
	What Happened to Peg	1932	RTS

Plate Rack

HANN, Mrs A C Osborn (cont.)	*Captain*	1934	RTS
	Lieutenant, a Camping Story	1935	RTS
	The Redheaded Patrol	1936	Partridge
	The Torchbearer	1938	Lutterworth
	Jane's First Term (slight Guiding content)	1944	Lutterworth
	Chris at Boarding School (slight Guiding content)	1946	Lutterworth
	It's Fun in the Guides	1951	Lutterworth
	Five in a Family	1951	Lutterworth
HANN, Mrs A C Osborn & OWSLEY, Sibyl B	*The Guides' Kit Bag*	1931	J F Shaw
	The Guides' Kit Bag	1932	J F Shaw
	(two collections of short stories published in successive years)		
	Three Guides Adventuring	1934	J F Shaw
HARRIS, Mary K	*Henrietta of St. Hilary's*	1953	Staple Press
HAVERFIELD, E L	*The Happy Comrade*	1920	OUP
HAYES, Nancy M	*The Plucky Patrol*	1924	Cassell
	Meg-All-Alone, a Girl Guide Story	1925	Cassell
	The Caravan Patrol	1926	Cassell
	The Guides at Calamity Hill	1927	Cassell
HERBERT, Joan	*Lorna's First Term*	1932	Sheldon
	With Best Intentions	1935	RTS
	The Trail of the Blue Shamrock	1937	RTS
	The Three Halves	1937	RTS
	The Wrights are Left	1938	A & C Black
	One's a Pair	1939	A & C Black
	Just an Ordinary Company	1939	Pearson
	Penelope the Particular	1939	Pearson
	A Tenderfoot's ABC	1940	Brown, Son & Ferguson
	Jennifer Gay (reissued as *First-time Jennifer*, 1959)	1944	Lutterworth
HOPE, Pauline	*Pamela Ventures Abroad* (minimal Guiding content)	1934	GOP
HUDDY, Delia	*Blackbirds' Barn*	1965	Constable
IRELAND, Doreen	*Lynette of Carisgate and Other Stories of School Life and Adventure*	1937	Epworth
	Margery the Mystery	1938	Epworth
IRVINE, A M	*Nora, the Girl Guide; or, from Tenderfoot to Silver Fish*	1913	Partridge
	Naida the Tenderfoot	1919	Partridge
	The Girl who Ran Away	1921	Partridge
JOHNSON, Cris	*The Rising of the Larks*	1960	Collins

KEITH, Felicity	*The Oakhill Guide Company*	1933	Blackie
LAKE, Edna	*The Mystery of Tower House School*	1928	Warne
LANGDON, Dorothy	*A Wider World*	1936	GOP
LEAN, Mary	*Joan of Glen Garland, a Canadian Girl Guide Story*	1934	GOP
LENNARD, Selma Nellie	*Stories on the Girl Guide Laws*	1932	Scott
LLOYD, Joanna	*Betty of Turner House*	1935	Hutchinson
	Catherine Goes to School	1945	Blackie
LYNCH, Theo	*Adventures of the Eastmere Guides, a Girl Guide Story*	1937	Partridge
MANSELL, C R	*The Ragtail Patrol*	1948	A & C Black
	The Littlest Guide	1949	Lutterworth
	Curlew Camp	1954	Lutterworth
	The Swallows See it Through	1955	Lutterworth
MARCHANT, Bessie	*Norah to the Rescue*	1919	Blackie
MARSHALL, May	*Twenty-Six Guide Stories*	1935	Sheldon
MARSHALL, Vera (M Vera Armstrong)	*The Quest of the Sleuth Patrol*	1931	Cassell
MARTEN, S E	*Girls of the Swallow Patrol* (stories, some non-Guides)	1927	Epworth
MASTERMAN, Margaret	*Gentlemen's Daughters*	1931	Ivor Nicholson & Watson
MATTHEWMAN, Phyllis	*Josie Moves Up*	1943	Lutterworth
McCLELLAND, Helen	*Visitors for the Chalet School* (First published Bettany Press 1995)	2000	Collins
McGARRY, Kevin	*The Monkey Puzzle*	1965	World Distributors (Manchester)
	Blue Goose East	1965	World Distributors (Manchester)
METHLEY, Violet	*The Bunyip Patrol, the Story of an Australian Girls' School*	1926	Pilgrim Press
	The Windmill Guides	1931	Pilgrim Press
	Mystery Camp	1934	Blackie
	The Queer Island	1934	Blackie
MIDDLETON, Ivy	*The Adventures of the Scarlet Pimpernel Patrol*	1937	Sheldon Press
	Kay of the Pimpernels	1938	GOP
	Triumphant Pimpernels	1939	RTS/Lutterworth
	The Fourth Musketeer	1940	Lutterworth
	The Musketeers and Wendy	1941	Lutterworth
	Red Trefoil	1944	Lutterworth
	Chris Temple, Patrol Leader	1964	Victory Press
	A Challenge for the Poppies	1965	Victory Press
	The Poppies and Mandy	1966	Victory Press

MIDDLETON, Margaret	*The Guide Camp at Herons Bay*	1927	Blackie
	The Guide Adventurers	1929	Blackie
	The House of Golden Hind	1930	Nelson
	Three Girls and a Car	1931	Blackie
	(Ranger Guide related)		
	The Island Camp	1935	Blackie
MOORE, Dorothea	*Terry, the Girl-Guide*	1912	Nisbet
	Guide Gilly, Adventurer	1922	Nisbet
	(very minimal Guiding content)		
	Greta of the Guides	1922	Partridge
	Brenda of Beech House	1927	Nisbet
	Judy, Patrol Leader	1930	Collins
	Judy Lends a Hand	1932	Collins
	(first third of *Judy, Patrol Leader*)		
	Sara to the Rescue	1932	Collins
MOSS, Robert Alfred	*The Challenge Book of Guide Stories*	1969	Purnell
	The Wild White Pony, and other Girl Guide Stories	1976	Collins
MOSSOP, Irene	*Hilary Leads the Way*	1933	Warne
MUMFORD, Elisabeth	*Judy Joins the Jasmines*	pre 1934	CSSM
	The Wonderful Fortnight	1934	CSSM
	(not really Guide but features the Jasmines)		
NASH, F O H	*How Audrey Became a Guide*	1922	Sheldon Press
	Audrey in Camp	1923	Sheldon Press
	Audrey at School	1925	Sheldon Press
	Richenda and the Mystery Girl	1928	Sheldon Press
	Merrie Brandon	1929	Warne
	Audrey the Sea Ranger	1931	Sheldon Press
	Kattie of the Balkans	1931	Warne
	Richenda in the Alps	1936	Sheldon Press
	Hopefuls Adrift	1936	Sheldon Press
	Lucy of the Sea Rangers	1943	Blackie
	Guides of the Glen School	1948	Warne
	Second Class Judy, a Story of the Girl Guides	1952	Warne
NEWMAN, Marjorie W	*Sybil Makes Good*	1936	Sheldon Press
NORRIS, Phyllis I	*The Mystery of the White Ties*	1937	Sheldon Press
O'BRIEN, Deirdre	*The Three at St Christopher's*	1944	Hutchinson
OHLSON, E E	*Pippa at Brighton*	1937	Nelson
	(aspirational Guide only)		
	Pippa in Switzerland	1938	Nelson
	(aspirational Guide only)		
OLDMEADOW, Katherine	*The Pimpernel Patrol*	1925	Collins

OWSLEY, Sibyl B	*M is for Mary*	1923	RTS
	That Tiresome Lower Fifth	1926	J F Shaw
	An Absent-Minded Schoolgirl	1928	J F Shaw
	Dulcie Captains the School	1928	Sampson Low
	The Guides of North Cliff	1928	Blackie
	The School that was Different	1932	J F Shaw
	The School Knight-Errant	1933	J F Shaw
	Greylees for Ever	1934	J F Shaw
	Nicolette Goes Guiding	1934	Blackie
OWSLEY, Sibyl B &	*The Guides' Kit Bag*	1931	J F Shaw
HANN, Mrs A C Osborn			
	The Guides' Kit Bag	1932	J F Shaw
	(two collections of short stories published in successive years)		
	Three Guides Adventuring	1934	J F Shaw
OXENHAM, Elsie Jeanette	*The Tuck-Shop Girl*	1916	Chambers
	The School of Ups and Downs	1918	Chambers
	Patience Joan, Outsider	1922	Chambers
	Ven at Gregory's	1925	Chambers
	The Camp Fire Torment	1926	Chambers
	Patience and her Problems	1927	Chambers
	The Crisis in Camp Keema	1928	Chambers
	Deb at School	1929	Chambers
	The Abbey Girls Play Up	1930	Collins
	(minimal Guiding content)		
	The Camp Mystery	1932	Collins
	The Reformation of Jinty	1933	Chambers
	Jinty's Patrol	1934	Newnes
	Peggy and the Brotherhood	1936	GOP
	A Divided Patrol	1992	Woodfield
PAGE, J M	*The Three Elizabeths*	1950	Blackie
	The Twins on Trial	1951	Blackie
PARES, Diana	*The Hawthorn Patrol*	1930	Blackie
	The Guides of Fairley and		
	Other Stories of School Life and		
	Adventure	1936	Epworth
PEPPARD, Tess	*Seven Robins*	1930	Sheldon Press
PIKE, Isabel	*At the Grey Farm*	1934	RTS
	At Bruckendale Manor	1937	GOP
POCOCK, Doris	*Ann the Odd Number*	1938	GOP
PROUT, G	*Sea Rangers at Sloo*	1949	Blackie
PYKE, Lilian M	*The Lone Guide of Merfield*	1925	Ward Lock
RHODES, Kathlyn	*A Schoolgirl in Egypt*	1937	Harrap
ROWE, Maud	*The Guides of Pexton School*	1927	RTS
ROWE, Mrs John G	*The Girl Guides of St Ursula's*	1926	Pilgrim Press
ROYCE, Marjory	*Eileen, the Lone Guide*	1924	Harrap

Steaming

SCOTT, Winifred	*Girl Castaways*	1950	Pickering & Inglis
SHREWSBURY, Mary	*All Aboard the 'Bundy',*		
	a Sea Ranger Story	1934	Pilgrim Press
SMITH, Madge S	*Guide Margery*	1931	OUP
SOWERBY, M	*Guides and Brownies*	not traced	OUP
SYKES, Pamela	*Juliet Joins the Guides*	1984	Hodder & Stoughton
TALBOT, Ethel	*Peggy's Last Term*	1920	Nelson
	Betty at St. Benedick's	1924	Nelson
	The Girls of the Rookery School (very slightly Guides)	1925	Nelson
	Jill, Lone Guide	1927	Pearson
	Jan at Island School	1927	Nelson
	Ranger Rose	1928	Nelson
	Skipper and Co, a Story of Sea Rangers	1929	Warne
	Ranger Jo	1929	Pearson
	The Peppercorn Patrol	1929	Cassell
	Anne-on-her-Own	1933	Ward, Lock & Co
	Sea Rangers All	1935	Warne
	Sea Rangers' Holiday	1937	Warne
	Pioneer Pat	1937	Ward, Lock & Co
	Guide's Luck	1938	Pearson
	Rangers and Strangers and Other Stories	1938	Nelson
TAYLOR, Marjorie	*With the Speedwell Patrol*	1938	Blackie
	Prior's Island	1939	Blackie
	The Highland School	1940	Epworth
TEETGEN, A B	*Open Patrols, a Story for Catholic Guides*	1925	Heath Cranton
WALMSLEY, Elizabeth	*Mary Court's Company*	1925	Pilgrim Press
	The Wishing Chair	1926	Pilgrim Press
	Blacklead Island, a Story for Sea Guides	1926	Pilgrim Press
WHITE, Constance M	*Kay of Kingfishers*	1954	Hutchinson
WHITE, Heather	*The Extravagant Year*	1929	Brown, Son & Ferguson
	Shirley's Patrol and Other Stories	1930	Triad Library
	Daffodil Row	1937	RTS
WHITE, Madge Torrence	*Chum, the New Recruit, a Story of Camp for Girl Guides*	1928	Warne
	Puck of the Priory Guides	1935	Hutchinson
WRIGHT, Mary	*Sugar and Spice*	1988	Puffin Books
	(A story of Australian Guides set in the 1920s)		
WYLD, Doreen	*The Girls of Queen's Mere*	1950	Blackie

REFLECTOR OVEN

WYNNE, May	*The Guide's Honour*	1929	Warne
	The Girls of the Pansy Patrol	1931	Aldine Publishing Co
	The Camping of the Marigolds	not traced	Marshall, Morgan & Scott

THE AUTHORS

Mary Cadogan was born in 1928 and thus spent her girlhood in the heyday period of girls' fiction. She left school at sixteen during the Second World War and went to work at the BBC before doing rehabilitation work and training to teach remedial movement and dance. In 1957 she began working with the spiritual teacher J Krishnamurti and remains a Governor of the Krishnamurti Foundation. Since the 1970s she has been writing, lecturing and broadcasting about children's literature and popular culture, and last year she was awarded an honorary Doctorate (D Litt) by Lancaster University. She has been married for fifty-nine years to Alexander Cadogan and has a daughter, Teresa, who is a primary school teacher.

Although she enjoyed reading Girl Guide stories as a child, she never joined the movement because she preferred to spend her very limited money on tap-dancing lessons. Her favourite Guide story, without a doubt, is Catherine Christian's *The Seventh Magpie*.

Máiréad Campbell was a Brownie (a Pixie, and rose to the dizzying heights of Sixer) and then a Guide (a Robin, with a modest sleeveful of badges; anyone who knows her now would laugh heartily to hear that one of those badges was Housekeeper). She didn't read Guiding fiction but she does recall a short story in a non-Guiding collection in which an urban working-class Guide called Florrie was sent to camp with a middle-class Guide Company as a sort of Scholarship Girl and became a heroine when she saved a baby from starving to death after its mother fell down the stairs and broke her leg.

Hilary Clare was born and brought up in Lincolnshire. She was a Brownie from the age of seven and a Guide from ten and a half to fifteen, when pressure of 'O' levels kicked in. Despite huge incompetence at practically everything she became PL of the Blackbirds, but achieved no other distinction. Her best Guiding experiences were taking part in the 50th Jubilee celebrations, and going on a trip to Switzerland. She has enjoyed Catherine Christian since youth, and particularly appreciates Winifred Darch in old age.

Adrianne Fitzpatrick came from a Scouting family: her mother was Akela of a Cub group for a number of years, and her father a Cub leader. Apparently Adrianne went to Brownies for a few weeks but didn't like it—she has no recollection of this, but her mother insists it's true! However, the Guides met at the same time as the Cubs, and Adrianne joined in their activities and was soon adopted as the Guides' Mascot. She remembers enjoying many games and holding her own amongst the older girls. By the time she was old enough to join them officially, her parents had given up Cubs so involvement in Guides was not encouraged.

Judy Lee Harris is from Adelaide, South Australia, and was a Brownie and a Guide in the 1980s. As a child, she avidly read the Brownie books by Verily Anderson and Pamela Sykes, as well as *The Marigolds Make Good* by Catherine Christian. In 1995, Judy agreed to become a Brownie Guide leader 'just for a year'. Nearly fifteen years later she is a Guide leader, has led groups of girls of all ages, and has been a member of various State and National Guiding committees. She is currently a member of the Girl Guides Australia International Committee, and in 2008 was appointed to the WAGGGS World Centres Committee as Centre Team Leader for Sangam. Judy also volunteered at Our Chalet in 2007 and has visited all four World Centres.

In Judy's 'spare time' she is a lawyer and a teacher. She also collects Girl Guide fiction, having begun the collection in the mid 1990s when the title of Dorothea Moore's *Judy, Patrol Leader* caught her eye in a second-hand book catalogue. Judy's favourite Girl Guide fiction books include the *Peg* series by Mrs A C Osborn Hann, especially those books with photo plates still intact!

Wendy Ingle sewed her first special badge on to her Brownie uniform to mark Guiding's fiftieth anniversary. She was in the Fairy Six until she became a Pixie Sixer. Then she flew up to become a Nightingale. Transferring to a new Guide Company, she eventually rose to the lofty heights of PL of the Scarlet Pimpernels. She became a Ranger at the time when Air, Sea and Land Rangers were rolled into one as Ranger Guides. She has since been a Guide and Ranger Guider, a District Commissioner, and has worn various adviser hats. Currently she is Outdoor Activities adviser, which suits her, she feels. The post she aspires to is Archivist, the history and ephemera of Guiding being a passion. It is not easy for her to pick a favourite book. She has grown fond of *Terry, the Girl-Guide* as she read and re-read it, but her vote goes to *Seven Wild Swans*. She bought the book expecting to mock the plot and quickly grew to love those earnest young women who lived the Law so fully.

Ruth Jolly grew up in inner-city Nottingham, where she was a member of the 55th Nottingham Brownies and Guides. She was Sixer of the Elves and PL of the Speedwells, and later Tawny Owl, though she never obtained her warrant. Ruth's family was very active in the early days of Guiding. Her Aunt Vera was a Girl Scout before the formation of the Guides (see picture on page 76) and wore a Scout hat and carried a pole. Her Cousin Lois ('Robin') belonged to a very early school company which had its own system of awards and badges, different from those which were ultimately adopted by the Girl Guides. Robin always, to her dying day, slept with her feet higher than her head, 'because B-P said so'. Ruth's father was a Wolf Cub in Dinard, northern France. His Akela was a near relative of Baden-Powell, so everything had to be done perfectly. His little sister was also a Cub, there being no Brownie Pack! Ruth's mother, a Yorkshire schoolgirl in the 1930s, was a tremendously keen Guide who helped to form a wartime Sea Ranger unit in land-locked Leeds, and later became Ruth's Guide Captain.

Alison McCallum was a 4th Edinburgh Brownie and Guide and helped to start a Land Ranger Company with her friends when she was sixteen. She represented Scotland at a Swedish camp in 1968 and went on to become Guide Captain of the 4th Edinburgh (St Serf's) Guides. She started the 4th Edinburgh Rainbow Guide Unit in April 1989 and is still Guiding with both these units. In 1998 she went with a party of Guides from Edinburgh to visit the Lechtal valley in Austria and spent a night in a mountain hut. She still enjoys camping with Guides and loves the camping chapter at Kittiwake Cove in *The Wrong Chalet School* by Elinor M Brent-Dyer.

Claire Smerdon discovered Brownies in 1961 in Toronto, where the 102nd Brownie Pack skipped in circles and sang, while paying homage to a papier-mâché owl perched on a wobbly cardboard toadstool. A clumsy and self-conscious Leprechaun, Claire always worried that she would shout too early, leap too late or skip in the wrong direction, and attempted to compensate for her ineptitude at hopping, throwing-and-catching and other essential skills by becoming highly proficient at knots. But where were the magic pools, woodland glades and lavish iced cakes of the Brownie stories? Long before attaining her Golden Bar, she realised that no loyal chums would join in her madcap adventures, they would never go on rambles, ride in charabancs, sing around camp fires or rescue puppies. Her beloved Brownie books provided a far more satisfactory—and magical—experience than the Pack, so she deserted the Leprechauns and headed for the Public Library.

Antonia Syson was brought up in a family whose traditions of anti-imperialism and atheism stretch back more than three generations, and was firmly steered away from joining Brownies: instead, as a member of the Woodcraft Folk she learned to sing 'Can You Hear the H-Bombs Thunder?'

Tig Thomas was a Brownie (Imp, Pixie Second, Elf Sixer) and then a bored Guide member of the Swallow Patrol. The lacklustre games she played in the Guide hut each week seemed to have no connection to B-P's vision and she left Guides soon afterwards, but has remained a devotee of B-P all her life, and of wild camping and campcraft (she can weave a grass rope, forage for wild mushrooms and make bread on a hot stone in the ashes of a camp fire). Her favourite Guiding books are E M Channon's *The Honour of a Guide*, Catherine Christian's *Cherries in Search of a Captain* and, a recent discovery, Margaret Middleton's witty *The Guide Camp at Herons Bay*.

Helen Vincent burst into tears when at the age of six she was told she had to wait a year before joining the Brownies. Eventually she rose to the giddy heights of Second in the Pixie Patrol and still washes dishes according to the instructions in her Brownie Guide handbook, which featured a memorable illustration of dishes in order (glasses at the front, saucepans at the back) marching towards the sink. Sadly her Guiding experience never lived up to the standards of her favourite Guide story, *Cherries in Search of a Captain* by Catherine Christian, in which the Cherries work through *How Girls Can Help Build the Empire*, rabbit-skinning and all. She has never been camping, thank heaven—a disappointment to her father, who represented Northern Ireland at the 1947 World Scout Jamboree.

ACKNOWLEDGEMENTS

The editor would like to thank many people who have helped in preparing this book, in particular all the contributors: Mary Cadogan, Máiréad Campbell, Hilary Clare, Adrianne Fitzpatrick, Judy Harris, Wendy Ingle, Ruth Jolly, Alison McCallum, Claire Smerdon, Antonia Syson and Helen Vincent. Many of the contributors offered extensive further help to the book beyond writing their individual chapters, and she would like to give additional thanks to Hilary Clare for suggesting and writing the chapter on Catherine Christian, help with book research and the bibliography; Máiréad Campbell for reading other chapters, researching for the bibliography in the British Library, and taking on extra work at very short notice; Claire Smerdon for suggesting the title; Mary Cadogan for information, ideas and suggestions; Wendy Ingle for checking the glossary and bibliography; and Adrianne Fitzpatrick and Ruth Jolly for a great deal of invaluable editorial work. She is also very grateful to Karen Stapley, the Archivist of Girlguiding UK, for her patient help with many queries and for help with the bibliography and glossary; to Joan Firth for contributions to the bibliography; to Barbara Dryden, Susan Dunnachie, Rosalie Greaves, Barbara Harris, Judy Harris, Ruth Jackson, Kirsty Lowson, Kathryn Payne and Joy Wotton for checking the bibliography; to Louise Benson, Gill Bilski, Alexander Cadogan, Mary Cadogan, Sue Sims, Janet Stow, Imogen Thomas and Jennifer Wardle for help with supplying books, quotations and pictures; and to Adam Thomas for reading the MS several times and making many useful suggestions. The portrait of Baden-Powell on the frontispiece is © The National Portrait Gallery, London.

Guiding Around the Globe
Judy Harris and Tig Thomas would like to thank the many people who contributed to the 'Guiding around the Globe' chapter, including Barbara Robertson for help contacting New Zealand Guiding experts; Pam Airth in South Africa; Margaret, the Guide Archivist in South Africa; Wendy Davis in South Australia; Ann Lee in South Australia; Miss Priyanthi Hemamali Rajapaksa in Sri Lanka; Joan Lees in New Zealand; and the members of the Church Corner Trefoil Guild, Christchurch, New Zealand.

The Story of a Company
Alison McCallum would like to acknowledge the help given by the contributions of Ann Redman and Margaret Roberts.

'Kicked Out'
Antonia Syson would like to express her thanks to Tig Thomas as editor for helping make it possible to write this chapter, and for many observations that improved it. Equal gratitude goes to many other members of the Girlsown email list, whose insights into Antonia Forest have coloured and enriched her understanding of the novels over the last ten years.

INDEX